MYSTERIUM CHRISTI

CHRISTOLOGICAL STUDIES
BY BRITISH AND GERMAN THEOLOGIANS

EDITED BY

G. K. A. BELL, D.D.
BISHOP OF CHICHESTER

AND

D. ADOLF DEISSMANN, D.D.
PROFESSOR AT THE UNIVERSITY OF BERLIN

WITH FOUR ILLUSTRATIONS

LONGMANS, GREEN AND CO.
LONDON · NEW YORK · TORONTO
1930

Made in Great Britain

PREFACE

On August 29, 1925, at the World-Conference of the Churches at Stockholm, one of the two signatories to this introductory statement, being then Dean of Canterbury, expressed the desire and the hope that sometime in the future a group of representatives of different countries and Churches might meet together for some common intellectual task under the shadow of his cathedral. He himself enabled this idea to be realised in April 1927, when in association with the Chairman of the Stockholm Theological Commission, Dr. Deissmann, he organised the First British-German Theological Conference at Canterbury. This conference brought together for a whole week thirteen British and German theologians in discussion of the great subject, which the Stockholm meeting had made a matter of universal concern—' the nature of the Kingdom of God, and its relation to human society.' In August 1928 almost the same group of theologians met on the Wartburg above Eisenach for the Second British-German Theological Conference, and once more spent a week, this time on the problem of Christology. Reports of both these conferences can be found in the pages of *Theology* (London) and of *Theologische Blätter* (Leipzig), May 1927 and October 1928.

The close scientific and personal contact which was experienced during both conferences, and greatly enriched all who took part, led to the determination to give literary expression to the common theological task. The result is the present volume, which is appearing simultaneously in an English and a German version. In order to make as clear as possible, even superficially, the identity of both editions, we have adorned the volume with the phrase which the Apostle inscribed upon his banner *Mysterium Christi* (Col. iv. 3 ; Eph. iii. 4).

Though it is the outcome of a strong and growing feeling

of friendship, this book is not a manifesto for which, as a whole, all the contributors take responsibility. Nor is it vouched for by any Church or other organisation. Nor are the editors responsible for the contents, but each writer is entirely responsible for his own contribution. This personal independence of the contributors is further revealed in the fact that neither in method nor in results has a complete agreement been achieved. Limitations of space are responsible for the slightness of treatment which was all that could be given to a number of points.

The special editorial work has, at the request of the contributors, been undertaken by Dr. Mozley and Dr. Frick, who have laboured untiringly in connection with the articles, in providing for their translation, in proof-reading and the compilation of the index. We are all deeply indebted to our two friends for this great service. And we should all wish to express our united gratitude to our two publishing firms, Messrs. Longmans, Green & Co. of London and the Furche-Verlag of Berlin, for their great practical understanding and their friendly spirit.

We send the book out with the aim and hope that it may be a small contribution to the elucidation of the greatest question which has been offered to the consideration of Christendom—'What think ye of Christ?' (Matt. xxii. 42).

G. K. A. BELL.
ADOLF DEISSMANN.

CHICHESTER AND BERLIN.
Passiontide 1930.

CONTENTS

CONTENTS

LIST OF ILLUSTRATIONS

ALPHABETICAL LIST OF CONTRIBUTORS

ALTHAUS, PAUL, Hon. D.theol. (Göttingen), Professor für Dogmatik, Apologetik, Dogmengeschichte an der Universität, Erlangen.

BELL, GEORGE KENNEDY ALLEN, D.D., Bishop of Chichester.

CREED, JOHN MARTIN, D.D., Ely Professor of Divinity in the University of Cambridge and Canon of Ely.

DEISSMANN, ADOLF, Hon. D.theol. (Marburg), Hon. D.D. (Aberdeen, St. Andrews, Manchester, Oxford), Hon. Litt.D. (Wooster, Ohio), Professor der Neutestament-lichen Wissenschaft an der Universität, Berlin.

DODD, CHARLES HAROLD, M.A., Hon. D.D. (Aberdeen), Rylands Professor of Biblical Criticism and Exegesis in the University of Manchester.

FRICK, HEINRICH, Hon. D.theol. (Marburg), Dr. phil. (Giessen), Professor für Systematische Theologie, Religionswissenschaft und Missionskunde an der Universität, Marburg/Lahn.

HOSKYNS, Sir EDWYN CLEMENT HOSKYNS, Bart., M.A., Fellow, Dean and Lecturer in Theology, Corpus Christi College, Cambridge.

KITTEL, GERHARD, Hon. D.theol. (Kiel), Professor für Neutestamentliche Exegese an der Universität, Tübingen.

MICKLEM, NATHANIEL, M.A., Professor of New Testament Literature and Criticism at Queen's Theological College, Kingston, Ontario, Canada.

MOZLEY, JOHN KENNETH, D.D., Warden of St. Augustine's House, Reading, and Lecturer of Leeds Parish Church ; sometime Fellow, Dean and Theological Lecturer of Pembroke College, Cambridge.

THE NAME 'JESUS'

BY ADOLF DEISSMANN

I

THE NAME 'JESUS'

I

In his book entitled *Der Vorchristliche Jesus*, the American scholar William Benjamin Smith advocates a theory which Paul Wilhelm Schmiedel recapitulates as follows in his preface to the German edition [1]:

'The doctrine concerning Jesus was a pre-Christian one, a cult which at the meeting of the centuries (100 B.C. to 100 A.D.) was widespread among the Jews and especially among the Hellenists, more or less in secret and veiled in "mysteries"'; Christianity originally proceeded from many centres, and only according to a later theory from a single centre, from Jerusalem. 'From the beginning Jesus was nothing other than a divinity . . . namely as the redeemer, the guardian, the saviour.'

Then William Benjamin Smith has incidentally referred to me in his book [2]: it is 'noteworthy that Deissmann has recently been very favourable to the conception of the "monotheistic Jesus-cult" and has used the term as a favourite expression. See *Die Urgeschichte des Christentums im Lichte der Sprachforschung*, pages 23, 27, 25, 29.' That is a sufficient reason for my discussion of the American's theory.

Among the evidence used by Smith is found the great Paris Magic Papyrus verse 3019 f [3]:

ἐξορκίζω σε κατὰ τοῦ θεοῦ τῶν ʽΕβραίων ʼΙησοῦ· ʼΙαβα· ʼΙαη etc.

---

[1] William Benjamin Smith, *Der Vorchristliche Jesus Vorstudien zur Entstehungsgeschichte des Urchristentums* (2nd edn., with a Preface by Paul Wilhelm Schmiedel), Jena, 1911, p. 111. The English edition was not accessible.

[2] German edition, p. xxvii.

[3] Not 3920, as is stated in the German edition of Smith, p. xxvii, nor 3113 f., as Smith has given on p. 38.

Here he sees an instance of the use of the name *Jesus* in very early, pre-Christian times for the exorcism of daemons.[1]

This theory of the American's can be concisely stated thus : the name *Jesus* was an ancient cult-name, long before the rise of Christianity ; it originally denoted, not an earthly-human personality but a divinity, and originated in the Diaspora. It was associated with the ancient Jewish divine name *Christ*, and in the combination *Jesus Christ* the essence of Early Christianity is contained and expressed.

In discussing this theory the problem of the origin of Early Christianity may be formulated in the alternative : did a historical personality who bore the name *Jesus* afterwards become the central figure in a cult, or from an ancient pre-Christian cult-god of the Diaspora, Jesus, was a figure created who, in the New Testament tradition, appears as the man Jesus of Nazareth ?

In this way it deals with one of the greatest problems of the internal history of Early Christianity, which is lastly a problem of religious semasiology and is to be solved only through a serious study of the history of language and of cult.

II

First of all we may say that no instance whatever of the use of the name *Jesus* as a cult-name before our era has been established. The papyrus cited by Smith undoubtedly employs the name as a cult-name. But it was written about the year 300 A.D.[2] and, although it certainly contains formulas considerably older, the very lines cited by Smith contradict him in that they refer, not to a cult in the Diaspora, but to a cult existing in Palestine. The

---

[1] P. 38.

[2] Compare the facsimile and the transcription in my book, *Light from the Ancient East*, new and completely revised edition, London, 1927, pp. 256 ff. The papyrus must now be cited from the critical edition by Karl Preisendanz, *Papyri Graecae Magicae*, vol. i. Leipzig, 1928, p. 170. A *Jesus*—passage in the Leyden Magical Papyrus has likewise been misinterpreted ; Carl Schmidt has now set the matter right (*Theol. Lit.-Ztg.* 47 (1922), *col.* 469 f.). For the whole question *cf.* also W. W. Graf Baudissin, *Kyrios*, ii. Giessen, 1929, p. 120.

word *Hebrews* in ancient usage always denotes the Aramaic-speaking Jews of Palestine,[1] and it supplies no proof whatever that the formula of the papyrus is earlier than the second century A.D.; it is no evidence whatever for the cult history of pre-Christian times.

When we examine the authentic documents of the pre-Christian period we find, in Palestine and in the Diaspora, innumerable instances of the name *Jesus* being used as a masculine personal name (and once as a place-name).[2] But there is not a single instance of the pre-Christian use of *Jesus* as a cult-name.

The Greek name Ἰησοῦς is a Greek transcription of יֵשׁוּעַ (*Jeshua*) supplied with a Greek ending. *Jeshua* is the shortened form of the old name *Jehoshua* (*Joshua*) and became the usual form after the Exile; the abbreviation was adopted in order to avoid the proximity of the two vowels ô–û. This shortened form is already found in the later books of the Old Testament, and it is still in common use to-day in the Jewish idiom.[3]

The Semitic name means : *he whose salvation is Yahweh, God's salvation*, σωτηρία κυρίου, as Philo correctly translates it.[4] In its longer form we first find it as the name of Moses' successor whom we call *Joshua*, and already at an early time we find his name with its meaning fully appreciated and referring to the divinely blessed work of Joshua. It is noteworthy that another bearer of the name *Jesus*, the son of Sirach (Jes. Sir. 46, 1), says of Joshua : κραταιὸς ἐν πολέμοις Ἰησοῦς Ναυῆ καὶ διάδοχος Μωϋσῆ ἐν προφητείαις. ὃς ἐγένετο κατὰ τὸ ὄνομα αὐτοῦ μέγας ἐπὶ σωτηρίᾳ ἐκλεκτῶν αὐτοῦ, ἐκδικῆσαι ἐπεγειρομένους ἐχθρούς, ὅπως κληρονομήσῃ τὸν Ἰσραήλ.

Here again we have no cult interpretation of the name. Neither has σωτηρία as yet acquired the apostolic meaning *salvation*, but refers to the deliverance of the nation from severe oppression through the military exploits of Joshua.

---

[1] Compare my book, *Paul²*, London, 1926, p. 90.

[2] *Jeshua*, Neh. xi. 26, in southern Judah.

[3] For example : The modern name of Jesus in the Yiddish of Alsace-Lorraine is *Jeshu*, יֵשׁוּ (*cf.* E. Weill, *Revue des Études juives*, vol. 71, 1920, p. 76).

[4] *Nom. Mutat.* § 21.

We see here what is rather a pious explanation of the name as an omen, the beginning of that edifying explanation of names, as they were later drawn up in long lists by Philo, Origen, and Jerome for the practical purpose of preaching and instruction; and occasionally they were also used as amulets.[1]

III

As the name *Jeshua* found its way into the world of the Diaspora it was, like the majority of other Semitic names, adapted to the usage of that world by being Graecised or Latinised. We have what is probably an exception in a tomb inscription from Venusia (Southern Italy) where the name is simply transcribed : *Gesua* (Genitive : *Gesues*).[2] As a rule the name was adapted to the world's languages.

The name *Jeshua* was Graecised and later Latinised mostly in such a way that a name in -οῦς arose through the addition of a sigma,[3] an ending which is not unusual in Greek masculine and especially feminine personal names.

The Greek name 'Ιησοῦς thus formed was declined in various ways. The most convenient was the inflection -οῦς, -οῦτος, etc., on the analogy of the above-mentioned names in -οῦς. This inflection of the name is actually found in the papyri and ostraca. On the other hand, in the Greek Bible the name is generally [4] inflected thus : -οῦς, -οῦ, -οῦ, -οῦν, an inflection of which there are examples with other Graecised names outside the Greek Bible.[5]

---

[1] See further *Light from the Ancient East*, pp. 405 f.

[2] See Oehler, ' Epigraphische Beiträge zur Geschichte des Judentums,' in *Monatsschrift für Geschichte und Wissenschaft des Judentums*, 53 (1909), p. 445.

[3] Analogies of this are found in LXX ('Ελιοῦς, Σαμμοῦς, 'Ελεισοῦς, Θεησοῦς, cf. Henry St. John Thackeray, *A Grammar of the Old Testament in Greek*, vol. i. Cambridge, 1909, p. 165) and elsewhere (cf. 'Ιεδδοῦς, mentioned below).

[4] Occasionally the Dative in the LXX is 'Ιησοῖ (cf. Thackeray, p. 165).

[5] A good example is the Jewish name 'Ιεδδοῦς (Accusative 'Ιεδδοῦν) in the Zenon Papyrus, No. 4 (259/250 B.C.). See Edgar, *Annales du Service des Antiquités de l'Egypte*, 18 (1918 ff.) ; this name is the Graecised form of the transcribed (not Graecised) form 'Ιεδδουά from LXX 2 Es. xxi. 21 (Neh. x. 22).

And further, we must reckon with the possibility that the name *Jeshua*, when it entered the Greek world, was not transcribed but replaced with a name of similar sound : I regard the common Jewish name *Jason* as a substitute for *Jeshua*.[1]

Of special importance with regard to the use of the personal name *Jeshua* in Palestine itself are two ossuary inscriptions from Jerusalem, for knowledge of which we are indebted to Ch. Clermont-Ganneau.[2] They probably belong to the early Imperial period. One comes from the vicinity of the Cedron Valley; it only gives the name *Jeshua* in Hebrew, ישוע (*cf.* Figure 1), and affords an admirable idea of the writing of the name in the trilingual title on the Cross (and likewise of a contemporary form of Yod, named in the Sermon on the Mount (Matt. v. 18), as the smallest letter of the alphabet). The other comes from the Hill of Offence near Jerusalem and gives the words *Shimeon bar Jeshua*, also in Hebrew script : שמעון כר ישוע. With this should be compared Βαριησοῦς of Acts xiii. 6.

Another Greek ossuary inscription, also published by Clermont-Ganneau,[3] comes from the Hill of Offence near Jerusalem : Ιεσους Ιεσους. For a long time I hesitated with regard to this and had some misgivings as to its genuineness : at first the writing of the name with ε and a cross sign before the Greek line appeared to me somewhat strange. But even these very signs occur elsewhere in inscriptions of Jewish ossuaries. I may mention the ossuary of the Alexandrian Jew Nikanor,[4] the famous founder of the gate of Nikanor in the Temple of Herod, known to us from Acts iii. 2 as θύρα ὡραία. But then with regard to the name Ιεσους itself I found that here we had, not a Graecised form of *Jeshua* but of either *Jishwi* or

---

[1] For this use, up to the present day, of foreign surnames with Jewish names *cf.* my *Bible Studies*³, Edinburgh, 1923, p. 315.

[2] *Arch. Researches*, i, London, 1899, pp. 437 and 394 (with facsimile). It would be of great advantage to me to learn where this ossuary and the following now lie.

[3] *Op. cit.* p. 409 (with facsimile).

[4] *Cf.* the facsimile of the ossuary discovered about 1902 near the house of Mr. Gray Hill on the north end of the Mount of Olives : Palestine Exploration Fund Quarterly Statement 1903, *cf.* the memorandum on such cross signs, p. 331.

Jishwa, two masculine names from Gen. xlvi. 17 (*cf.* also Num. xxvi. 44; 1 Chron. vii. 30; 1 Sam. xiv. 49) which are transcribed with ε in all cases by the LXX : *Jishwi* there becomes 'Ιεσού and 'Ιεσονεί, or 'Ιεσσονέ and 'Ιεσσονί or 'Ιεσσιούλ and 'Ιεσσιού ; *Jishwa* becomes 'Ιεσονά. It is only that the ossuary inscription from Jerusalem has the name in a more Graecised form than the LXX : by appending a sigma it gives it a Greek ending. Its genuineness is beyond doubt.

The number of persons called by the name *Jesus* known to us from literary sources is very considerable ; here our most important sources are the LXX, New Testament, and Josephus. Nearly all of these literary instances come from Palestine. I need not treat each of them separately.

The numerous instances from Josephus will be conveniently found in the large edition of that author by Benedictus Niese, who, in the index, specifies about twenty instances of persons called by the name *Jesus*, ten of them being contemporaries of Jesus ; among them a number of priests. The evidence of Josephus alone would be sufficient to prove the frequency of the name. The New Testament instances which had a peculiar fortune in the history of the text will be dealt with separately at a later stage.

But to these instances of *Jesus* as a personal name in literature is to be added now a large number from non-literary sources. I have already mentioned the Palestinian ossuaries. The Egyptian papyri, ostraca[1] and inscriptions are adding many bearers of the name in the Egyptian Diaspora,[2] the majority of them belonging to the end of the first and the beginning of the second century A.D. One instance of the papyri comes even from the first century B.C.[3]

---

[1] I wish to give but one specimen (*cf.* Figure 2) : the ostracon printed in Preisigke's *Sammelbuch*, M. 5822, from Apollinopolis Magna (Egypt), A.D. 110, being a receipt concerning Jews' tax for the Jew Sambathion Jesus (*cf.* line 1 : Σαμβαθίων ὁ κ(αὶ) 'Ιησοῦς).

[2] Most of them will be found in Friedrich Preisigke, *Namenbuch*, Heidelberg, 1922, col. 148.

[3] The Oxyrhynchus Papyri No. 816 (vol. iv. p. 257).

Fig. 1. The name *Jeshua* upon an Ossuary
from Jerusalem. Early Imperial Period.

Fig. 2. The name *Jesus* upon an Ostracon from Egypt. 110 A.D.

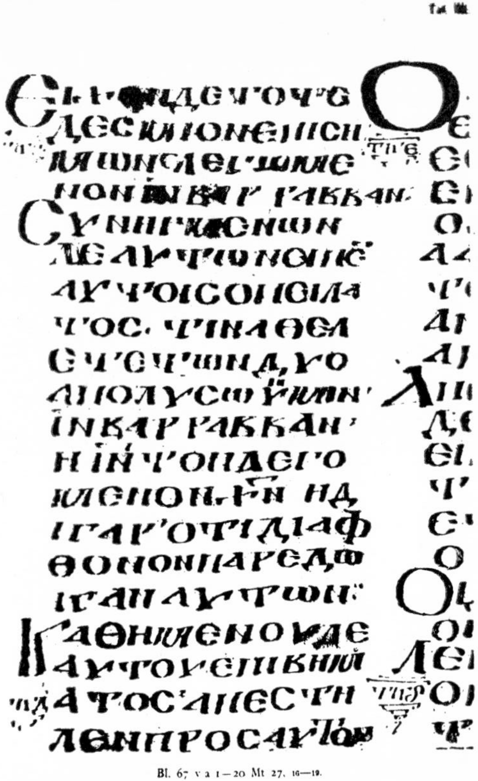

Fig. 4.   The *Jesus-Barabbas* Passage, Matt. 27, 16-17
(cp. lines 4 and 11) of the Codex of Koridethi; IX cent. A.D.

Fig. 3.   The *Jesus*-Inscription
from Leontopolis in Egypt.   Augustan Age.

IV

Of these numerous instances I only wish to discuss briefly what is perhaps the most interesting one of all. It has not yet been mentioned by Preisigke.

It occurs in one of the newly discovered inscriptions from Tell-el-Yahoudieh in Egypt, published a few years ago by C. C. Edgar [1]—nearly three dozen Greek inscriptions from the Jewish necropolis of the ancient Leontopolis which is so famous in the religious history of late Judaism owing to the Temple of Onias. These newly discovered inscriptions of the Leontopolis Jews, nearly all of which belong to the time of Augustus, show a high degree of Hellenisation of the Jews, especially by the fact that in them an attempt has been made, with varying degrees of success, to imitate Hellenic poetry—evidently the influence of the Greek tomb epigrams.

The Jesus-inscription [2] (*cf.* Figure 3) is indeed remarkable. Supposing a mutilated papyrus leaf were found containing lines similar to the following : *I am Jesus, I went to Hades, Thou art my child*, at first sight one could easily think that he had before him a fragment of a lost Gospel, probably of a Gnostic Gospel. ' I am Jesus ' sounds like a quotation from the account of Christ's epiphany on the road to Damascus (Acts ix. 5). ' I went to Hades ' has the appearance of an allusion to Christ's descent into Hades, and ' Thou art my child ' could easily be an echo of the narrative of the baptism of Jesus.

The text could be interpreted in that way, especially when read with the eyes of William Benjamin Smith eager to find traces of a cult. But really we are still in the pre-cult period, and it deals, not with the hero of a cult, but with an otherwise unknown Jew, Jesus of Leontopolis, whose memory is preserved in an epigram composed in the ' I '-style :

$$\epsilon \grave{\iota} \mu \epsilon \grave{\iota} \; \grave{\epsilon} \gamma \grave{\omega} \; ' I \eta \sigma o \hat{\upsilon} \varsigma, \; \acute{o} \; \phi \grave{\upsilon} \varsigma \; \delta \grave{\epsilon} \; \varPhi a \mu \epsilon \hat{\iota} \varsigma, \; \pi a \rho o \delta \epsilon \hat{\iota} \tau a \cdot$$
$$(\grave{\epsilon} \xi \eta \kappa o \nu \tau a \acute{\epsilon} \tau \eta \varsigma) \; \mathring{\eta} \lambda \theta o \nu \; \delta' \epsilon \grave{\iota} \varsigma \; ' A \epsilon \acute{\iota} \delta a \nu.$$

---

[1] *Annales du Service des Antiquités de l'Egypte*, xix. and xxii.

[2] *Annales*, xxii. p. 10 f. It has the number 22. I give the text with its errors.

κλαύσατε δὴ ἅμα πάντ⟨ε⟩ς τὸν ἐξαπίνης μεταβάντα
εἰς μυχὸν αἰώνων ἐν σκοτίᾳ διάγειν.
καὶ σὺ δέ, Δωσίθεε, κατάκλαέ με· σοὶ γὰρ ἀνάνκη
δάκρισι πικροτάτοις τύμβῳ ἐμῷ προχέειν.
τέκνον ἐμοὶ εισν, ἐγὼ γὰρ ἀπῆλθον ἄτεκ⟨ν⟩ος.
κλαύσατε πάντες ὁμοῦ Ἰησο⟨ῦ⟩ν δυσμενέα.

I am Jesus which begat Phameis, O passer-by !
   Sixty years old I went into Hades,
Therefore let everyone weep together for him who has
   departed so suddenly
   In the innermost part of the aeons to live in darkness.
And thou especially weep for me, Dositheos, for to thee
   it is necessary
To shed bitter tears on my tomb.
Thou art my child, for I went away childless.
Bewail all together Jesus, the enemy.

It is clear at first sight that the text of the conclusion
is not in order. Instead of δυσμενέα some synonym for
unfortunate or *poor* must have been intended, perhaps
δυστυχέα. The text of the last line but one, regarded by
Edgar as incurable, is probably not so difficult to restore.
To me τέκνον ἐμοὶ εἶ σύ is beyond doubt the proper text
though corrupted by an error in writing, and we are to take
the sentence as an adoption formula ; it coincides in contents and form with the well known phrase of Psalm ii
and echoes in the pericope of the baptism of Jesus : ' Thou
art my son.' Dositheos will have been the adopted son of
Jesus of Leontopolis and is indicated as such in the tomb
inscription. The father of the Jew Jesus of Leontopolis
bore a name that is obviously Egyptian : Φαμεῖς, which
is probably the same as the name Φαμῆς shown by Preisigke
to occur in the third century B.C. Of great interest are the
words used for the life to come, especially the use of αἰῶνες
in a local sense. Hades, which had long been adopted by
Hellenistic Judaism, is also mentioned, but then it is interpreted as ' the innermost part of the aeons.' Here the
influence of the Septuagint seems recognisable : the Wisdom
of Solomon xvii. 14 uses the phrase ἐξ ἀδυνάτου Ἅιδου
μυχῶν ἐπελθοῦσαν.

Of course the phrase ' I am Jesus ' was not intended in

any cult-sense. It therefore contrasts characteristically with the above-mentioned phrase of Acts ix. 5, where we meet the *I am* formula in the sense common in ancient times of the self-manifestation of a deity. For the history of the *I am* formula I may refer to my book [1] and to the researches of Eduard Norden.[2]

V

Thus when in the New Testament a Galilean Jew bore the name *Jesus* it was only one instance among dozens of authenticated similar cases and among hundreds of others. At first his name had only the character of a plain personal name, just as in the other instances of its occurrence in the New Testament : in the genealogy of Jesus, Luke iii. 29 as the name of one of his ancestors ; Matt. xxvii. 16 and 17 as the name of the insurgent and murderer, Barabbas ; Acts xiii. 6 as the name of the father of the magician Elymas from Cyprus ; Col. iv. 11 as the name of one of Paul's fellow-workers, Jesus Justus ; in addition, the Old Testament Jesus-Joshua is twice mentioned, Acts vii. 45 and Heb. iv. 8. In all these cases we deal with a very common, ordinary personal name.

Jesus first became a cult-name when Jesus of Nazareth, after his exaltation, was given divine reverence as the Kyrios, that is, after the rise of the cult of Jesus Christ in the Early Church.[3] We have from the early days of the Kyrios-cult, in Matt. i. 21, what is probably the first instance of the elevation of the name *Jesus* into the sacred cult-sphere : in the words of the angel, καὶ καλέσεις τὸ ὄνομα αὐτοῦ Ἰησοῦν· αὐτὸς γὰρ σώσει τὸν λαὸν αὐτοῦ ἀπὸ τῶν ἁμαρτιῶν αὐτῶν.

Here, quite differently from the interpretation of the name *Joshua* by Philo,[4] the name *Jesus* as a *nomen sacrum*

---

[1] *Light from the Ancient East*, pp. 137 f.

[2] *Agnostos Theos*, Leipzig and Berlin, 1913.

[3] A first step is seen in the use of the name *Jesus* in exorcism by the disciples, Mk. vi. 13, Matt. vii. 22, and Jewish exorcists (Mk. ix. 38 = Luke ix. 49) ; here, however, Jesus is not yet conceived of as God, but as a powerful divine exorcist.

[4] *Cf.* above, p. 5. The conception of σωτηρία in this early Christian interpretation became quite different from that of Philo.

is canonised into the sphere of the cult and obtains a cult-interpretation : it has become the banner-sign of the cult of the Saviour ; *Jesus* now signifies, as, at a later time, the magical formula of the Paris papyrus [1] correctly felt, *the God of the Hebrews*, that is, the cult-deity of a Saviour-cult of Palestinian origin.

The canonisation of *Jesus* as a cult-name in Early Christianity was evidently effected very soon, so soon that the rapidly developing feeling of the uniqueness now attached to this name gave rise to certain phenomena at a very early time, traces of which are perceptible through the centuries down to the present day.   They appear on the one hand in the practice of name-giving among Jews and Christians, and on the other hand in the far-reaching interferences with, and alterations of, the text of the New Testament.

VI

Among Jews and Christians the name *Jesus* after it had become a cult-name began to disappear rapidly as a personal name and was as good as abandoned, among the Jews because of an intelligible feeling of antagonism, among the Christians because of an equally intelligible aversion to profane the beloved, most holy name.   With this I touch upon an important episode in the history of inward piety that has never been worked out systematically.   Adolf von Harnack with his most valuable treatise on Jewish and Christian names [2] could long ago provide the stimulus for the work on this significant chapter.

In the present state of the investigation I cannot, on my part, give a statistical account with unqualified certainty.   But in general there can be no doubt that the personal name *Jehoshua—Jeshua—Jesus*, which was still such a favourite in the Diaspora about the end of the first century and the beginning of the second A.D., gradually disappeared.   I have consulted many Jewish experts

---

[1] *Cf.* above, p. 3 f.

[2] *Die Mission und Ausbreitung des Christentums in den ersten drei Jahrhunderten*, i[4], Leipzig, 1924, pp. 436 ff. (Eng. trans.[2], 1908, pp. 422 ff.).

concerning the matter and have always received an answer in agreement with my own observations, that after about the second and third centuries the name became scarcer and scarcer.[1] It seems to be an exceptional case that in the eleventh century we find two Karaites, Jeshua ben Jehudah and Aron ben Jeshua,[2] and in the fifteenth century a Spanish Rabbi Jesua.[3] It is possible that the statistics vary in different Jewish communities. But it will be difficult to indicate any district where the name is used other than in exceptional cases. I give one example.

There exists an official list of the Jews of Alsace in the eighteenth century[4]; it contains about 20,000 Jewish names, masculine and feminine. Among them there are only two instances of the name *Joshua*: in the village Reichshoffen a Joshua Feisel and a Jochel Josué. Also in modern Alsace the name is not used; at one time there was a Jewish family of the name *Schue* in Hattstadt having come from Flehingen in Baden whose name may possibly be claimed as an abbreviation of *Joshua*.[5]

I am grateful for any information on the matter; but, so far as our present knowledge goes, the name, though it was frequently used down to the second century A.D. as one of the greatest of Old Testament names, became a *nomen ingratum* among the Jews both of Palestine and of the Diaspora through their reaction against its canonisation in Christianity.

But in the life of the early Christian communities its profane use as a personal name was as good as completely lost from the beginning. And generally speaking it has

---

[1] *Cf.* Samuel Poznanski, *Revue des Études juives*, vol. 54 (1907), p. 276 f.; he gives very few examples for *Jeshua* from the Geniza-texts of the eleventh century. After him S. Krauss, one of the best experts, emphasised the rareness of the name *Jeshua* in Jewish circles of the Christian era, *Revue des Études juives*, vol. 55 (1908), p. 148.

[2] Poznanski, p. 278.

[3] Here belong also the examples given by Leopold Zunz, *Namen der Juden* (*Gesammelte Schriften*, II. Berlin, 1876), p. 52.

[4] *Dénombrement général des Juifs qui sont tolérés en la Province d'Alsace*, Colmar, 1785. I am indebted for this account (through the kind help of Siegmund Feist) to the expert, Dr. Ernest Lévy of Strassburg.

[5] I am also indebted to Dr. Ernest Lévy for this information. Neither he himself nor the authorities of whom he made inquiries know of an instance in Alsace to-day.

remained so throughout the centuries. If in Nubia the formula *Jesus is the son of Mary* is attested as a feminine name,[1] it is not an instance of the name *Jesus* being again taken as a personal name ; it belongs rather to the numerous class of examples of the use of short powerful religious phrases in names, the separate parts of which cannot be isolated and taken as the name proper. The Nubian women who seek to protect themselves with such names are no more named *Jesus* than a man with the name *Fuerchtegott* is named *Gott*. Neither does the somewhat similar custom among believers in the Middle Ages and later of adding *a Jesu* or *de Jesu* or even *a Jesu Maria* to their names mean that the name *Jesus* is again adopted as a personal name : just as Johann von Gott did not have the name *Gott*, so Didacus a Jesu and Thomas a Jesu had no desire to be taken as bearers of the name *Jesus*.

Only in special districts does the attempt seem to have been made to use *Jesus* as a personal name. In Spain the name is common as a second Christian name but not as a name by which a person is called,[2] and this explains the instances of *Jesus* as a personal name which are found in districts which were at one time under Spanish domination : one example is found among the leaders of ' The United Evangelical Church in the Philippines,' Mr. Jesus Dineros.[3] One may respect this peculiar custom of name-giving among the Spanish, Mexicans, and also among the young Filipino Christians, without regarding it as worthy of emulation. But further, by its very peculiarity, this custom can bring out clearly for us the lines of general Christian practice elsewhere with its characteristic reverence.

[1] *Cf.* A. Alt, *Zeitschrift des Deutschen Palaestina-Vereins*, 51 (1928), p. 223. I may say that this custom may also perhaps throw a light on an enigmatic passage in a Greek Inscription given by Gustave Lefebvre, *Recueil des inscriptions grecques-chrétiennes d'Egypte*, Le Caire, 1907, No. 634 : line 5 [η] μακαρια ιησους with an abbreviation line on the last four letters.

[2] Communication from Ernst Gamillscheg, January 13, 1930.

[3] *Cf.* *The Christian Century* (Chicago) for May 29, 1929, p. 724. The name is also common in Mexico ; Erich Seeberg drew my attention to the notice in the *Berliner Lokalanzeiger*, No. 17, for January 10, 1930, p. 1.

VII

Quite different from the possibilities of the use of the name *Jesus* in Judaism and Christianity were those in Islam. Jesus was and is considered in Islam to be one of the greatest prophets. Here his name was neither hated so that it had to be avoided with disgust, nor was it, as a prophetic name, surrounded with that divine halo of the cult that prevented its further application to men. Thus we find it, like the names of other Biblical prophets, used without restraint in Islam as a personal name in the form *'Isā*. Franz Babinger [1] refers me to the Arab Grammarian and Koran Reader 'Isā ibn 'Omar (died 149 H. = 766 A.D.), the 'Abbāside 'Isā ibn Mūsā ibn Muhammed (died 167 H. = 783 A.D.), the Arab Emir 'Isā ibn Muhannā (735/1334) ; and later in the fourteenth and fifteenth centuries the name was very common, also among persons of high rank. The wonderful mosque of Sultan Isa I. of Aidin, built in 1375 close under the hill of the Church of St. John the Divine at Ephesus, though it is not a ' Jesus-Mosque ' is yet the ' Sultan Jesus-Mosque.' A son of Bajesid I. was also called 'Isā (died 1405). And only a few decades ago the name occurred in the Ottoman empire. That it has lately receded more and more in Turkey is explained by Babinger as due to the influence of a changing fashion in names. Does that indicate something of a new political antipathy towards the ' Christian ' powers ? I simply raise the question without being able to answer it.

VIII

The strongest influence of the canonisation of the name *Jesus* as a cult-name is seen in the history of the text of the Bible, especially that of the New Testament.

First of all, externally, in the distinctive manner of writing the name which occurs in the polyglot traditions in two forms : in the Greek abbreviations $\overline{\text{IHC}}$ and $\overline{\text{IC}}$, all

---

[1] Letter, Berlin-Wilmersdorf, January 4, 1930.

relative material being collected by Ludwig Traube,[1] and in the Latin abbreviation I̅H̅S̅ which bears still clearer the character of a sacred rune and therefore became still more popular ; for this Wordsworth and White in their Vulgate edition on Matt. i. 1 offer a wealth of materials.[2] These facts of writing which, however, have far more than a graphical significance, are universally known and it is not necessary to explain them at full length.

Less noticed and, in any case, hardly recognised in their inner homogeneity are the other facts of textual history which can be brought together in the formula : a Christian tendency of no inconsiderable degree of strength has been effective to obliterate or at least to make unrecognisable the name *Jesus* where it occurs in the true text of the New Testament writings as the ordinary name of another person. Clearly it was felt to be a scandal, and that in early times, that there should have been other men of the name *Jesus*, especially men who for certain reasons were repugnant to Christian sentiment.   Thus we find that in all other cases where the name *Jesus* occurs in the New Testament there have been interferences with the text, by means of which other persons were deprived of the sacred name with varying degrees of success.   That these interferences did not arise from the mistakes and caprice of ' the copyists ' but were officially sanctioned is highly probable.

---

[1] ' Nomina Sacra : Versuch einer Geschichte der christlichen Kürzung ' (*Quellen und Untersuchungen zur lat. Philologie des Mittelalters*, Band II.), Muenchen, 1907, pp. 113–116, 149–164, 271 ff. This abbreviation starting from the Greek text is extended in many manuscripts to the name *Jesus* in the cases where it occurs as the name of other persons in the Bible.

[2] Pars 1, fasc. 1, Oxonii 1889, pp. 41 f. From the Greek-Latin codices Bezae and Augiensis comes the positive proof that in this Latin abbreviation the sign H which appears in the Latin as a large *h* is really the Greek η of the abbreviation I̅H̅C̅ taken over, and this seems to have been necessary because the Latin had no means of indicating the two different *e*-sounds. The abbreviation I̅E̅S̅ was rightly avoided. (Then later I̅H̅S̅, which was adopted in the Latin Church, was often taken by popular exegesis to stand for *in hoc signo*.) From similar motives the name *Jesus* in modern editions of the Bible is often printed in capitals.

IX

Let us take the separate passages.

1. The interferences are already found in Luke iii. 29, where a Jesus the son of Eliezer is named among the ancestors of Jesus Christ. The passage belongs to that section of the Lucan Genealogy which has no Old Testament parallel and was therefore more open to interferences than the names confirmed by older genealogical lists. Here the textual tradition [1] shows a large number of variants for the undoubtedly original *'Ιησοῦ* : *Ιησω, Ιωση* (*Iose*), *Iozes, Zoses, Iosez, Iessu* (Codex R). Of these *Ιωση* (*Iose*) is by far the commonest. Since it deals with an ancestor of the Saviour there was really no compelling reason for altering the text. That in spite of this there is such great variance in the text proves for us how deeply was felt the uniqueness of the name *Jesus* as a cult-name.

2. In Acts vii. 45, where the Old Testament Joshua is called *Jesus*, we also see at least one of the above-mentioned variants : the remarkable form *Iessu*. It occurs in Codex D and, like Luke iii. 29, exhibits a remarkable alteration of the name.

3. A third case in which there was no immediate necessity for altering the text is found in Col. iv. 11, where Paul conveys the greeting of *Jesus which is called Justus*.[2] Here the textual tradition seemed to have been quite uniform from that time onwards. But recently the long lost commentary of Pelagius on the letters of Paul was again made accessible by Alexander Souter.[3] This commentary was written by the great heretic in Rome, 406–409. Its Old Latin Pauline text can be restored with

---

[1] For the evidence I refer to Tischendorf's *Octava critica major* and Wordsworth-White.

[2] An instance of the common practice of naming by adding a similarly sounding worldly name to the Semitic name.

[3] Pelagius's *Expositions of the Thirteen Epistles of St. Paul*, II. *Text and apparatus criticus*, by Alexander Souter. *Texts and Studies*, edited by J. A. Robinson, vol. ix. Cambridge, 1926, p. 472. To what extent the Latin Vulgate tradition had something similar I cannot ascertain, as the great edition of the Vulgate has not yet reached to the letter to the Colossians.

certainty, and for the first time affords certain evidence of
a variant which likewise originated in cult reverence for
the name : codices E and S of Pseudo-Hieronymus, which
belongs to the Pelagius tradition, omit the words *et Iesus
qui dicitur*, and the disciple of the Apostle is thereafter
called simply *Justus*. To the originator of this omission the
name *Jesus* belonged exclusively to the Saviour.

Souter [1] could also point out that Codex D of the
Vulgate gave the name *Jesus* here in the peculiar form
(two occurrences of which we have already found) *Iessus*.
This is, of course, no accident.

4. Now comes a passage where it becomes evident that
the occurrence of the name *Jesus* was felt to be offensive
and the name was therefore altered. In Acts xiii. 6 Paul
and Barnabas have come into conflict with the magician and
pseudo-prophet *Barjesu* at Paphos in Cyprus. There is no
doubt that the father of this diviner was called *Jesus* and
was one of the many who bore that name as we have
already seen. There can be no doubt as to the genuineness
of the tradition.[2] But the name *Son of Jesus* as the name
of a man whom Paul afterwards (xiii. 9) calls *Son of the
Devil* was clearly a scandal in the eyes of the Christian
reader at an early period ; how could such a villainous
fellow be called *Son of Jesus* ! And the textual tradition [3]
then shows a multitude of various attempts to remove the
name or to make it unrecognisable.[4]

To begin with, the ending *-ov*, which the linguistic
instinct of the Greek Christians recognised as a genitive
usage and therefore especially offensive, was abandoned
and Βαριησους or Βαριησουν was written. But this being
still an offensive form, it was again either altered in another
and more radical manner or replaced, so that Βαριησουαν,[5]

---

[1] See above.

[2] I do not enter here into the question whether the name *Elymas*
which is mentioned in xiii. 8 was the particular name which he used, as
was often the case, combined with the name of his father.

[3] *Cf.* again Tischendorf and Wordsworth-White.

[4] Hans Hinrich Wendt has already pointed this out correctly in his
work on Acts (*Meyer* III [9], Goettingen, 1913), p. 202.

[5] *Cf.* also the form *Varisuas* in the so-called *Opus imperfectum in
Matthaeum* (about A.D. 400), Th. Zahn, *Acta Joannis*, Erlangen, 1880,
pp. lxiii. f.

Bariesuam, Bariesuban, Barieu, Berieu, Barshumo were
written.

But further : concerning this passage we have what is
very old and clear evidence for the conscious rejection of
the original reading disclosed thus far purely by the
condition of the text. Jerome [1] openly declared the
reading Βαριησου to be corrupt (*nonnulli bariesu corrupte
legunt*) and gave *Berieu* [2] as the correct form, which he
interpreted *maleficum sive in malo.* And four hundred
years later Bede [3] in dependance on Jerome again
declared the reading *Bariesu* to be corrupt and sought to
explain its origin by saying that the original *Barieu* was
wrongly taken for an abbreviation of *Bariesu*, ' for it is
not fitting that such a wicked fellow, a diviner, should be
named *Son of Jesus*, that is *Son of the Saviour.*'

It is now probably clear from such connections why,
at a later time, the name *Barjesu* also, where it occurred
as the name of a Christian, could not remain. The
Synaxarium Ecclesiae Constantinopolitanae [4] gives the name
of a Bishop Barjesu of Damascus for February 28 ; but his
name is altered to Βάρσος [5] in some other calendars.

5. Yet more energetically this naïve text criticism,
judging solely from religious antipathy, went to work
on another passage which was even more open to the
influence of this feeling of aversion : Matt. xxvii. 16 and
17. Here again the motive for the interference with the
text is made quite clear by a very old authority.

We have here a case where a group of evidence, though
smaller in number, is overwhelming on account of its age
and authority and, against a mass of evidence for a
mutilated text, has saved the original. It is the problem

---

[1] *De interpretatione nominum Hebraicorum,* III. 99 (written A.D.
389).

[2] This form is also attested in the Vulgate tradition, *cf.* Wordsworth-
White.

[3] I quote Beda 60 from Tischendorf II, p. 107 ; *corrupte legitur bariesu,
cum barieu, id est maleficus sive in malo legi debeat, credo quia nomen Iesu
iisdem litteris sed nota superposita scribatur.   Non enim convenit hominem
flagitiosum et magum filium Iesu, id est salvatoris, appellari, quem e contrario
Paulus filium diaboli nuncupat.*

[4] Edited by Delehaye (see below, p. 26), p. 495, 27.

[5] *Op. cit. Barsos* occurs also as the name of a Bishop of Edessa.

of the name of a criminal whom we know from the current text solely by the name *Barabbas*, a murderer whom Pilate set with Jesus before the people for them to choose. Here it has long been known that the minuscules 1*, 118, 209*, 241**, 299**, [1] together with the Syriac Evangeliarium of Jerusalem and the Armenian version have the name as *Jesus Barabbas* either in both places or in one of them. Then in addition to this came, through recent discoveries, the evidence of the Greek uncial codex Θ of Koridethi [2] (*cf.* Figure 4) and of the Sinaitic Syriac.[3]

What is still more important concerning the antiquity of this tradition is the testimony of Origen,[4] that he found in ' very old ' manuscripts that Barabbas was also called *Jesus*, so that Pilate had to put the alternative thus : ' Whom of the two do you want me to release, Jesus *Barabbas* or Jesus who is called *Christ* ? '

' Very old ' Gospel manuscripts in the hand of a scholar of the third century must have been manuscripts of the second or first century. This notice by Origen then leads us right up to the primitive tradition.

We are thus placed in a position to see one passage of the Passion narrative in its original form. If there is anywhere a certain criterion for distinguishing between primary, secondary and tertiary readings, we have here a classic example of an original text being preserved under innumerable strata of corrupt forms from later times. It is altogether unthinkable that the addition *Jesus* should have been subsequently made to a text which only had *Barabbas*. It is rather more than probable that the

---

[1] Kirsopp Lake has here ascertained the marks of a connected group, *cf.* Nestle—von Dobschuetz, *Einführung in das griech. N.T.*⁴, Goettingen, 1923, p. 52.

[2] G. Beermann and C. R. Gregory, *Die Koridethi-Evangelien* Θ 038, Leipzig, 1913, p. 134. Our Figure 4 reproduces Plate III of this publication. The Codex (as others) writes the name Βαρραββαν.

[3] *Cf.* Adalbert Merx, *Die vier kanonischen Evangelien nach ihrem ältesten bekannten Text* II. 1, Berlin, 1902, pp. 400 f. Merx also names other Syriac evidences.

[4] In the scholia, Gallandi, p. 81, *cf.* Th. Zahn, *Das Evangelium des Matthaeus ausgelegt* ², Leipzig, 1905, p. 702, who traces the scholion back to Origen himself ; so also Erich Klostermann in Lietzmann's *Handbuch zum N.T.* 4², Tuebingen, 1927, p. 220.

imprisoned murderer really had the common personal name
Jesus, and Pilate made use of this coincidence of names to
make his question more forcible : Which Jesus do you
want ? Jesus *Barabbas* or Jesus *Christ* ?

This text, just because it was later felt to be an unbearable scandal and was altered, mocks every hypothesis
of the unhistoricity of Jesus of Nazareth. This original
text, this ' Ur-Text ' with its naïve pre-cult unaffectedness,
is a piece of primitive rock on which the historian can as
confidently build as on any other tradition anywhere in
the history of the world. From the gloomy subordinate
figure of Jesus Barabbas a sufficient ray of light falls on
the historical reality of Jesus Christ and his martyrdom.
The fact that early Christendom afterwards was horrified
at this original text and nearly destroyed it is a safe
argument that its existence is not due to Christian in-
vention but that it is a ' survival,' a ' relic ' of the facts.
This piece of original text should be confidently restored
to its place in modern revisions of the Bible—even though
the simple Bible reader with his pious aversion from the
text may still feel difficulties.

How old this aversion is we can also determine in this
case. Origen,[1] although he had found the original text in
very old manuscripts, emphasises that the name *Barabbas* was
not found with *Jesus* in many manuscripts and ' perhaps
rightly, so that the name *Jesus* be not associated with one
of the unrighteous.' With this ' perhaps ' the great textual
scholar soothed his conscience : he left a small opening for
the real original text ; but the necessity of protecting the
majesty of the name *Jesus* was already too strong for him.

---

[1] In the commentary on Matthe wser. lat. 121 : ' *in multis exem-
plaribus non continetur quod Barabbas etiam Iesus dicebatur, et forsitan
recte, ut ne nomen Iesu conveniat alicui iniquorum. In tanta enim multi-
tudine scripturarum neminem scimus Iesum peccatorem, sicut in aliis
nominibus invenimus iustorum, ut eiusdem nominis inveniantur esse etiam
iniqui* ' . . . ' *non autem conveniebat esse tale aliquid et in nomine Iesu. Et
puto quod in haeresibus tale aliquid superadditum est ut habeant aliqua
convenientia dicere fabulis suis de similitudine nominis Iesu et Barabbae.
Existimo enim in istis verum aliquod mysterium demonstrari.*'

X

While in every one of the passages discussed above
more or less distinct traces of interferences in the original
text have been left in the textual tradition, in two passages
complete purging of the text was attained, without leaving,
at least until recently, the minutest marks of the original
in the critical apparatus.

6. One passage is Mark xv. 7 : ἦν δὲ ὁ λεγόμενος
Βαραββᾶς μετὰ τῶν στασιαστῶν δεδεμένος. Everywhere,
in the Greek original and in the versions, that was the text
unanimously transmitted. But whoever is familiar with
the usages of the language knows that the frequently
occurring form ὁ λεγόμενος, etc., is used everywhere else
in the New Testament in connection with a thing or person
mentioned in the text [1] and is especially frequent in the
cases of double names.[2] Therefore to him this awkward
ἦν δὲ ὁ λεγόμενος Βαραββᾶς will appear at once to be a
mutilation : he will miss the other name or at least
the indication of a person before ὁ λεγόμενος. Therefore
Erich Klostermann [3] was quite correct when he asked
in this connection whether ἦν δὲ ‹Ἰησοῦς› ὁ λεγόμενος
Βαραββᾶς was not the earliest form of the text. He could
have confidently answered in the affirmative ; the usages
of the language and linguistic feeling make it highly
probable. But in addition it happens that the Barabbas
passage in Matthew depends on Mark. If therefore the
original text of Matthew had *Jesus Barabbas* then this
double name was used also in Mark.

7. The other passage is Philemon 23 and 24. At the
end of this letter, which was contemporaneous with the
letter to the Colossians and was addressed to Colossae, Paul

---

[1] Besides in the N.T. ὁ λεγόμενος, etc., always comes after the designation of the person or thing, with the exception of Luke xxii. 47, where the
designation of the person follows ; *cf.* also John xix. 17. In the former
passage perhaps ὁ λεγόμενος refers back to xxii. 3.

[2] Matt. i. 16 ; iv. 18 ; x. 2 ; xxvii. 16 ; xxvii. 17 ; xxvii. 22 ; John iv.
25 ; xi. 16 ; xx. 24 ; xxi. 2 ; Col. iv. 11. Likewise the use of ὁ καλούμενος
with double name is always the same : Luke vi. 15 ; viii. 2 ; xx. 3 ;
Acts i. 23 ; xiii. 1 ; xv. 22 ; xv. 37.

[3] *Loc. cit.*

conveys the greetings of his fellow-workers who were in the vicinity. In the letter to the Colossians there are six men, in the letter to Philemon, according to the unanimous evidence of the text, there are only five. This difference appears very striking, especially when one is aware of the importance that was laid in the ancient East (as also to-day) on the correct conveyance of greetings : the ceremoniousness of the greetings in the papyri letters and also the long Pauline greetings are good instances of this.

When the two lists are compared it is found that in the letter to Philemon only Jesus Justus is omitted of the men :

Philemon 23 and 24 :	Colossians iv. 10–14 :
ασπαζεται σε Επαφρας ο	ασπαζεται υμας Αρισταρχος
συναιχμαλωτος μου εν	ο συναιχμαλωτος μου και
Χριστω Ιησου Μαρκος	Μαρκος . . . και Ιησους
Αρισταρχος Δημας Λουκας	ο λεγομενος Ιουστος . . .
οι συνεργοι μου.	Επαρρας . . . Λουκας ο
	ιατρος . . . και Δημας.

A real reason for the omission of Jesus Justus does not make itself apparent ; negligence on the part of the Apostle is also very improbable, in particular since Timothy collaborated with him in composing the letter.[1] Therefore the conjecture is strongly suggested that the name *Jesus* originally stood in the text, but for some reason or other it was removed at a later time.

It is to the great credit of Theodor Zahn that, already a generation ago, he put forward this conjecture and argued convincingly for it solely from the irrefutable logic of the situation in which the letter was written.[2] And it says much for the compelling force of the conjecture of Jesus Justus being mentioned also in the original letter to Philemon, that ten years later, independently of Zahn, whom he evidently did not know, Ernst Amling likewise proved it.[3]

The conjecture is pressed on us now with new force when we include the Philemon passage in the significant

---

[1] Philemon i.
[2] *Einleitung in das N.T.*, Leipzig, 1897, p. 319. So also in the later editions.
[3] *Zeitschrift für die neutestamentliche Wissenschaft*, 10 (1909), pp. 261 f.

series of the *Jesus*-passages of the New Testament. What Zahn and Amling held to be probable on internal [1] and palaeographical [2] grounds without admitting any additional motive now finds a stronger support when we consider it in connection with the other *Jesus*-passages and their fortunes, because we now recognise the true motive for altering the text : as, in the letter to the Colossians, at least, the very last finger-marks of the hand that anxiously altered the text are recognised in the tradition,[3] so it may now be asserted here with greater confidence, although no external traces of the alteration are visible, that in the original copy of the letter to Philemon the name *Jesus* or *Jesus Justus* [4] stood before *Mark* (verse 24).

The alteration undertaken from cult-motive, as we have already ascertained in the other New Testament cases, was effected in a very simple manner : the Ἰησοῦ which originated through the omission of the sigma was connected with the preceding formula ἐν Χριστῷ.

From this formula comes yet again another not un-important support for our conjecture. It seems to have been the general custom of the Apostle when mentioning brothers, and especially fellow-workers, to add just ἐν Χριστῷ or ἐν κυρίῳ as a distinguishing formula.[5] Of course the textual tradition for this passage occasionally shows variant readings with the longer form ἐν Χριστῷ Ἰησοῦ ; but the evidence for it stands in the background. And elsewhere the short formula ἐν Χριστῷ is favoured by Paul, and particularly in Colossians (i. 2 ; i. 28) and in Philemon (8 and 20) it is the predominant form.[6] This suggests that also in Philemon 23 the short formula ἐν Χριστῷ would be the most probable.

---

[1] The parallelism of the letter to the Colossians.

[2] At the end of verse 23 after ἐν Χριστῷ Ἰησοῦ an original Ἰησοῦς could easily disappear through haplography.

[3] *Cf.* above, pp. 17 f.

[4] Since in the short letter to Philemon the names in the greetings are all given quite briefly without the characteristics of the letter to the Colossians, the simple form *Jesus* is much more probable.

[5] *Cf.* my treatise *Die neutestamentliche Formel ' in Christo Jesu,'* Marburg, 1892, pp. 118 ff., where, however, the passage Philemon 23 is cited, of course, in the longer form.

[6] Naturally the longer form is occasionally attested even here.

And in fact, the hitherto general and uniform attestation of the longer form ἐν Χριστῷ Ἰησοῦ in this passage has recently received a set-back through the discovery of new material, and again through Souter's publication of the commentary of Pelagius [1]; Souter gives the text of Pelagius in the short form : *salutat te Epafras concaptivus meus in Christo.*   Only A H G V Cas (as in the Vulgate) have here the addition *Iesu.*

Consequently I have no doubt that the original greeting list of the letter to Philemon was as follows : ἀσπάζεταί σε Ἐπαφρᾶς ὁ συναιχμάλωτός μου ἐν Χριστῷ, Ἰησοῦς, Μάρκος, Ἀρίσταρχος, Δημᾶς, Λουκᾶς οἱ συνεργοί μου.

Whoever felt himself compelled to alter the text here had an easy task ; there was no need to do more than omit a sigma and a text came into existence which, entirely free from visible scars, held its ground undisputed for nearly two thousand years :—until a modern scholar (a man without any heretical stain) disturbed it with ingenious internal criticism.

That Erwin Nestle, who cautiously and with deep religious feeling continues the work of his father Eberhard Nestle, has adopted the conjecture of Theodor Zahn, at least as a conjecture, in the apparatus of the thirteenth edition of the Stuttgart Greek New Testament, 1927, is, it is to be hoped, only the first step towards the rehabilitation of good Jesus Justus in the text of Philemon, and that also above the line.

This apostolic worker, so highly praised by Paul,[2] who had the fortune or misfortune to be called by the same name as the Saviour, has been badly treated elsewhere. One could almost speak of a *damnatio memoriae* when hearing that the hagiographic tradition (which has willingly allowed its ivy to creep luxuriantly about almost every name in the New Testament) has preserved no tradition of Jesus Justus, and neither the Greek menologies nor the Latin martyrologies mention him.[3]   But this statement needs one qualification.   At least the *Synaxarium Ecclesiae*

[1] *Loc. cit.* p. 539.   [2] Col. iv. 11.
[3] Franz X. Poelzl, *Die Mitarbeiter des Weltapostels Paulus*, Regensburg, 1911, pp. 338 f.

Constantinopolitanae [1] mentions him, on June 21, 22 and 30, as well as on October 20 and 30 : in all cases in a fixed list of persons in which he always stands between Markos and Artemas.   But even in this tradition his name has been mutilated at least in one passage : on October 30 he is deprived of the name *Jesus*, and must be content with only the name *Justus*. [2]

But the faithful ' fellow-worker unto the Kingdom of God,' who was a ' comfort ' to the Apostle of the Gentiles (Col. iv. 2), comes forth again from the *silentium saeculorum* and imperceptibly takes his old place, even in the letter to Philemon, in the list of his companions which Paul himself has drawn up with a feeling of comradeship.

XI

The book here submitted is a collection of Christological studies by scholars from different countries and various Churches.   I hope no one will find that this essay on the name *Jesus* falls outside the sphere of the ' Christological.' This historical-philological study will rather be of help to Christological thought.   If the Christian reflection on Jesus Christ is not to degenerate into an extravagant, phantastic gnosis then it must be reflection on Him who was Jesus of Nazareth in history.

First of all, it seems to me to be at least a by-product of my study that it brings out anew the historicity of Jesus of Nazareth from apparently remote corners, in particular through the critical investigation of the Barabbas tradition.

But, as a whole, by following the lines of development from the personal name *Jesus* to the cult-name *Jesus*, we may have seen the path traversed by the early history of our religion.

The ingenious American with whose thesis we began believed in a retrograde movement from an alleged primary

---

[1] Edited by H. Delehaye (*Propylaeum ad Acta Sanctorum Novembris*), Bruxellis, 1902.

[2] Delehaye, p. 180, 38.

cult-name to a secondary and unhistorical personal name. The path of history leads from a historical personal name to a cult-name, from the Gospel of Jesus of Nazareth to the cult of Jesus Christ the Lord. This path is also the path for Christology and must remain the path of Christology.

THE JESUS OF HISTORY
BY GERHARD KITTEL

II

THE JESUS OF HISTORY

I

THE SCANDAL OF PARTICULARITY

A HALO of reverence and devotion encircles the historical career and person of Jesus of Nazareth. When a mother tells her children the stories about the Saviour, she speaks to them of that which occurred in past history; when the Christian congregation repeats on Good Friday the clause in the Creed 'Suffered under Pontius Pilate' and sings the hymn 'When I survey the wondrous Cross,' [1] it takes part in a liturgical action so directed as to emphasize that which once took place as an event. Nor are modern ethical and social reformers who endeavour to shape human life externally in accordance with the teaching of Jesus, or those modern authors who are moved inwardly by what they feel to be tragic or heroic in Him, able to escape wholly from that historical happening which took place in a particular locality within the Roman Empire during the years which immediately preceded and which immediately followed the thirtieth year of the first century A.D.

When once this is said, the scandal emerges. The scandal is the problem of history. Can a particular historical happening be peculiar? Can it be significant *sub specie aeternitatis*? And above all, can this particular occurrence be either peculiar or significant?

What is a historical happening? Somewhere in the course of centuries something has once occurred. Yes, but that which we name humanity and human history is

---

[1] In the German text the author refers to the *Choral* 'O Lamm Gottes, unschuldig,' and in particular to the line 'All Sünd' hast du getragen.'

just a formless mass of innumerable lives which have run their course, and it resembles a great heap of sand. Can we dare to select one grain of sand and claim for it uniqueness and particularity? And yet that is precisely what we in fact do. In itself this constitutes a problem. But it becomes more than a problem when the nature of that event which is the Jesus of History is made evident. It is impossible to maintain that His life and death are obviously of universal significance. Neither the land in which He lived nor the people among whom He dwelt was marked as the centre of a mighty empire or of a brilliant civilisation. The famous Roman historians regarded Judaea as one of the most obscure corners of the Empire, and Galilee was even more obscure. And if a Jew suffered a martyr's death by crucifixion in Jerusalem, well, the Romans erected many crosses, and both then and always there have been many martyrs, the majority of whom were, in their deaths, humanly speaking, far more heroic, far more noble, than He who died with the miserable cry upon His lips, *My God, my God, why hast thou forsaken me?* In order to escape this difficulty His teaching rather than His death has been selected as constituting what is unique, peculiar and eternal. But the more the history of religion and of systematic spiritual thought be candidly and exactly investigated, the less is it possible to award even this praise with confidence. The teaching of Jesus is embedded in a passionate eschatology; and, for this reason, though it contains much that is otherwise valuable, from the point of view of the history of human perception, the ethic of the Stoic philosophers was far more complete and rounded off, the wisdom of Plato was far more perfect, the achievements of the great lawgivers, Hammurabi, Moses, and Solon effected far more for the public good, and the insight of Buddha was far more penetrating. Even if that which seems to be the noblest element in His teaching be detached—the command that men should love their enemies— is it so certain that human life has not been sentimentalised rather than enriched by it? And if it be sound moral teaching, did not the Chinese thinker 500 years before demand that men should 'Repay enmity with love'?

May it not then be merely fortuitous that this particular and in itself indifferent happening has been separated from thousands and thousands of other similar and repeated occurrences and exalted upon a pillar of peculiarity ? Thus a new illustration is provided of that process, so familiar to the historian, by which that which is insignificant and hardly worthy of mention becomes fraught with mighty results.

If the life and death of Jesus be considered merely as an event in history, the historian is able to contribute little more than this resigned and trivial judgment. And yet in the New Testament the claim is confidently uttered that this happening, with all its contingency and insignificance, is the ground of Salvation, and in very truth the Revelation of God to men. It is not *one* of the many revelations of God by which men of peculiar spiritual insight believe themselves enabled to divine the action of Providence in the general spiritual movements of mankind, or in the details of the progress of history, or in the insignificance of their own lives. It is declared to be *The Revelation of God*, and its characteristic mark is that there is none like it. It is that *Revelation of God* of which it is said, *And in none other is there salvation. Neither is there any other name under heaven, that is given among men, wherein we must be saved.* Could anything be more ridiculous, more nearly verging on madness, than the claim which is made in an obscure place in the midst of all this contingency—*No one cometh unto the Father, but by me* ? If this absurdity be challenged, the New Testament can only answer, ' Yes, humanly spoken and according to the *wisdom of this world* (I Cor. i. 20) it is completely scandalous, completely foolish ; aye, it is complete madness.' This is, and has been, and always must remain the normal historical judgment of human understanding. We have no right to tone down this judgment any more than the New Testament does.

And yet, the New Testament adds something to all this. *The foolishness of God is wiser than men* (I Cor. i. 25). Here is declared the singularity of the New Testament message ; and this is the miracle of which it speaks from the first page to the last. The New Testament tells of

D

nothing that is obviously comprehensible. It tells of a
' miracle ' in the strict and proper sense of the word. *The
Word became flesh*, that is to say, what is eternal became
historical, accidental, and miserably insignificant, and this
poor and trivial contingency contains that particularity
which only One can claim—God Himself.

II

THE NEW TESTAMENT AND THE PROBLEM OF THE JESUS OF HISTORY

The phrase ' The Jesus of History ' expresses a modern
theological conception. Consequently it is apt to be set
aside as unnecessary theologising by those whose piety is
rooted in the New Testament. They set it aside all the
more readily because they know, or, moved by a delicate
instinct, they suspect that this phrase carries with it a
number of problems which raise not only questions of
merely historical interest, but also questions which may
affect the very essence of faith. It requires, however, but
little reflection to show that, though the phrase is provocative in its modern usage, it is also a fair expression of
that which is not at all modern. Christology and the
problem of the historical Jesus have belonged together ever
since there have been Christians and ever since there has
been a Christology. The New Testament takes account of
no Christology which is not related primarily to the
Historical Jesus. That is at once obvious when it is
recognised that the whole New Testament Christology rests
upon the historical fact of Jesus of Nazareth. Neither Paul,
nor John, nor the author of the Epistle to the Hebrews uses
the term ' the Christ ' to express a general doctrine. It
never occurs to them to use the term except in relation to
that which occurred under Pontius Pilate *without the gate*
(Heb. xiii. 12), and at a particular point in the development
of history.

This general statement does not, of course, touch the
heart of the ' Problem of the Jesus of History,' but it is
capable of even greater precision. From the very be-

ginning Primitive Christianity was concerned to substantiate
not merely the general picture of Jesus, but also its particular features. The narrative of the choice of the twelfth
apostle (Acts i.) is instructive in this connection. Two
men were selected as especially suitable, and between these
two the lot—that is, God Himself—was to decide. The
choice of these two was made, strangely enough, not because
either of them possessed especial qualifications of general
efficiency or of peculiar spiritual gifts. The only qualification which was considered adequate was that they had
been continuous eye-witnesses during the whole period
*that the Lord Jesus went in and went out among us, beginning
from the baptism of John, unto the day that he was received
up from us* (Acts i. 21, 22). This selection marks the
nature of the apostolic leadership of the Christian community. An apostle was a leader because, and in so far
as, he was able to answer questions concerning the Jesus
of History.

One of the strongest and most impressive proofs of the
urgency and vital importance of the question concerning
the Jesus of History among the early Christians is the
existence and preservation of the Gospels. The prologue
to the Third Gospel makes clear the origin of these
traditions. They are the traditions of men who *from the
beginning were eye-witnesses*. It was considered important
to preserve and treasure these traditions, *to trace the course
of all things accurately from the first* and *to write them down
in order*, because in this historical tradition lay the certainty
of faith and the ground of instruction. The process of
testing can be detected in the Palestinian and in the
Hellenistic communities, in the Jewish-Christian as well as
in the Pauline churches. Each of the Gospels betrays the
fact that the tradition was fixed where Aramaic was the
spoken language—that is, in Palestinian-Jewish-Christian
circles. But it is also clear, especially from the Gospel of
Luke, the companion of Paul, that the same interest
dominated the Christian world which lay outside Palestine.
The burning and vital interest in the History of Jesus is
thereby established. How otherwise can it be explained
that Primitive Christianity was anxious to repeat particular

sayings of Jesus and to record particular incidents in His life, and even to ask whether their authority was that of an eye-witness, thus raising the question of authenticity? *The certainty of those things, wherein thou hast been instructed* (Luke i. 4) does not mean that they were busied with a particular Christological sequence of ideas or with a system of dogma, or with a mythological speculation: they required simply an answer to the questions, What had Jesus of Nazareth said? What had He done? What was His history?

Nor was it a matter of chance that the Primitive Christians felt themselves bound to the History of Jesus and linked to a particular historical occurrence. In this relationship they expressed the essence of Christian piety and marked its contrast with the world outside them. Of this distinction Paul provides an admirable illustration. Paul belonged to two worlds. He belonged to the world of Palestinian Judaism with its expectation of the Messiah; he belonged also to the world of Oriental-Hellenistic syncretism. As a pious Jew he possessed a Messianic dogmatism; but the whole was fulfilled in that which was entirely removed from timeless Messianic dogmatic generalities: it was concentrated in a statement about a person who had been born *of the seed of David according to the flesh* (Rom. i. 3). It can be proved that Paul was familiar with the speculation concerning the 'Heavenly Man' (Rom. v., 1 Cor. xv. 21 f., and perhaps also Phil. ii. 7)—a speculation which was widespread throughout the East and was known also to the authors of the Jewish Apocalyptic Literature. But when he alludes to this speculation, his whole attention is fixed upon the concrete historical fact of the Death and Resurrection of the one 'Man'—Jesus. Paul must also have been aware of the myths of dying and rising deities, and with that form of piety in which salvation was sought in mystical communion with the fate of one of these divinities. Nor can it be doubted that many of those who composed the Christian communities had been devotees of some such piety, or that Paul, who knew well this state of mind, made use consciously or unconsciously in his letters of expressions moulded by that piety. But the phrase *crucified with him* makes it perfectly clear to the reader of Rom. vi. 2 ff. that behind these allusions there is set that which completely transforms them. For Paul mystical communion depends upon no mythical speculation or aesthetic divorced from history: it depends upon the history of Him who was crucified under Pontius Pilate, and it has no other ground. This is the paradox of Pauline mysticism, and it may be questioned whether the word ' mysticism ' ought to be used in this connection.

Nowhere does Paul state so precisely where the emphasis in his teaching lay as in the words, *of whom the greater part remain until now* (1 Cor. xv. 6). In this passage he roundly states that the fact of the Resurrection can be authenticated simply by going and asking the eye-witnesses. He might have referred to the same authorities for corroboration when he declared the command to the married to be not his command, but the Lord's (1 Cor. vii. 10), or when he spoke of the Cross or of the Death of Jesus. But in these cases he did not require corroborative testimony, simply because neither the authenticity of the command nor the fact of the death of Jesus upon the Cross was open to doubt. Some fifty years later when Docetism began to cast doubt upon the reality of the Death of the God-Man, John at once emphatically declares that its reality was undeniably attested by an eye-witness (John xix. 35). This attestation is exactly parallel to the Pauline, *of whom the greater part remain until now.*

At the end of the Apostolic Age there burst forth again in the Johannine writings the passionate insistence upon the necessity of maintaining the link with the Jesus of History. With a harshness which cannot be surpassed the mark of those who possess the Spirit of God is declared to be their confession that Jesus Christ is come in the flesh (1 John iv. 2 f.). This involves the reference of the Christology simply to the Historical Jesus. Its denial is apostasy from God and possession by the spirit of anti-christ. That *The Word became flesh* is the ground theme of the Johannine writings. The Eternal became *Historia* ; and this *Historia* is—Jesus of Nazareth.

The myths and speculations and philosophies of the period familiarised men with Saviours and with the idea of Salvation. But none of those who trusted in them paid the slightest attention to historical realism, whether they were devoted to a god like Osiris, or to a demi-god like Hercules, or to a series of Gnostic messengers from heaven. These Saviours were removed from the categories of time. It need not be seriously discussed whether the events to which the myths referred had or had not taken place in some remote past. This was a matter of complete indifference. The perfect gift of salvation was secured by partaking in liturgical rites regarded as symbols of the timeless verity of the myth. With the Johannine sentence (every word of which is significant in spite of its familiarity), *The Word was made flesh, and dwelt among us, and we beheld His glory* (John i. 14), the reader is translated into a wholly different world. The recognition that the Christ who now meets the believer is identical with the Historical Jesus involves the Sonship of God, and Salvation is to encounter Him whom the eye-witnesses saw as the Jesus of History.

III

THE APPLICATION OF METHODS OF HISTORICAL INVESTIGATION

Primitive Christian piety was thus linked indissolubly with the History of Jesus. And this link was no trivial or incidental element in the piety. It constituted its very essence, since the piety was rooted in the History. This being so, no one who regards primitive Christian faith as in any sense normative can contemplate the severance of the link by which Christian piety is related to the History as involving anything less than the destruction of that piety. In other words, there is no avoiding the question concerning the Jesus of History. Judged by the standard of the New Testament, we not only have the right, but the duty of conducting strict historical research according to the best methods available for us to use. Now historical investigation must be a critical investigation. It is impossible to proceed without being prepared to examine whether a tradition is true or false, credible or incredible. Tradition cannot be accepted simply because it is tradition.

The peculiar conclusion which emerges from handling the New Testament material is that in the course of its investigation it becomes clear that it is itself the product of a criticism of tradition. The New Testament is the product of criticism according to the proper meaning of the word. ἡ κριτικὴ τέχνη means skill in judgment and in decision. It was precisely with the application of this critical skill that the Primitive Christians were concerned. An apostle was not marked as an apostle because he was good or pious, that was taken for granted. He was marked as an apostle because his person provided a standard of judgment and a means by which the community could exercise its critical judgment. An Evangelist did not compose his gospel simply by putting together anything that was told him about Jesus without any plan and without the exercise of any critical judgment. He submitted the material to the test of authenticity. Whether he did this adequately or inadequately according to our standards is another matter. Paul did not direct the attention of his converts to his visions or to his own inner experiences ; even his own conversion, which was to him more than an experience, he places last in his list of testimonies to the Resurrection (1 Cor. xv. 8). Nor did he consider the matter established because *someone* had recounted it, or because it was widely accepted in the Church. He enumerates witnesses whom he has selected and judged critically.

The Problem concerning the Jesus of History is a real problem. It is not a matter which may not be touched. The question must be put seriously. In the Apostolic Age it occurred to no one to regard such a question as profane. When once the right to proceed with the investigation is granted, it is obvious that each generation must apply its own methods to its solution. The attempts of the Primitive Christians were assuredly undertaken with complete sincerity. They were far too deeply convinced that the action of God was visible in a particular history not to have undertaken its investigation to the best of their ability. But, since they belonged to a wholly different age, their critical methods were not the same as ours. During the eighteenth and nineteenth centuries a method of historical investigation was evolved far more complicated and involving far greater precision of observation than any which had preceded it. This new method cannot now be neglected without sinning against the commandments of sincerity.

The early Christian writers, with the healthy instincts of simple men, were not aware of the historical problem as a problem. They were concerned solely with the reality of that upon which their faith was based. This does not mean that their method of procedure was bad or useless ; for, after all, the insistence upon eye-witnesses, which was the only test they were aware of, must remain for every historical investigation one of the prime means of ascertaining what did or did not take place. The inadequacy of their procedure does, however, mean that the sifting of the tradition by the early Christians was insufficient to produce a final result, and cannot absolve us from formulating historical questions afresh. If the Primitive Christians had possessed our refined and improved methods of historical investigation, they would no doubt have employed them. If therefore we apply our *criteria* as earnestly and with the same severity as they did theirs, we do but follow in their footsteps. We ought then to regard their primitive historical work as a valuable *prolegomenon* to ours. Their work must be re-examined and retested. But at the same time we should clearly recognise the peculiar importance of their work as the source of our knowledge, and as a valuable source because they stood so close to the events and to the eye-witnesses of those events. When Paul appeals to the brethren of whom *the greater part remain until now*, and when Luke appeals to the *autoptai*, we are faced by attestations of the most serious nature which cannot be lightly disregarded by those engaged upon historical research in the twentieth century. And yet, even so, we cannot avoid the necessity of testing each fragment of the tradition in order to discover whether the confidence which the Primitive Christians placed in the tradition was justified or not according to our standards of historical evidence. For it must be borne in mind that, when once an approach by means of historical investigation be accepted, its acceptance involves the recognition that it is undertaken by men endowed with no more than human capacity, and consequently error in the application of criticism is unavoidable. There are no ' final ' critical results. Had the Primitive Christians not reckoned seriously with the possibility of error, they would not have taken such care to guard themselves against it. It should also be noted that it is quite clear from the New Testament that the early Christians were not satisfied with the statement that *someone* had said this or that, or that *someone* claimed to know this or that. They were concerned only to know what had actually occurred. *Their whole religious possession was grounded upon what God had wrought in the presence of eye-witnesses.* If the real historical occurrence was inaccessible to them, if it was obscured, blurred, or falsified, then everything they supposed that they possessed was in fact illusion. For that piety therefore which is directed by the piety of the New Testament, the cry ' It is written ' pales into insignificance before the terrible question, ' Was it real ? What was that History which claims to be the Revelation of God ? ' Consequently, the question concerning the Jesus of History remains vital and unavoidable for each generation.

IV

THE UNCERTAINTY OF HISTORICAL RECONSTRUCTION

The interest required by the Christian Religion in questions concerning the Jesus of History does not belong to the periphery of its activity. The historical interest belongs to the essence of the Christian Religion. Since these questions are historical questions, they are subject to the laws of historical investigation for their elucidation.

These conclusions involve one of the greatest problems which can be presented to those endeavouring to live the Christian life. Christianity is thereby invested with all the uncertainty and relativity which attaches to all historical knowledge. Christianity is bound to that which is open to

doubt. To say this about a religion which composes its
' Song of songs ' upon the themes ' We are at peace with
God ' and ' I am persuaded ' is surely an intolerable
paradox, when it is recognised that the Peace and the
Persuasion exist only because the historical fact of Jesus
is regarded as something given. This fact of history is the
ground and pledge of all Christian certainty. And yet this
same fact, precisely because it is a fact of history, is enclosed
in all the doubt and uncertainty which is inseparable from
history. At this point it is possible perhaps for us to
appreciate most fully the truth of the words *He took upon
him the form of a servant.* The Revelation of God was not
presented to men as an unchangeable and unquestionable
message, as though it were a book fallen from heaven. It
was a happening which took place at a particular point in
human history. It is particular and incidental, blown
about by the wind, a small fragment of the past : *The
Word became flesh.*

The situation in which we find ourselves is then in no
sense simple. In the first place, everything lies in suspense ;
there is no absolutely fixed point ; everything is open to
discussion and nothing can be abstracted from this discussion. In our particular field of historical investigation
there is, for example, no single *Logion* of Jesus, no single
recorded action of His, which is not open to doubt. There
are, of course, degrees of historical certainty and probability, and it is the aim of historical research to record
these degrees ; but even so, not even the modern historian
is able to extinguish uncertainty. It may be questioned
whether Jesus ever lived ; and, however improbable and
unbalanced such scepticism may be, its existence was and
is perfectly logical, precisely because the naked fact of His
existence, being a fact of history, is for that reason an object
of critical investigation. And such investigation has to
judge between credibility and incredibility. Even the
most conservative theologian, in so far as he recognises
historical problems at all, is unable to state *a priori* that
this or that passage is removed from critical questioning.
Each fragment of the life of Jesus is open to critical attack,
because the story of His life as it actually occurred belongs

within the succession of historical events. Even among
the early Christians it would have been quite possible for
an eye-witness to arrive and declare with reference to some
generally accepted and supposedly fundamental *Logion* or
action of Jesus : ' You are mistaken and wrong. He did
not speak thus, at least not as you have put it. His action
was not at all as you have described it.' The congregation would no doubt have tested this criticism. But if the
eye-witness could have substantiated it neither in the
Palestinian community, nor in Pauline circles, would there
have been any hesitation in deleting the *Logion* or the action
from the tradition ? They would have been bound to yield
to historical criticism, if it were proved reasonable.

Is then anything certain ? Can any positive statement
be made ? Or, does criticism mean simply negation ?
It must often appear as though criticism were purely
negative, since it has often seemed to have produced only
negative results, and has often shown marks of the most
trivial dilettantism. There is a critical method of procedure, which operates according to a supposedly historical
method, but which is in fact completely unhistorical.
Those who employ it imagine that the original history can
be discovered by accepting a radical scepticism. All but
a small fragment of the tradition is thus discarded, and
what remains is simply summarised. They then claim
that this method of procedure represents the pinnacle of
historical investigation. They do not perceive that the
resultant historical reconstruction is just a caricature of
history, and that, whatever may be the truth, this cannot be.

We are bound to recognise that a number of elements
in the tradition, which appear open to considerable doubt,
do in fact belong to the true historical picture. A matter
is not unhistorical because it is open to doubt. Nor should
everything that may be unhistorical be simply deleted
from the historical picture. If one thing may be regarded
as certain, it is that the real historical happening was
infinitely richer, infinitely more comprehensive, than that
which survives when all critically doubtful passages are
removed. If the competent historian is very seldom able
to pronounce a *Logion* or an action ' certainly ' genuine, it

is also true that he is very seldom able to pronounce it
' certainly ' spurious. Isolated features do not bear the
marks of credibility in themselves. They bear the marks
of credibility as parts of a whole picture. This generalisation is capable of illustration. Every ' Son of man '
passage, if taken in isolation, resembles a leaf blown hither
and thither by the wind, and its authenticity is exceedingly
questionable. But if all the ' Son of man ' passages be put
together, they betray a common peculiarity which causes
their deletion to raise an infinitely more serious historical
problem than their retention. Or again, each miracle
narrative in the Gospels, if treated in isolation, must be
pronounced incredible, and every historian would judge it
to belong in all probability to the realm of legend. But
if it be placed within the context of the whole evangelical
record, the careful critic must own that, whatever interpretation may ultimately be assigned to these displayed
powers, it is exceedingly difficult to detach certain actions
of Jesus from the historical picture simply because they
lie outside the horizon of ordinary human experience and
because they were regarded by contemporaries as
' miraculous.' Or again, it would seem most natural to
treat the isolated *Logia* in which Jesus foretold His death
as *vaticinia ex eventu*. But if these *Logia* be taken together
and placed upon the background of the Deutero-Isaiah
' Servant ' passages, the whole matter looks different, and
it becomes in the highest degree probable that these *Logia*
belong to the most characteristic features of the true picture
of Jesus.

Thus it is possible for the historian who exercises his
critical powers with care to reconstruct a picture which is
composed of many particular features, but which when
regarded as a whole bears all the marks of probability.
And yet, precisely because the picture remains incomplete,
it is impossible to draw the outline so clearly that what is
historical can be sharply distinguished from what is unhistorical. It is not as though, having delineated the
picture of the Jesus of History, we could stand back and
say, ' There He is, precisely as He was.'

Can faith then be adequately grounded upon a historical

reconstruction produced in this manner ? It is easy to understand the revolt which discards all this historical uncertainty, since, though it may be interesting to the investigator, to the pious mind it is useless and hopeless ; and it must appear as a liberation of thought to escape to the purer and more serene sphere which lies beyond all history. The writer, who most passionately defended the thesis that Jesus never lived was, as is well known, moved primarily by philosophical considerations.[1] He believed he could prepare the way for the emergence of genuine Christianity only by detaching it from its slavery to history. The suggestion may perhaps be hazarded that the exaggerated historical scepticism which appears in some theological treatises upon New Testament subjects also has its ground ultimately in the longing to escape from history. To formulate this in a provocative form, it might be stated that, whereas previously modern Theology was concerned only with the Historical Jesus, and was frankly puzzled by ' Christ ' and ' The Word,' now ' The Word ' presents no difficulties, and it is the Jesus of History who is treated as of little importance. Many who once engaged in the search for the Historical Jesus have returned from the search convinced that it is fruitless, because, when they thought they had grasped something firm, it slipped through their fingers ; and so they surrendered the investigation of the past to the experience of the present. Having drunk the last drop from the cup of history and found that it left only a nasty taste of relativity, they will have no more of this beverage and will seek purer draughts from the timeless truths of aesthetics and liturgical worship, in myths and symbols, where they are disturbed by no history. Such a flight is, however, forbidden the man who knows himself bound to the New Testament. In any case there must be no illusion.

[1] Arthur Drews, *Die Christusmythe*, 1st edn., 1910. The author writes at the conclusion of the Preface : ' As a religious idea, as the symbolical personification of the essential union of God and man, Jesus Christ can be great and worthy of reverence, since upon belief in this idea the possibility of " Redemption " depends. If, however, Jesus be regarded as a mere historical person, as the Liberal theologians have presented him, he sinks to the level of other great historical personalities, and becomes from the religious point of view as irrelevant as they are— nay, he becomes even more trivial.'

The essence of Primitive Christianity is lost when the link with the Jesus of History is broken. The way marked out for us is no smooth road. The whole description which has been given of the burden of history remains without any easement. But God did not will it otherwise when He set His Revelation in this particular History, and I am unable to recognise this Revelation except by recognising this History. The road runs along the sharp edge of a knife. On the one side the dogma of Verbal Inspiration beckons to me. There, where the Word and the Letter have been given, is security. It remains only to read what has been written, and to believe it. But this road is forbidden, because it falsifies that to which the New Testament bears witness. To proceed along that road means that New Testament History is no more history ; it is no longer that which took place in the succession of earthly happenings ; no longer that which was attested and handed down by real men with all their human incapacity. This is to refuse to take seriously either that *He took upon him the form of a servant*, or that *The Word became flesh*. On the other side there beckons a flight into the sphere of meta-history. And this leads straight to Docetism. There remains therefore only the middle path. If its undertaking is harsh and fraught with renunciation, yet it holds the promise that he who is not ashamed or put out of humour by setting his hand to an earthly vessel—to him belongs the treasure.

V

THE JESUS OF HISTORY—THE CHRIST OF FAITH

And yet, the question still remains : What is the value of all this historical investigation ? Even if it be granted that an accurate and certain picture of the Jesus of History has been reconstructed by patient research : Is this the Salvation of which the New Testament speaks? It must be owned that in point of fact we have gained nothing but the miserable contingency of an event which took place in the distant past. The process of historical reconstruction may have given pleasure to the critic, and the result may display a touching and even elevating example of the tragedy of human life ; it may be that there has been extracted from the history a human teaching possessing permanent value ; but, to speak the cruel truth, it may be that we have only unearthed the story of a religious fanatic or of a poor dreaming idiot.

It may be so, and we have no right to be annoyed with those who judge the matter thus. We are not, however, at liberty to say that this is the message of the New Testament. In the New Testament we are presented with two points of view, with two ways of looking at the matter, as far removed from one another as winter is from summer. These two were both perfectly familiar to the writers of the New Testament. They tell in one breath of those who murmured and left Him, and of those who confessed : *Lord, to whom shall we go ? thou hast the words of eternal life.* They describe the majority of the contemporaries of Jesus as men who saw nothing but the Jesus of History. They claimed Him as the popular hero encouraged by the crowds who wished to make Him their king. They feared Him as a man who incited to dangerous revolution, whom it were therefore better to destroy before He accomplished irreparable damage. They despised Him as the dreamer who helped others but could not help Himself, or they beheld the tragic figure whose fate moved women and sensitive men to tears. All these are but different modes of expressing a single attitude to Him. There are, however, men in the New Testament whose judgment of the same history is completely different. In the same occurrence they beheld the Gift of God, the Ransom, the Atonement, the Justification, and the Forgiveness of our debt to God. They did not name the occurrence Salvation because they saw in it a symbol of the heroism or tragedy of human life. To them the Event itself was Salvation. It was not only that they were ' taught ' by the Event to trust in the goodness and mercy of God—the story of the Crucifixion leads rather to an opposite conclusion—they perceived the occurrence itself, the actual historical happening, embedded in contingency, strangeness, and uncertainty, and found it to be *in itself* the redeeming act of the mercy of God.

Once again we stand finally before the scandal and madness of the New Testament claim. Who can comprehend it ? The New Testament gives but one answer : *We believed*. When these words have been spoken, there arises from the dead and distant phenomenon of the History of Jesus an immediate present ; for instead of an incidental occasion there emerges in history the plan of God, and the event in the past has its goal in the present reality of my life.

And there is more to be said. Hitherto everything has been grounded upon an abstraction. The New Testament never intends to regard the story of the Jesus of History *only*. The Apostles did not tell the story to the community in order that they might be edified or moved, but that they might believe and be saved. Not one of the Evangelists wrote his narrative because he was interested in the accurate telling of a story. It has been rightly pointed out that the experience of Easter Day controls the whole narrative of the life of Jesus in the Gospels. No early Christian wrote a sentence about Jesus which did not proceed from the conviction that He had risen from the dead and was present in their midst. As far as the early Christians were concerned, if it were only a matter of knowing *Christ after the flesh*, He could be left to perish, in spite of His heroism and in spite of the tragedy of His life. If there were nothing more, they were *of all men most pitiable* (1 Cor. xv. 19). When this is understood, not only does the historical picture gain life and content, but it becomes real and true. The application of the historical method *only* has the effect of bringing into the foreground of the History of Jesus a number of strange, impossible, irrational fragments, and the more detached the historian is the more clearly he perceives the impossibility of harmonising these disparate elements. At best he can do no more than own that he is in the presence of a riddle to which he does not possess the key. Now we have reached the point where we can understand why this should be so. The mere historian is, as it were, endeavouring to describe a colour his eyes have not been constructed to perceive. He attempts the delineation of a history which is conceived of as only historical. But in fact there is no historical reality to correspond with it. Consequently, though he is able to compose the outward features, the picture inevitably lacks that life which is its essence. The mere historian can perceive this life no more than the crowds or the Pharisees of the Gospel story. He may attempt an interpretation of the Jesus of History ; but whether his interpretation moves in terms of heroism or tragedy or folly, it must always be wrong. Faith is the only possible key to the riddle of the Jesus of History. If the Jesus of History were in very truth the Christ of God, then His History with all its humiliation and contingency was the Revelation of God, and faith alone has the eye to perceive this. Only in the actual confession *My Lord and my God* can the claim of Christ be acknowledged. Only the believer can exercise the final judgment as to whether the identification *Jesus is the Christ* (1 John v. 1) is true or not, that is, whether the History of Jesus is veritably God's completed act of salvation. Only faith can interpret this identification and complete the work of historical criticism.

The Jesus of History is valueless and unintelligible unless He be experienced and confessed by faith as the living Christ. But, if we would be true to the New Testament, we must at once reverse this judgment. The Christ of faith has no existence, is mere noise and smoke, apart from the reality of the Jesus of History. These two are utterly inseparable in the New Testament. They cannot even be thought of apart. There is no word about Christ which is not referred to Him who suffered under Pontius Pilate, and which is not at the same time intended as the Gospel applicable to all men of every time and in every place. Anyone who attempts first to separate the two and then to describe only one of them has nothing in common with the New Testament.

E

JESUS AS TEACHER AND PROPHET
BY CHARLES HAROLD DODD

JESUS AS TEACHER AND PROPHET

I

IT is not the least remarkable feature of the Gospels as historical documents that although they all—even Mark— are written under the influence of a ' high ' Christology, yet they all—even John—represent Jesus as a teacher with His school of disciples. Both His adherents and others give to Him in the Gospel stories the courtesy title commonly given to Jewish teachers of the Law, ' Rabbi,' whether in its original Aramaic form transliterated ('Ραββεί, 'Ραββουνί) or translated into Greek as Διδάσκαλε, 'Επιστάτα. There is evidence in the Talmud that Jesus was known to Jewish tradition as a Rabbi of the Tannaic period. Thus Eliezer ben Hyrcanus, according to Aboda Zara (16b–17a), had talked with ' one of the disciples of Jesus of Nazareth ' (*talmidhe Jeshu ha-Notsri*) ; and as the Gospels give lists of his μαθηταί so a Baraita (Sanhedrin 43a) says, ' Jesus had five *Talmidhim* : Mattai, Naqai, Netser, Buni and Todah.'

It is fully in accordance with this representation of Jesus that His teaching is handed down largely in the same forms as contemporary Rabbinic teaching—in the form of aphorisms or in the form of short dialogues leading up to aphoristic sayings. (See Bultmann, *Geschichte der synoptischen Tradition*, 1921, pp. 20–23, 64, etc.) Sometimes indeed it happens that the same, or closely similar, sayings are attributed to Jesus in the Gospels and to other Rabbis in Jewish tradition. Thus the maxim that the Sabbath exists for the sake of man is attributed to Jesus in Mark ii. 27, and (in a very slightly different form) to Simeon ben Menasiah in Mechilta Ex. (109), and Jonathan ben Joseph in Joma (85b) ; the saying ' sufficient unto the day

is the evil thereof ' is cited in almost the same words (בשעתה
דיה לצדה) from Jacob ben Abina quoting Huna of Sep-
phoris ; ' knock and it shall be opened to you ' is applied
to the study of the Mishna by Banna'a ; and so forth.
The question of priority in such cases is not easily to be
answered,[1] and is in any case secondary. The point is
that a comparison of Jewish and Christian tradition makes
the teaching of Jesus and the teaching of the Rabbis appear
as varieties of a common type.

As a Rabbi, Jesus is represented in the Gospels as
disputing with other Rabbis upon points arising out of the
interpretation of the Torah or the unwritten tradition.
Thus we have debates, sometimes initiated by Jesus,
sometimes by others, on particular points of practice such
as the observance of the Sabbath, Fasting, ritual Cleansing,
Divorce, the Payment of Tribute ; on more general points
such as the relative importance of Commandments and the
validity of Tradition ; and on points of a more speculative
interest such as the Resurrection, the Life of the Age to
Come, and the Doctrine of the Messiah. Echoes of similar
debates among Rabbis are to be found in the Talmud.
The implication is that up to a point at least the disputants
found common ground from which to argue, and recognised
each other's methods. Matthew indeed represents Jesus
as instructing His disciples to regard the Pharisaic Scribes
as authoritative teachers of religion, and as affirming
without qualification the eternity of the Torah, small
(' light ') and great (' heavy ') commandments alike, in the
spirit and manner of Pharisaic orthodoxy.[2] There is,
however, reason to suspect that this Gospel has at some
stage been under the influence of a kind of Christian
' Rabbinism ' which has given it a colour more Jewish than
that of the earlier tradition. Nevertheless in the oldest
strata of the Gospels Jesus affirms that no part of the Torah
can pass while the present world order endures [3]—a state-

---

[1] The tacit assumption is commonly made by writers of a certain
tendency that in all such cases the Jewish form or attribution of the
saying is original, and that either the Gospel saying is not to be accepted
as ' authentic ' or that Jesus ' borrowed.' This assumption is as little
justified as the contrary assumption would be.

[2] Matt. xxiii. 2–3, v. 17–20.   [3] Matt. v. 18 = Lk. xvi. 17.

ment which if interpreted in any literal sense is hard to reconcile with His actual treatment of some parts of it, but which must surely represent a reverent attitude to the Law. More clear and significant is His expressed agreement with a questioning Rabbi that the two great commandments of the Law are those of love to God and Neighbour.[1] It is on all grounds probable that Luke is right in giving to the 'lawyer' the credit of formulating the twofold summary : if he was of the school of Hillel it would be perfectly harmonious with what we know of that Rabbi's teaching. In any case, whether Mark or Luke be followed, the enthusiastic agreement of Jesus and the unnamed Rabbi is important, and should be kept in mind in reading the severe strictures on Pharisaism, or some of its features, in other parts of the Gospel. In interpreting the second of the Two Commandments Jesus is recorded to have followed Hillel's *Golden Rule*, though with a characteristic modification.[2]

II

It is, however, evident that the issue of the disputes was to leave the Pharisaic Rabbis more conscious of the difference of Jesus from themselves than of what they had in common. It was not simply that within the field of legitimate discussion they found His teaching at variance with that of orthodoxy ; for within this field there was a large amount of tolerated difference of opinion at this period. It was that they discerned in Him an attitude in religious matters which was fundamentally inconsistent with their presuppositions. He was after all not a person with whom you could argue. The Talmud preserves the statement that Jesus of Nazareth 'practised sorcery and led the people astray' (Sanhedrin 43a). Similarly the Gospels (Mark and 'Q' here probably agreeing)[3] state that the Pharisees accused Him of acting under diabolic inspiration : 'he has Beelzebul, and by the prince of demons

[1] Mk. xii. 28–34 ; Lk. x. 25–28.
[2] On Hillel, the Two Commandments, and the Golden Rule, see Abrahams, *Studies in Pharisaism and the Gospels*, First Series, pp. 18–29.
[3] Mk. iii. 22 ; Matt. xii. 24 ; Lk. xi. 15.

he casts out demons.' Thus their quarrel with Him was
not simply on the score of unauthorised teaching on dis-
puted points, but represented a radical divergence of
religious principle. He explicitly renounced the 'tradition of the Elders,' and claimed to interpret the Torah
independently. His 'interpretations' sometimes amount
to reversals of express provisions (*e.g.* on divorce and
on oaths), and there is at least one saying which (except
on a forced and unnatural exegesis) amounts to a repudia-
tion of the written Law (Mk. vii. 15). Thus, although the
passage on the Law in Matt. v. 21–48 as it stands must be
regarded as a literary elaboration rather than a transcript
of His teaching, yet its antithesis, ' it was said to them of
old . . . but I say unto you . . . ' represents not unfairly
the extremely independent position taken by Jesus towards
Law and Tradition, whether in particular cases He approves
or disapproves their precepts. Thus the attitude He
adopted towards Law and Tradition was felt to be inconsistent with the position of a Rabbi, as a teacher of
Torah. ' He taught them like a sovereign, and not like
the Rabbis ' (Mk. i. 22 : ὡς ἐξουσίαν ἔχων perhaps כְּשַׁלִּט,
in any case not simply ' like one authorised to teach ').
The question of His authority, however, was raised even
more decisively by what He did than by what He taught.
His high-handed assumption of control over the Temple
courts was clearly an act that lay outside the rôle of a Rabbi.

III

There are many passages in the Gospels which indicate
that Jesus was regarded by the populace as a prophet, and
that He claimed to be accepted as such. At Nazareth He
is reported to have cited a proverb about the prophet who
is without honour in his own country (Mk. vi. 4 ; Lk. iv. 24).
According to Mk. vi. 15, viii. 28, He was widely held in
Galilee to be ' a prophet like one of the (Old Testament)
prophets.' The same idea appears in secondary passages
like Lk. vii. 16, xxiv. 19 ; Matt. xxi. 11, as well as in the
important saying Lk. xiii. 33, which is generally regarded
as from an early source. It is equally implied in the attitude

attributed to His critics in certain narratives. Thus when Jesus is mocked after His arrest (Mk. xiv. 65) He is called upon to ' prophesy ' with veiled face (? *cf.* Num. xxiv. 3). Similarly in Lk. vii. 39 His claim to be a prophet is held to be under suspicion because He does not show a prophetic insight into character. We may further adduce the universal postulate of the Synoptic Gospels and the early chapters of Acts, that Jesus was ' full of Holy Spirit,' or ' anointed with Holy Spirit ' ; for ' prophet ' and ' inspired person ' (אִישׁ הָרוּחַ) are ancient equivalents.[1] And from this point of view the hostile judgment of Him as ' demon-possessed ' carries a similar implication ; for if ' Holy Spirit ' makes a prophet, an ' unclean spirit ' makes a ' false prophet.'

We may therefore ask, What was there in the external or more obvious aspects of the ministry of Jesus which caused men to rank Him with the prophets ?

(i.) First, we must recall that note of sovereign authority in His teaching which led the populace, with sure instinct, to distinguish Him from the Rabbis with whom they were familiar, in spite of His superficial resemblance to them. Where they cited tradition, He spoke words which carried their own authority within them—' a new teaching, with authority ' (Mk. i. 27). His pronouncements had the same absoluteness which the Old Testament prophets indicated by their formula, ' Thus spoke Jahweh.' He does not, however, appear to have made common use of any such formula, though we probably have one example in Lk. xi. 49 : ' The Wisdom of God said . . .' Such a periphrasis for the divine Name is in the manner of the period, for the Talmud has similar expressions : ' The Righteousness of God saith . . .' ' the Holy Spirit saith . . .'[2] But the form of His sayings more commonly

---

[1] Hosea ix. 7, etc.

[2] See Strack-Billerbeck *ad loc.* It has been fashionable to treat the formula of Lk. x. 49 as indicating a quotation from a ' lost Wisdom book,' or alternatively as representing the identification of Jesus with Wisdom in the sense of Paul's Christology. But why may Jesus not on occasion have used the prophetic formula in a slightly ' Rabbinised ' paraphrase ? Or, indeed, may not the Wisdom-Christology itself have found a starting-point in sayings which He spoke ' in the name ' of the Wisdom of God ?

expresses a more than prophetic immediacy of authority :
' (Verily) I say unto you . . .'

(ii.) In a great part of the reported utterance of Jesus
there is a definitely poetical character which recalls that
of the prophetic oracles, and sets it apart from most
Rabbinic teaching as known to us from the Talmud. In
judging this poetical element the undefinable ' feeling ' for
the difference between poetry and prose necessarily plays
a part. But it is possible also to appeal to definite formal
tests. C. F. Burney (*The Poetry of our Lord*) showed by
elaborate analysis and comparison that the distinctive
types of rhythm and parallelism employed by the Hebrew
prophets reappear in large sections of the Gospels, and
must be regarded as characteristic of the original utterance
of Jesus. It is noteworthy that one such poetic passage
(Matt. xi. 25-27 ; Lk. x. 21-22), in which Burney recognises
a poem in three-beat measure, rhyming regularly in couplets
and making typical use of antithetic and other parallelism,
is noted by Luke (x. 21) as a ' pneumatic ' or inspired
utterance, and this may well reflect the impression made
by the public speech of Jesus on many occasions.

(iii.) There is a suggestion of other ' pneumatic ' traits
associated with prophecy, such as vision and audition. It
is true that such traces of the ' ecstatic ' are rare—as indeed
they are rare in prophets like Isaiah and Jeremiah, in
comparison with Ezekiel or the early *nebi'im* ; and like
them Jesus seems to have spoken little of the ' Spirit.'
Yet in the Gospels as we have them there are passages
which undoubtedly imply the belief that Jesus was in the
more popular sense a ' man of the Spirit.' Some critics
regard such narratives as that of the Baptism as intrusions
of mythical material into the Gospels. But in view of
other elements in the Gospel picture which recall prophetic
traits, it seems natural to accept the vision and the voice
at the Baptism, the Temptation, and the vision of Satan
fallen from heaven (Lk. x. 18) as parallel with similar
experiences of Old Testament prophets, so far as their
form is concerned (their content is another question).

(iv.) It was part of the popular conception of a prophet
that he should utter predictions. The Gospels offer

sufficient evidence that Jesus was believed to have uttered many predictions. Radical criticism tends to treat these as *vaticinia ex eventu* read back into the tradition. But there are some predictions at least which do not readily admit of such treatment. The forecast of the desolation and ruin of the Temple, in its earliest forms (Matt. xxiii. 38 = Lk. xiii. 35 ; Mk. xiii. 2, xiv. 58), does not seem to owe anything to historical reminiscence of the events of A.D. 70. Again, the warning about the sword of Rome and the collapse of the towers of Jerusalem in the form given in Lk. xiii. 1–5 does not suggest a *vaticinium ex eventu*. The forecast of His own death at Jerusalem is linked in Mk. x. 39 with a definite prediction that two of the disciples at least should share His fate—a prediction which was not fulfilled.[1] Thus without going into the debatable question of the eschatological element in the Gospels, there seems to be sufficient ground for saying that Jesus, like the Old Testament prophets, predicted coming events in the field of history.

(v.) One of the most curious features of Old Testament prophecy is the practice of performing symbolic actions, as when Jeremiah wore a yoke to signify the subjugation of the nations to Babylon, or Ezekiel shaved himself with a sword, treating the hair in peculiar ways, to signify the fortunes of his people after the Babylonian conquest. Of such symbolic actions Dr. Wheeler Robinson says, ' They are not simply dramatic illustrations of a rather feeble kind ; they are partial realisations of that which is to come, and to its coming they themselves will contribute in their own degree. Their complete fulfilment may bring the greatest grief to the prophet, as it did to Jeremiah ; yet

---

[1] James indeed perished some few years after the Crucifixion. The theory of an early martyrdom of John rests on an uncertain inference from statements in late writers, and an ambiguous entry in a Syrian Martyrology. This scarcely seems sufficient to overthrow the almost constant tradition that he survived to old age and died a natural death. But in any case the prediction of Jesus, taken in its natural sense, surely implies that the brothers are to share His own martyrdom then and there, and not that a somewhat similar fate will befall them years after, in different circumstances. The prediction in the Gospels should not be used to support a theory of the early martyrdom of both sons of Zebedee which has otherwise left no trace in our primary sources.

it is the will of Yahweh, and he must both declare and
further that will by every means in his power. . . . Any
theory of prophetic symbolism which fails to do justice to
its realistic element must be rejected.' [1] Now the Gospels
represent Jesus on at least one occasion as performing acts
which seem to partake of this ' realistic ' symbolism : when
He broke bread, saying ' This is My Body,' and gave His
disciples a cup, saying ' This is My Blood of the Covenant.' [2]
It is very probable that other incidents in His life are open
to a similar interpretation, though their significance is
partly obscured in the record.   Such are the ' Cursing ' of
the Fig-tree (the rejection of Israel), and the Feeding of
the Multitude (a ' sacrament of the Kingdom of God ').
The Johannine interpretation of the miracles as ' signs '
(cf. the use of מוֹפֵת, אוֹת in the prophetic books) may in
some cases at least be true to their original intention.

All these are traditional prophetic traits, and might
account for the popular estimate of Jesus as προφήτης ὡς
εἷς τῶν προφητῶν.

IV

The resemblance of the ministry of Jesus to that of the
Old Testament prophets goes deeper than these external
traits. The purport of His teaching recalls in many
essential respects that of the prophets.

(i.) He is represented as appealing to Isaiah (Mk. vii. 6),
Hosea (Matt. ix. 13, xii. 6), Deutero-Isaiah and Jeremiah
(Mk. xi. 17), against the formalism of contemporary
Judaism. Whether or not such citations are accepted as
in the strictest sense His own, it is clear from the whole
Gospel narrative that whereas among contemporary Rabbis
religious devotion, often splendid in its purity and strength,
takes the form of zeal for the strict observance of a Law
in which ethical and ceremonial precepts are not clearly
distinguished, in the teaching of Jesus the emphasis is

---

[1] *Old Testament Essays*, edited by D. C. Simpson, Griffin, 1927, ' Essay
on Prophetic Symbolism,' p. 10, p. 12.
[2] For similar actions on the part of Christian ' prophets,' see
Acts xxi. 11.

placed once more where the great prophets had placed it (compare Matt. xxiii. 23 = Lk. xi. 42, with Micah vi. 8). This fact sets His ethical teaching in strong contrast with that of His contemporaries, in spite of frequent agreement in detail. For the prophets the will of God is that which is seen to be right by the native faculties of the human spirit—as the ox knoweth his owner (Is. i. 3) and the stork in the heaven her appointed time (Jer. viii. 7). In developed Judaism it had come to be that which could be learned from Scripture and tradition. Jesus appealed afresh to the ' single eye ' (Matt. vi. 22 = Lk. xi. 34), or healthy moral instinct. ' Why do you not judge from yourselves what is right ? ' He asked (Lk. xii. 57), and that appeal to insight underlies His dealing with casuistical questions such as those of fasting, of the Sabbath, and of the claims of the moral as against the ceremonial law.

(ii.) The tendency of His eschatology is in harmony with that of the prophets. Amos, Isaiah, Jeremiah, and their fellows attacked the unethical optimism of the ' false prophets,' for whom the ' Day of Yahweh ' was a day of triumph for their people, unqualified by any ethical conditions. Jesus similarly dissociated Himself from the national hope of His day. The challenge of Amos, ' Are ye not as the children of the Ethiopians unto me, O children of Israel ? saith Yahweh. Have not I brought up Israel out of the land of Egypt, and the Philistines from Caphtor ? ' finds an echo in the words of the Gospel, ' It shall be more tolerable for Tyre and Sidon in the judgment than for you. . . . It shall be more tolerable for Sodom in that day than for that city ' (Matt. xi. 23 = Lk. x. 14, Matt. x. 15 = Lk. x. 12 ; cf. also Is. i. 9–10). Since Jeremiah there is nothing like the stern pronouncement of judgment on Jerusalem in the Gospel. Further, if it be true that the prophets took the fantastic eschatological conceptions of their time (based on primitive popular mythology), and reinterpreted them rationally in terms of political and historical realities (the menace of Assyria and Babylon),[1] we may probably recognise a similar treatment of

[1] As is held, e.g. by Gressmann (Ursprung der israelitisch-jüdischer Eschatologie).

apocalyptic fantasies in the reference to the Roman menace in the prophecies of Jesus. Though not all His prophecies can be given a historical application (since He shared in certain ways the transcendental outlook of Apocalyptic), yet His realistic treatment of current history has definite affinities with classical prophecy rather than with Apocalyptic.[1]

(iii) Like the prophets, Jesus announced the Reign of God in the face of the power of evil in the world. The actual phrase of the Gospels ' the βασιλεία (*malkuth*) of God ' (or ' of Heaven ') is indeed not a prophetic expression. It is, however, found in the Targums in renderings of expressions like ' Yahweh is king,' and the root idea, that God is the King whose glory fills earth and heaven (*cf.* Is. vi. 1–5), and that His kingly rule will be manifested to the confusion of all evil, is the burden of all prophecy. The exact sense in which Jesus used the term ' the Kingdom of God ' is a question too large to be treated here, but certainly His manner of ' proclaiming the Kingdom of God,' as a fact of tremendous moral import and challenge, has the true prophetic note, in contrast both to Apocalyptic and to Rabbinic legalism.

(iv) This leads to the further observation, that Jesus appears in the Gospels much more as a preacher of ' repentance ' than as a teacher in the ordinary sense. His μετανοεῖτε is an echo of the prophetic שׁוּב. His aim is to set before men the momentous issue between good and evil, and to bring them to a decision. This more than anything else is the *differentia* of the prophet as a religious phenomenon.

V

The affinity of Jesus with the Old Testament prophets may further be recognised in certain personal traits.

[1] There is ground for the view that in some of the ' apocalyptic ' passages of the Gospels (as notably in Mk. xiii.), the traces of a realistic reference to the terror of Rome which survive represent the original tone of what Jesus may be supposed to have said better than the traditional eschatology with which it has been fused in the evangelical tradition.

(i) As we have seen, Jesus is said to have received, like the Old Testament prophets, a special calling or designation in a ' pneumatic ' experience. But even if this be treated as legendary, His sayings imply a vocation amounting to predestination (*cf*. Jeremiah i. 5, etc.). Thus He speaks of being ' sent ' by God (Mk. ix. 37, Matt. xv. 24 ; *cf*. Is. vi. 8 ; Lk. iv. 18–26 expressly associates the ' sending ' of Jesus with that of the prophets).[1] The fortunes of His ministry are founded in the divine εὐδοκία (Matt. xi. 26 = Lk. x. 21). His forebodings of death are couched in terms implying the fulfilling of a destiny laid upon Him by the divine will (Lk. xii. 50, and so the δεῖ of Mk. viii. 31), and His prayer in Gethsemane is an acceptance of that destiny (Mk. xiv. 36).[2] If in other passages He uses the language rather of personal choice (' I came . . .,' ' the Son of Man came . . .,' Mk. ii. 17, x. 45, etc.), we may perhaps trace here the same transition from the prophetic to the more-than-prophetic which is marked by the difference between ' Thus saith the Lord ' and ' I say unto you.'

(ii) The prophetic vocation involves the possession of a divine revelation received in intimate communion. So Jesus ' knows ' God and is ' known ' by Him, and ' all things (that He teaches) are delivered unto ' Him by God, Matt. xi. 27 = Lk. x. 22. It is unnecessary to invoke Hellenistic parallels to explain this language, for it has direct precedent on the prophetic books ; *cf*. Jer. i. 5, ix. 24, Amos iii. 7, etc. If it affirms a more unique intimacy than the prophets are wont to claim, we may regard it as one more example of the ' more-than-prophetic ' supervening on the prophetic.

(iii) Hence, like the prophets, He is the representative of God ; to follow His teaching is to do the will of God ; to reject Him is to reject God (Mk. ix. 37, *cf*. 1 Sam. vii. 7 ; Ezek. xxxiii. 30–33, etc.). Here we have the inner side of

---

[1] The Fourth Gospel lays special emphasis on the ' sending ' of Jesus, no doubt under the influence of a particular theological development, but surely not without reference to the more primitive idea of a prophetic calling.

[2] The figure of a ' cup ' is so inseparably associated with His death as involved in His calling that we may profitably compare Jer. xxv. 15–17 Is. li. 17, Ezek. xxiii. 31–33.

that note of 'authority' which the populace marked in His teaching.

(iv) Like the Old Testament prophets, the Jesus of the Gospels has a mission to Israel, and His words and deeds are related to the national destiny. That this should be made so clear in our records is the more remarkable since they all, in the form in which we have them, belong to the Greek-speaking and mainly Gentile wing of the Church. The explicit statement, indeed, that Jesus was sent only to 'the lost sheep of the house of Israel' (Matt. xv. 24) occurs in a passage which is perhaps secondary. But apart from it the evidence is sufficient. The choice of twelve disciples to 'sit upon thrones judging the twelve tribes of Israel' (Lk. xxii. 30 = Matt. xix. 28) may fairly be considered one of those symbolic acts to which reference was made above. Further, the whole account of the journey to Jerusalem and the events and sayings connected with it, implies the intention in one way or another to appeal to the nation at its political and religious centre. The parable of the Vineyard in Mk. xii. 1–12, with its 'Q' counterpart, Matt. xxiii. 34–36 = Lk. xi. 49–51, represents this appeal as the climax of a historic series of prophetic appeals. When the appeal failed, He pronounced the doom of the Temple and of Jerusalem, quite in the spirit of the earlier prophets, and then, like Isaiah (viii. 16–18), separated His disciples, as the 'Remnant' of Israel. His last supper with the Twelve, with its Paschal setting and its reference to the 'covenant' (surely not without allusion to such ideas as those of Jeremiah xxx. 31–34), may be regarded as the inauguration of a New Israel in view of the coming of the Kingdom of God.

(v) The Hebrew prophets thought of themselves as not merely declaring the Word of God, but as playing a part in the fulfilment of that Word. This is the sense of the 'symbolic action' to which reference has been made. Behind the sometimes bizarre symbolism lies the conviction that the prophet is by his words and deeds an instrument in God's hand for the accomplishment of His purpose. 'I have set thee this day over the nations and over the kingdoms, to pluck up and to break down, and

to destroy and to overthrow; to build and to plant'
(Jer. i. 10). No interpretation of such expressions does
justice to them which does not admit that the prophet
believed that his ministry had actual consequences in
history, under God's Providence. It is possible that in
the consciousness of the prophets themselves this was their
most clearly marked distinction from the mere teacher. In
the light of this it is surely significant that Jesus frequently
speaks as though His own ministry was in fact the critical
event in history, and in particular that He seems to have
expected from His death some momentous consequence.
He foretells that death, not as an accident that may happen
to Him individually, but as an item in a series of events
by which the glory of God is manifested in the salvation
of man (as an ' eschatological ' event).

(vi) We may add that in His personal religion (so far
as this is accessible to us in the records) Jesus stands in
the succession of the prophets, while He goes beyond them.
Out of the prophetic sense of a calling in relation to the
purposes of God grew a definite type of prophetic piety,
best displayed in Jeremiah and after him in many of the
Psalmists. Their communion with God is direct, personal,
childlike. They bring to Him the urgent senses of need
arising out of a concrete situation, and appeal to Him with
an unshakable faith in His goodness and power as a ' living
God.' Their prayer issues in a serene acceptance of His
will, whether it call them to do or to suffer. So Jesus,
repudiating the idea of prayer as a meritorious religious
exercise, insists that it is essentially converse with ' your
Father who is in secret,' and bids His followers ' ask . . .
seek . . . knock,' with as realistic a reference to the urgent
need of the moment as a man shows who calls his neighbour
from sleep to beg for bread, and with a firm faith that with
God all things are possible. His own prayers, in lonely places
at crises of His ministry, surely are of this kind. His final
prayer in the Garden, reasserting faith in the boundless
power of God, craving help in desperate need, and rising
to unreserved acceptance of His will, represents the ideal
to which all prayer of the prophetic type tends.

VI

Jesus recognised in John the Baptist ' a prophet and more than a prophet.' In the foregoing discussion we have found ourselves compelled again and again to pass from the category of the prophetic to that of the ' more than prophetic.' To ask what Jesus Himself was, ' more than a prophet,' lies outside the scope of this chapter. But it seems necessary to indicate the point at which the prophetic element in His ministry naturally leads beyond itself. He sees in His own ministry something which does not merely revive prophecy but ' fulfils ' it. Prophets and kings (or righteous men) have desired to see what His disciples now see, and have not seen it (Matt. xiii. 16–17 = Lk. x. 23–24). Something greater than Jonah (the prophet) and than Solomon (the wise king) is here (Matt. xii. 41–42 = Lk. xi. 31–32). The time is fulfilled (Mk. i. 15), the roll of the martyrs is closed (Matt. xxiii. 35–36 = Lk. xi. 50–51), the servants of the Lord of the Vineyard have all done their errand and met their fate, and his Son has come (Mk. xii. 1–12). In a word, the Kingdom of God is no longer merely imminent : it has come—ἔφθασεν ἐφ' ὑμᾶς.[1] Thus, while the content of the prophetic message is present in the teaching of Jesus, it is present in a form which passes from anticipation to realisation. This carries with it a profound change in the religious character and value of the teaching itself, and it has important implications in regard to His Person.

---

[1] Observe that ἐγγίζω (Mk. i. 15), and φθάνω (Matt. xii. 28 = Lk. xi. 20) are in the LXX alternative translations of נגע, מטא. The sense therefore of ἤγγικεν ἡ βασιλεία should probably be determined by that of ἔφθασεν ἡ βασιλεία.

JESUS, THE MESSIAH
BY EDWYN CLEMENT HOSKYNS

IV

JESUS, THE MESSIAH

Est animal quod dicitur ibex, duo cornua habens, quorum tanta vis est ut, si ab alto montis dimissum fuerit ad ima, totum corpus sustentetur illaesum his cornibus. Significat autem eruditos homines, qui duorum Testamentorum consonantia quidquid adversi eis acciderit, quasi quodam salubri temperamento temperare solent, et velut duobus cornibus fulti bona quae perpetrant, veteris ac evangelicae lectionis attestatione sustinant.

' There is an animal named " Ibex " which possesses two horns of so great strength that, if it be thrown down from the top to the bottom of a mountain, the whole weight of its body is supported without hurt upon its horns. This signifies the wisdom of men who encounter any evil which may happen to them by strict adherence to the salutary congruence and agreement of the two Testaments, and whose actions are supported by the witness of the Old and New Testaments as by two horns.'—Physiologus *De Ibice* (Migne, *Patrologia Latina*, vol. clxxvii. p. 64.)

THE neglect of the venerable principle that the well-instructed Christian man must trust in the two Testaments, as the ibex relies upon the strength of his two horns, has caused so great a confusion in the interpretation of the New Testament and of the Synoptic Gospels in particular that modern exegesis has reached a point where the genesis of the Christian religion has been rendered almost wholly inexplicable. Modern criticism has been at pains to prove that the New Testament, having emerged from the Roman Empire in the first century A.D., must be interpreted in the light of ideas current within the empire and set upon the background of Hellenistic religion, or of contemporary Judaism, or of that intermingling of the two which is supposed to have produced the faith of the primitive Church. The effect of this general presupposition upon the study of the Synoptic Gospels has been to handle them as delicate instruments recording subtle movements within primitive Christianity, so that the main energy of historical exegesis has been directed towards the detection and description of these movements of faith and controversy.

In the course of this detailed examination certain sayings and actions of Jesus have, it is true, obstinately refused explanation as reflecting the later faith of the Church ; and these are sometimes thrown to the greedy eschatologists, or more often left in their detached and fragmentary form, and handed over to the humanitarians to use according to their taste. Meanwhile the technical New Testament scholar makes use of other material for the interpretation of primitive Christianity. It is this method and the resultant edifice, built according to this method, which is beginning to exhibit signs of almost intolerable weakness. In the end the weakness consists in attaching to the words and acts of Jesus a significance inadequate to support or explain the faith of the Primitive Church. The purpose of this essay is to provide some grounds for supposing no further progress in the understanding of primitive Christianity to be possible unless the ark of New Testament exegesis be recovered from its wanderings in the land of the Philistines and be led back not merely to Jerusalem, for that might mean to contemporary Judaism, but to its home in the midst of the classical Old Testament Scriptures —to the Law and to the Prophets. The consequent reconsideration of the New Testament literature should, moreover, begin with the Synoptic Gospels, since it is inadequacy of treatment there which tends to throw the interpretation of the other books out of gear and to render inexplicable the genesis of the Christian religion.

When the sayings and actions of Jesus recorded in the Synoptic Gospels are set upon the background of the classical Old Testament Scriptures, it soon becomes apparent that we are concerned less with the rehabilitation of the Old Testament than with its creative interpretation and with its fulfilment : that is to say, we are concerned with the sayings and with the actions of the Messiah. If this be proved to be the case, we must then abandon a merely tentative ascription to Jesus of Messianic claims, and be prepared to find that there is no event or utterance recorded of Him which does not wholly proceed from a conception of the Messiahship smelted and sublimed from the ore of the Old Testament Scriptures; and that this complete Christological control is not imposed awkwardly upon the material, but underlies and penetrates every fragment of it. The Gospels as they stand are no doubt formally the work of evangelists who were members of the Christian *Ecclesia*, but the creative activity rests with Jesus and not with the Church or with a series of editors. The material which the Evangelists handle is beyond their power of complete mastery, and, though they may endeavour to smooth it out into an orderly narrative, it continually breaks through their orderliness and refuses to be confined within the framework of their intelligence. The last generation discovered the editors and noted their characteristics; the present generation has to rehabilitate the Christ and mark the significance of the close interweaving of His teaching and acts.

The vigorous analysis to which the Synoptic Gospels have been recently subjected under the general title of *Formgeschichte* has set the seal on what was already implicit in the older analysis, and has established a negative conclusion from which it is extremely difficult to escape. The Synoptic Gospels provide no sufficient evidence by which the historian is enabled to trace in detail the movements of Jesus during the ministry or to compose an orderly narrative of His life. The connections of the incidents and the grouping of the *Logia* belong largely to the literary structure of the Gospels or to the parenetic and hortatory character of primitive Christian instruction out of which the Gospels were composed. This negative conclusion opens the way to a new analysis of the *Logia* considered as a whole and for a new examination of the works of healing considered as a whole, in order that, if possible, those delicate threads by which the teaching is related to the miracles and by which both teaching and miracles are related to the titles Son of Man and Son of God so as to lead irresistibly to the necessity of the Crucifixion, may be detected and brought into prominence. Here is the real problem of the historical interpretation of the Gospels, since if the titles be detached and considered by themselves, they are found to possess no precise meaning, and therefore provide no fixed point of exegetical departure ; nor is the Crucifixion the natural or easily intelligible climax of the ministry. The significance of the titles and the necessity of the Crucifixion are set hidden and embedded in the teaching and actions of Jesus, and emerge only when these are subjected to a careful and accurate analysis, the purpose of which is not so much to discover the literary technique of the evangelists as to recover the original meaning of the words and acts of Jesus. This is not to overthrow the earlier analysis, but to press beyond it ; and it is precisely the work of our immediate predecessors which makes this further pressure inevitable. The exegesis of this or that *Logion* or of this or that incident cannot now be safely undertaken with reference to the literary context in which it stands ; it needs interpretation from other *Logia* and from other incidents, and especially from those which belong to different literary strata. Thus a *Logion* in Mark should be set side by side with *Logia* found in Q or in special Matthew or special Luke, and if these widely disparate *Logia* be found to contain a common outlook or a common series of ideas, then the particular saying or incident must be interpreted from this common outlook and not from the notions of the evangelists which may turn out to be half misunderstood simplifications, resulting partly from their desire to collect and to order, and partly from the extreme difficulty and obscurity of the material they were called upon to handle. The main direction to which such a method of exegetical procedure points may be illustrated by a few examples.

If the narrative of the healing of the deaf and dumb man in Mk. vii. 31–37 be presented to a competent Greek scholar for his opinion, he will almost inevitably remark that the account is perfectly straightforward except for the word μογιλάλος. Yes, precisely, since the word is used by no classical Greek author, is found in no known Greek inscription, and occurs but once in the Papyri. It is true that it appears four times in very late Greek writers ; but it is an awkward and obscure word. To the Biblical scholar, however, not only does the word itself present no particular difficulty, but—and this is far more important—it suggests a familiar literary background. The Greek translators of the Old Testament use it in very significant passages to translate the Hebrew word אלּם. The word is used in the LXX translation of Is. xxxv. 4–6 : *Behold your God will come with vengeance, with the recompense of God ; he will come and save you. Then the eyes of the blind shall be opened, and the ears of the deaf shall be unstopped. Then shall the lame man leap as an hart, and the tongue of the dumb* (μογιλάλος) *shall sing* (LXX *shall be distinct*). Aquila, Symmachus, and Theodotion use the word in translating the passage where Moses complains that he is *slow of speech and of a slow tongue*, to which the Lord answered, *Who hath made a man dumb* (μογιλάλος) *or deaf or seeing or blind ? is it not I the Lord ? Now therefore go, and I will be with thy mouth and teach thee what thou shalt speak* (Ex. iv. 10–12). Aquila also uses it in translating Is. lvi. 10, which forms part of the description of the Shepherds of Israel when the salvation of the Lord is *near to come*, and His righteousness is *to be revealed*, and He is come to gather the *outcasts of Israel : His watchmen are blind, they are all without knowledge, they are all dumb* (μογιλάλοι) *dogs, they cannot bark, dreaming, lying down, loving to slumber.* The word μογιλάλος then betrays the relation between the New Testament works of healing and the Old Testament marks of the Messianic age. It may, of course, be objected that Mark's use of the word is casual and insignificant, or, alternatively, that he has so framed his narrative as to introduce an Old Testament allusion. But is Mark so casual or so strangely and subtly allusive ? The possibility must be reckoned with that the material behind Mark is more significant than he is altogether aware of, and that the word μογιλάλος points to the nature of this significance. This hypothesis is strongly supported by the Q *Logion* which contains the answer of Jesus to the messengers of John (Matt. xi. 2–5, Lk. vii. 18–23) : *Go your way, and tell John what things ye have seen and heard ; the blind receive their sight, the lame walk, the lepers are cleansed, and the deaf hear, the dead are raised up, and the poor have good tidings* (the gospel) *preached to them.* Here the words of Jesus do not rest merely upon the miracles of healing, but upon these miracles regarded in the perspective of Is. xxxv. 4–6 and lxi. 1 ; that is to say, they look beyond the physically healed to the presence of the Christ in their midst and to the appearance of the Messianic people of God, whose sins will be forgiven, who will walk in His law, behold His mysteries, hear his truth, and give it utterance clearly and without stammering. The physically healed men were the types and signs of the new order of which Peter and the disciples were to form the nucleus. The preparatory character of the works of healing is also suggested in the saying recorded by Luke only, and which apparently does not belong to the Q material : *Go and say to that Fox, Behold I cast out devils and perform cures to-day and to-morrow, and the third day I am perfected* (Lk. xiii. 32). It is extremely difficult to avoid the conclusion that the Lord Himself attached Messianic significance to His works of healing.

The older critics were worried by the problem of the historicity of the miracles. They quite rightly noted a tendency in the editors of the Gospels to heighten the miraculous, and they named such editing ' heightening the Christology.' But such a judgment is in the end wide of the mark, because just in proportion as the evangelists heightened the narratives so that they stood on their own feet as miraculous stories, they in fact depressed the Christology by tending to obscure the real significance of the works of healing as signs of the appearance of the Christ and of the Kingdom of God. It is this Christological, Old Testament aspect of the works of healing rather than the mere love of the miraculous which is of importance for the historian and for the theologian.[1]

Firmly embedded in the record of the works of healing is the emphatic association of such miracles with the publicity of a synagogue on the Sabbath day (*e.g.* Mk. iii. 1–6). This association does not merely provide a historical setting for a miraculous narrative. The association is a provocative association in which the initiative rests with Jesus, and results in a condemnation by the Pharisees so severe that they *took counsel against him, how they might*

[1] *Cf.* Adolf Schlatter, *Das Wunder in der Synagoge* (1912) ; *Theologie des N.T.* (1909), p. 277.

destroy him, and combined with the Herodians for this purpose (Mk. iii. 6). That the power of Jesus was exhibited in word and action precisely on the Sabbath, and that it was productive of controversy, is supported also from the Q material (Matt. xii. 11, Lk. xiv. 5) and by special Luke (Lk. xiii. 10–17, xiv. 16–30 ; *cf.* xiv. 1–6). It seems therefore impossible to throw upon the editors the responsibility for this emphasis, and their tendency to open a narrative with some such formal introduction as *He entered, as his custom was, into the synagogue on the sabbath day* (Lk. iv. 16) is occasioned not by a mere literary irrelevance, but by the peculiar importance attached to the Sabbath in the *Logia* of Jesus. There is a pressing problem here, which has been admirably perceived and stated by the writer of the article on the ' Sabbath ' in the *Jewish Encyclopædia*.[1] He says : ' In view of the spirit of philanthropy that, as Maimonides constantly asserts, underlies the Law, it is difficult to understand the controversies with Jesus attributed to the Pharisees in the New Testament.' If it be difficult to understand the violence of the controversy, it is even more difficult to understand how the action of Jesus on the Sabbath could provoke the Pharisees to demand and accomplish His destruction. Some peculiar incitement to punishment is required beyond that which is provided by the performance of manifestly good actions on an unsuitable day. The solution of the problem will not be found in an exaggerated description of the rigour of Sabbath observance among the Jews, nor in some romantic assertion of the paramount supremacy of human generosity over ecclesiastical regulations and in the heroism of those who maintain and act upon this supremacy. The solution of the problem is to be sought rather in the pregnant suggestions enclosed within the word ' Sabbath ' itself.

The Greek translators of the Old Testament reproduced the Hebrew root שבת and its synonyms by ἀνάπαυσις-ἀναπαύειν or by κατάπαυσις-καταπαύειν and denoted thereby not primarily naked human rest or peace, but the descending peace and mercy of God and the consequent freedom from the labour and trouble of this world. The

[1] Vol. x. p. 597 f.

translation of שבת and נוח or רבע (rest, lie down) by the same Greek word had the effect of linking the word ' Sabbath ' to the great passages in the prophets which look forward to the advent of the peace of God ; as for example Is. xiv. 3, *In the day that the Lord shall give thee rest from thy sorrow and from thy trouble and from all the hard service wherein thou wast made to serve* ; or Ez. xxxiv. 15, 16, *I myself shall feed my sheep, and I will cause them to lie down* (רבע, ἀναπαύειν), *saith the Lord God. I will seek that which was lost, and will bring again that which was driven away, and will bind up that which was broken, and will strengthen that which was sick ; and the fat and strong I will destroy ; I will feed them in judgment.*   The behaviour of the translators brings out, no doubt wholly unconsciously, the possibility of interpreting the observance of the Sabbath less as a characteristic mark of the faithful Jew or as a memorial of God's rest after the work of Creation than as a ritual anticipation of the advent of the Messianic age. Now if it be supposed that it was exactly this significance which Jesus attached to the Sabbath, not only is the provocative nature of His action and its sequence intelligible ; but the saying *The Son of Man is Lord of the Sabbath* and also the saying which Matthew associated with it, *A greater thing than the Temple is here* (Matt. xii. 6, 7), are both thrown upon their Messianic background.   With the advent of the Messiah and His mighty call to repentance the new order foretold by the Prophets has arrived, and the judgment of God hangs over those who refuse to recognise the call as His mercy rests upon those who accept it.   Thus the ritual observance of the Sabbath and the business of the Temple become occasions for the manifestation of their fulfilment, and, paradoxically, the instinct of mercy which caused the Jews themselves to break the Sabbath in order to save the life of a sheep (Matt. xii. 11, 12 ; *cf.* Lk. xiii. 15, 16, xiv. 5) is marked as a veritable anticipation of the mercy of God. The action of Jesus on the Sabbath and the miracles of healing together exhibit the presence of the Messiah, and the Pharisees, correctly detecting their meaning, proceed against Jesus for blasphemy.   It may be noted in passing that, if this exegesis be on right lines, the Matthean *Logion* which immediately precedes the record of a provocative Sabbath healing and of the Lord's rebuke of the Pharisees for condemning the disciples for plucking and eating ears of corn on the Sabbath is itself a Sabbath utterance. *Come unto me, all ye that labour and are heavy laden, and I will give you rest* (ἀναπαύσω). *Take my yoke upon you, and learn of me ; for I am meek and lowly in heart : and ye shall find rest* (ἀνάπαυσις) *unto your souls* (Matt. xi. 28–29). The saying has a wider background than is provided by a mere manipulation of Ecclesiasticus li. 23 ff.

Whether an eschatological significance was attached to the Sabbath in contemporary Judaism is exceedingly difficult to determine. In the second century A.D. Rabbi Jehuda interpreted the title of Psalm xcii. *For the Sabbath day* as a reference to the ' great Day of the world to come which was to be one perfect Sabbath.' [1] There are signs in the modern Jewish Liturgy of an attitude to the Sabbath as a foretaste of the world to come ; [2] but an argument from such indications back to Judaism before the destruction of Jerusalem is an exceedingly hazardous procedure, and in any case it is irrelevant because we have to deal not with the assigning of Messianic hope to the Sabbath, but with the fulfilment of that hope. The attitude of Jesus to the Sabbath is best explained as a creative Messianic interpretation of the Jewish observance of the Sabbath under the influence of the Old Testament prophecies of the Rest which God would provide for His faithful people, rather than as a mere adaptation of ideas already current among the Jews. The nearest approximation to the Synoptic Gospels is found in the New Testament itself. In the Fourth Gospel (v. 16–18) the persecution of Jesus is occasioned by His healing a cripple on the Sabbath day, and the author goes on to say that the Jews sought to kill him *because he not only brake the sabbath, but also called God his own Father, making himself equal with God* : that is to say, behind the action on the Sabbath and

[1] Cf. *Vita Adae et Evae*, li. 1 ; see James Moffatt, *Commentary on the Epistle to the Hebrews*, p. 52.

[2] *Jewish Encycl.*, article ' Sabbath,' pp. 589 and 601. For a similar interpretation of the Sabbath see Paul Levertoff, *Die religiöse Denkweise der Chassidim*, p. 90.

evident in it lay the claim to a peculiar relation to God, and this, not the mere breaking of the Sabbath, was the issue between Jesus and the Jews. The exegesis of Ps. xcv. 7–11 in the Epistle to the Hebrews (iii. and iv.) is also relevant. The argument is that the Christians are the household of God; Jesus, the Christ, the Son of God, being the Apostle and High Priest of that salvation to which Moses had borne faithful testimony. This Messianic order is then described as the fulfilment of the Sabbath hope. Joshua had failed to give rest to the people of God and David looked forward to a future Sabbath rest, but *we which have believed do enter into that rest* through Jesus the High Priest of the true Sabbath salvation. Is this Christian Midrash on the Psalm as far removed from the teaching of Jesus as modern commentators have supposed? and is not the precise note in the Fourth Gospel an admirable comment on the earlier tradition?

The preceding analysis, occasioned by the somewhat casual use of the Greek words μογιλάλος-ἀνάπαυσις-κατάπαυσις in the New Testament, suggests that modern reconstructions of the historical development within primitive Christianity, which proceed upon the assumption that the Christological penetration of the literature was initiated by the faith of the Church, are open to very severe criticism. The Messiahship underlies the miracles of healing and their accompanying *Logia*, and renders intelligible the severity of the controversy concerning the Sabbath; it is not introduced as a Christian interpretation of the ' personality ' of Jesus. The question now arises whether other elements in the synoptic tradition are not similarly conditioned by the claim of Jesus to be the Messiah.

Professor Gerhard Kittel devoted the major part of his book, *Die Probleme des Palastinischen Spätjudentums und das Urchristentum* (1926), to establishing the messianic background of the intensity of the moral teaching of Jesus. It is therefore unnecessary here to attempt what at best could effect nothing more than to dot his i's and cross his t's. One illustration will suffice to set this essay in complete agreement with him.

Mark, Q, and special Matthew, all contain sayings in

which rigid monogamy is rigorously and optimistically demanded (Mk. x. 1–12; Matt. v. 32 ; Lk. xvi. 18; Matt. xix. 10–12). The argument in Mk. x. 1–12, where the pronouncement concerning marriage is occasioned by a controversy concerning legitimate grounds of divorce, is sufficiently significant. Moses had permitted divorce (Deut. xxiv. 1–3), and, because of the hardness of the hearts of the people, Jesus recognises the necessity of this permissive legislation. But He reminds His hearers that behind the Mosaic enactment is set the judgment of God and His righteousness. A man shall *leave his father and mother, and shall cleave to his wife ; and the twain shall become one flesh* (Gen. ii. 24). The righteousness of God leaves no room for divorce. The moral demands of Jesus presume that the contradiction between the righteousness of God and the Mosaic legislation can now be resolved, and of this resolution the teaching concerning marriage is an admirable illustration. There is no suggestion that the Jews had reached a point in their moral progress where the Mosaic permission for divorce could be safely disregarded ; nor is there any suggestion of a criticism of Moses in the words of Jesus. The contradiction between the righteousness of God and the Mosaic Law is resolved not by a gradual moral progress among men, but by that purification of the heart which of necessity accompanies a genuine acceptance of the call of the Messiah. *Think not that I came to destroy the law or the prophets : I came not to destroy, but to fulfil* (Matt. v. 17). *Except your righteousness shall exceed the righteousness of the scribes and Pharisees, ye shall in no wise enter into the Kingdom of heaven* (Matt. v. 20). It is therefore not surprising that Jesus expects His disciples to understand His public teaching concerning marriage and divorce, and interprets it to them privately (Mk. x. 10–12). The Matthean *Logion* runs along similar lines. It is occasioned by the horror of the disciples at the rigour of the demand. They would prefer to remain unmarried. This results in an emphatic statement that this rigidity presumes vocation : *All men cannot receive this saying, but they to whom it is given* (Matt. xix. 10, 11). In other words, the general demand for a strict monogamy belongs within the messianic order,

which is the concretion of the righteousness of God.
Similarly the Q saying (Matt. v. 32; Lk. xvi. 18) belongs
to the general delineation of the new righteousness and is
not a detached piece of moral teaching.

The righteousness of God is then strictly attached to
the acceptance of the call of Jesus, the Messiah, and the
saying concerning the children, which Mark brackets with
the teaching concerning marriage (Mk. x. 13-16), is entirely
relevant. The point of the comparison between the
children and the true disciples does not lie in their common
innocence, but in their common movement towards Jesus.
The children come to Him, and such coming is the necessary
prelude to the righteousness of the kingdom; to follow
Jesus and to enter the kingdom are simply two means of
saying the same thing. In this connection the meaning of
the proverbially difficult question, *Why callest thou me
good? None is good save one, even God* (Mk. x. 17-31),
seems obvious enough; and yet modern commentators
persist in finding in it a relic of that gulf which separated
the true Jesus of history from His Father in heaven and
which sets Him firmly in the midst of His sinful human
brothers. But when once it is recognised that Jesus as the
Messiah brings the righteousness of God, and that Mark has
set the question of the rich man, *Good Master, what shall I
do that I may inherit eternal life?* in close proximity to the
saying concerning the children and to the teaching about
marriage, the question becomes provocative, and requires
some such answer as ' But thou art the Messiah, in whom
the goodness and righteousness of God is made concrete in
flesh and blood, and is available for men.' The rich man
refuses to follow Jesus, and thus loses the eternal life which
he had desired; and Jesus comments *How hardly shall
they that have riches enter into the Kingdom of God!* (Mk. x.
23). Matthew by a piece of very clumsy editing avoids
a false interpretation of the Lord's question, but entirely
fails to perceive its correct meaning. Discipleship of
Jesus, the righteousness of God, entrance into the Kingdom
of God, eternal life, are connected happenings which
together compose one whole. And this unity is not imposed
upon the tradition of the sayings and actions of Jesus, it

is not created by the literary form, it lies behind the whole
tradition and is implicit in each fragment, however detached
it may at first sight appear.

The recognition of the Christological unity by which
the various themes in the teaching of Jesus are held
together makes necessary a reconsideration of the technique
of the interpretation of the extended parables. Modern
exegesis of the parables depends directly or indirectly largely
upon Professor Jülicher's book *Die Gleichnisreden Jesu*,
the first part of which was originally printed in 1886, the
second part in 1899. Professor Jülicher put an end to
that undisciplined allegorising which was traditional in both
learned and popular treatments of the parables. For this
we cannot be too grateful. He then proceeded with great
elaboration to build up a system of interpretation which
had the effect of throwing upon the evangelists the whole
responsibility for the allegorising element in the parables
as they stand in the Gospels. He adopted the canon *Simplex
sigillum veri*,[1] and with its help extracted the original form of
the parabolic teaching of Jesus. The characteristic mark of
a genuine parable was that one simple truth was illustrated
by a story, the details of the story being conditioned by
its natural sequence uninfluenced by allegorical deflection.
Any unnatural break in a story is, he maintained, the sure
mark of editorial manipulation, since deflection turns a
parable into an allegory. Thus, for example, because the
parable of the Wicked Husbandmen (Mk. xii. 1-12) is not
a simple story illustrating the opposition of the Jews to
the messengers of God, but is disturbed by the distinction
between the Son of God and the slaves—that is, between
Jesus and the prophets—by the clear recognition of the
necessity of the death of the Son, and by the knowledge of
a new order coming into being as a result of that death,
Professor Jülicher judges the whole parable to be the record of
primitive Christian faith, and asserts that nothing has survived
which can be confidently attributed to Jesus Himself.[2] Similarly, the story of the Marriage Feast of the King's Son is
completely disturbed in the Matthean form by the conclusion

[1] *Op. cit.*, 2nd edition, vol. i. p. 322.
[2] 2nd edition, vol. ii. p. 406.

G

of the parable which relates the rough exclusion from the feast of the man without a wedding garment (Mt. xxii. 1-14); consequently, because the conclusion disturbs the natural sequence of the parable, Professor Jülicher rules it out as a Matthean addition due to the ethical interest of the evangelist. The whole literary critical procedure rests upon the assumption that the Christological nexus is superimposed by the evangelists and reflects the faith of the Church but does not compose the very essence of the teaching of Jesus. If, however, it be discovered, quite apart from the parables, that the claim to the Messiahship, a sharp distinction between Jesus and the prophets, His unique relationship to God as Son to Father, a categorical and Messianic demand for righteousness, a concrete situation in which the tension can be resolved only by the death of the Messiah, form elements, connected elements, governing the teaching and actions of Jesus, then their reappearance in the parables betray originality, not editorial manipulation. The disconnections and deflections in a story are in fact provocative Christological surprises. This is not for one moment to affirm that editorial manipulation is wholly absent. Matthew's editing of Mk. xii. 8 (Matt. xxi. 39) is almost certainly a *vaticinium ex eventu*. But the editing is not all in one direction. Luke seems to smooth out certain of the parables in order to secure precisely that unity of narrative which Professor Jülicher regards as the sign of originality. It is after all just as reasonable to suppose that Luke has removed the disturbance of the Man without the Wedding Garment (Lk. xiv. 16-24) as to imagine that Matthew has inserted it. Nor is a criticism of Professor Jülicher's canon of exegesis intended to open the way for a return to undisciplined allegorising. Only when a disconnection in a parable has the effect of securing its conformity with a surprising element in the teaching of Jesus, established apart from the parables, is it legitimate to claim that precisely such a disturbance is a mark of originality. The parables of Jesus are not merely illustrative stories, nor are they allegories. They are Messianic ' hard sayings ' which refuse to obey neat rules of literary form and do not admit

of drastic simplification in accordance with such rules—
I will open my mouth in a parable (משל, LXX παραβολή). *I
will utter dark sayings* (חידה, LXX προβλήματα : Ps. lxxviii. 2 ;
cited Matt. xiii. 35).

If the material which the Evangelists ordered and
arranged were in its original form completely and roughly
Messianic, a point of departure is secured for an examination of the significance of the titles Son of God and Son of
Man, and an opportunity is provided of explaining why the
whole is guided and directed towards the death of the
Messiah as the only firm foundation of an ultimate and
eschatological optimism. Through the various strata of
the earliest tradition there runs a persistent note of struggle
and tension associated with the conception of the Messiahship, and it is in connection with this tension that the
Sonship of Jesus and the Fatherhood of God and the title
Son of Man emerge into prominence. They define the
nature of the Messiahship of Jesus ; and yet the terms of
the definition are as elusive as that which they seek to
define. The Messiah, the Son of God, the Son of Man are
terms which, if they be detached from the concrete setting
of the teaching of Jesus, have no clear and precise meaning.
The truth is that we are in the presence of a creative interpretation initiated by Jesus Himself upon the foundation
of the Old Testament Scriptures.

Matthew concludes his record of the Flight into Egypt
with the comment *That it might be fulfilled which was spoken
by the Lord through the prophet, saying, Out of Egypt did I
call my son* (Matt. ii. 15). The Old Testament citation is
extracted from Hos. xi. 1, where Israel is named the Son
of God. It is, of course, easy to regard this procedure as
an illustration of the peculiarly Matthean method of
handling the Old Testament, and then to dismiss it as
trivial. But is the instinct which led Matthew first to
rivet the title Son of God to the Old Testament and then
to transfer it to Jesus trivial or peculiarly Matthean ? The
precision of the title Son of God and of its rider the Fatherhood of God is in fact an Old Testament precision. *Israel
is my son, my firstborn. . . . Let my son go* (Exod. iv. 22, 23).
Ye are the sons of the living God (Hos. i. 10 ; *cf.* Ps. lxxiii. 15,

lxxx. 15). *I am a father to Israel, and Ephraim is my first-born* (Jer. xxxi. 9). The King of the elect people of God is pre-eminently the Son of God. It is written of Solomon, *I will be his father and he shall be my son* (2 Sam. vii. 14), and of David, *Thou art my son ; this day have I begotten thee* (Ps. ii. 7). This background is presumed in the Gospels— and then the Sonship is torn away from the Jews and concentrated upon Jesus as the fulfilment of the Law and the Prophets, and the old claim of the Jews to be the holy, chosen, and peculiar children of God, set for the judgment or salvation of the Gentiles (Deut. xiv. 1), comes adequately to rest upon Jesus, the Christ, the Son of God. If this transference were a mere formal transference of title, it could be explained as a Christian interpretation, originating in Christian faith. But it is no formal transference of title. This becomes clear as we realise that the Sonship of Jesus underlies His teaching, and as we realise that the Sonship secures the precise definition of the Messiah as He who is not only wholly dependent upon God but must also obey His will to the uttermost. The isolation of Jesus, the tension between Him and the Jewish authorities, and between Him and the crowds, and between Him and His disciples, proceeds from and is conditioned by this unique Messianic Sonship. It underlies the insistent demand *Follow me* and the authoritative *But I say unto you* ; it appears in the radicalism of the new wine and the new wine-skins (Mk. ii. 22) and in the refusal to admit of the possibility of patching or reforming the old order (Mk. ii. 21) ; but it is given clearest expression in the Q *Logion, All things have been delivered unto me of my Father : and no one knoweth the Son, save the Father ; neither doth any know the Father, save the Son, and he to whomsoever the Son willeth to reveal him* (Matt. xi. 27 ; Lk. x. 22), with which may be compared the saying recorded only by Luke, *Fear not, little flock, for it is your Father's good pleasure to give you the kingdom* (Lk. xii. 32). In all this the Old Testament heritage is narrowed to its fulfilment in the obedience of Jesus, and expands from that isolated obedience into the new order of the sonship of His disciples which in the perspective of the Gospels still lies in the future. Jesus was no reformer of Judaism. He was the Christ who wrought out the Messiahship in the obedience of the Son of God—in flesh and blood. This concrete happening is denoted by the title Son of Man, which is no title, but rather a reinforcing, more precise, and far more staggering, definition of His inglorious yet perfected Messiahship.

The tension which results from the presence of the Messiah isolated in the midst of a hostile or ignorant human society, yet Himself flesh and blood and deprived of the glory which rightly belongs to Him, provides the background of the primary and creative use of the phrase *Son of man* in the *Logia* of Jesus. The phrase has its formal origin in the Old Testament, where it denotes the humiliation of a prophet to whom a divine mission has been entrusted (Ezek. *passim*), or points to the confident hope of a new order heavenly in origin and opposed to and victorious over the kingdoms of the world (Dan. vii. 13–28). In one passage the phrase bridges the gulf between humiliation and glory—*What is man, that thou art mindful of him : and the son of man that thou visitest him ? Thou madest him lower than the angels : to crown him with glory and worship* (Ps. viii. 4, 5). In handling the significance of *Son of man* in the Gospels it is tempting to seize upon its eschatological application and place there the weight of its interpretation, with the result that the emphasis in the teaching of Jesus is set upon the confident expectation of an imminent act of God which would obliterate a present failure. The suggestion of a tension between failure and an imminent act of God is, however, wholly foreign to the Gospels. The tension is between a victory over evil wrought out in flesh and blood, in humiliation, and the fruits of that redemptive victory, between an *opus operatum* and the reward of that act. The confident eschatological hope is grounded upon the obedience of Jesus : it in no sense proceeds from despair or redresses a failure. The eschatology is therefore secondary, derived, and dependent. It depends upon the work of Jesus, the Messiah, defined as the work of the Son of Man.[1]

---

[1] The influence of Is. liii. in this connection presents an exceedingly delicate problem, into which it is impossible to enter here. It should,

The temptation of the Son of God, His dependence upon faith and prayer, His incomplete knowledge, the fugitive nature of His mission, fit into no contemporary Messianic expectation ; but they are essential to the Messiahship of Jesus, and are imposed upon Him by a divine necessity. This divine necessity is recognised and expressed in the designation of the Messiah as the Son of Man. The whole course of the ministry of Jesus is thus directed by the paradox of the Christ—the Son of Man ; and the death of the Messiah is the necessary working out of the righteousness of God quite literally in flesh and blood. The necessity of His death belongs to the very fibre of His Messiahship, because by it the record of the persecuted and humiliated people of God in the Old Testament, and especially in the Psalms, is narrowed to its fulfilment. In the Old Testament the persecution of the people of God is in part at least merited by disobedience ; in the death of Jesus persecution is complicated by no such justification. Thus in the death of the Messiah sin is wholly and finally exposed and the righteousness of God is achieved in the concrete obedience of His Son. On this foundation the eschatology rests, since thereby the future is secured. His disciples must, it is true, take up their cross and follow Him, for this complete surrender to God securely marks the presence of the new Messianic people of God in the world. But the initial and normative victory was won by the Messiah without the aid of His disciples and in spite of their unbelief. They became the fruits of His victory, and to them its general redemptive proclamation was entrusted. The death of Jesus was not primarily effected by the secret and malicious planning of the Jewish authorities, nor was it the result of a sudden change of policy inaugurated by Jesus to cover the failure of His preaching in Galilee. It

however, be noted that Prof. Gerhard Kittel has detected in the Jewish apocalyptic literature a certain overlapping of Is. liii. and the title Son of Man (*Die Religion in Geschichte und Gegenwart*, 2nd edn., vol. iii. pp. 2120 f. ; *cf.* also Joachim Jeremias, *Deutsche Theologie*, 1929, vol. ii. pp. 106 ff.). If this can be established it would not be unreasonable to suppose that the sequence Messiah—Slave of God—Son of God—Son of Man belonged to the background of the *Logia* of Jesus, and that the necessity of the death of the Messiah was to some extent at least determined by a creative and messianic interpretation of Is. liii.

was involved from the beginning of His ministry in His creative definition of the Messiahship as the Son of Man. The initiative rested wholly with Jesus Himself. He provoked His death consciously and of set purpose, because its necessity was laid upon Him as the Messiah in order that the Old Testament Scriptures might be fulfilled. By this fulfilment of the righteousness of God in flesh and blood, and by the complete exposition of human sin which was the rider to the obedience of Jesus and occasioned His violent death, a new order was inaugurated into which the disciples were initiated at the Last Supper. Here is the origin of the Christian Ecclesia and the secret of its power—the active righteousness of God set in the midst of human society in active revolt against Him.

In an extended treatise upon the death of the Messiah it would be right at this point to consider whether the sacrificial cultus of the Old Testament is not consciously fulfilled in the death of the Messiah, and whether the necessity of its fulfilment does not underlie the necessity of the death of the Messiah as the Son of Man, thereby providing for the necessity of a new cultus based upon and centring round the sacrificial death of Jesus. Sacrificial language is used with great reserve in the synoptic Gospels. In fact it appears undoubtedly only in the *Logia* of the Last Supper. This does not mean, however, that when it is used it is trivial or superimposed. The words which make the death of the Messiah a sacrifice and which demand that the disciples must eat His Body and drink His Blood belong to the record of the solemn and final initiation of the disciples into the new order inaugurated by the death of Jesus. If it be a correct critical procedure, and the only adequate procedure, to read the record of the *Logia* of Jesus with ears ringing with the Old Testament as a whole, it is exceedingly difficult not to find in these final words a conscious superseding and fulfilment of the Old Testament sacrificial system. But, since they are Marcan, and Marcan only, a consideration of their historicity and meaning falls outside the scope of this essay.

The purpose of this essay has been to outline in a somewhat provocative form a critical reconstruction of the background of the ministry of Jesus and to claim the priority of the Christology. Only when the Christology is taken seriously and when its fundamental importance is fully recognised does Jesus emerge as a concrete figure in history. Only upon the background of the Christology do the great *Logia* which lie scattered about in the various literary strata of the Gospels cease to be disconnected fragments and come together as component parts of one messianic whole directed towards the crucifixion and towards the ratification by God of the obedience of the Messiah in the resurrection. *The foxes have holes and the birds of the heaven have nests ; but the Son of man hath not where to lay his head* (Q, Matt. viii. 20; Lk. ix. 57) ; *The Son of man came to seek and to save that which was lost* (special Luke, Lk. xix. 10) ; *The Son of man must suffer many things. . . . If any man would come after me let him deny himself and take up his cross and follow me* (Mk. viii. 29 ff.) ; *The Son of man goeth even as it is written of him* (Mk. xiv. 21) ; *This is my blood of the covenant, which is shed for many* (Mk. xiv. 24) ; *I have a baptism to be baptized with, and how am I straitened until it be accomplished* (special Luke, Lk. xii. 50) ; *Behold I cast out devils and perform cures to-day and to-morrow, and the third day I am perfected . . . for it cannot be that a prophet perish out of Jerusalem* (special Luke, Lk. xiii. 32, 33) ; *No man can enter into the house of the strong man* (Beelzebul) *and spoil his goods, except he first bind the strong man ; and then he will spoil his goods* (overlapping Mk. and Q, Mk. iii. 27 ; Matt. xii. 29 ; Lk. xi. 22). The saying rests upon and fulfils Is. xlix. 24 ff., *Shall the prey be taken from the mighty, or the lawful captives be delivered ? But thus saith the Lord, Even the captives of the mighty shall be taken away, and the prey of the terrible shall be delivered ; for I will contend with him that contendeth with thee, and I will save thy children . . . and all flesh shall know that I the Lord am thy saviour and thy redeemer, the Mighty One of Israel. I beheld Satan fallen as lightning from heaven* (special Luke, Lk. x. 18) ; *Art thou the Christ, Son of the Blessed ? And Jesus said, I am : and ye shall see the Son of man sitting at the right hand of power, and coming with the clouds of heaven* (Mk. xiv. 61, 62) ;

There is nothing hid, save that it should be manifested ; neither was anything made secret, but that it should come to light (overlapping Mk. and Q, Mk. iv. 22; Matt. x. 26 ; Lk. viii. 17, xii. 2).

This rehabilitation of the Christology is, however, not merely a piece of New Testament exegesis which challenges the adequacy of the ruling reconstruction of the development of primitive Christianity, and sets St. Paul and the author of the Fourth Gospel far nearer to the Jesus of History than is normally allowed ; it has implications for Christian Theology and for philosophy which vitally affect the doctrine of the Incarnation. The New Testament scholar, who is also a Christian, cannot patiently permit the dogmatist or the philosopher to expound the doctrine of the Incarnation on the basis of an analysis of human nature illustrated by the humanity of Jesus. He was unique ; and this particularity rivets the Christian doctrine of the Incarnation to the Christology and to the soteriology involved in the Christology, and presents an awkward material to the philosopher who is operating with a rigid doctrine of evolution. There are metaphysical implications in the Christology ; and the New Testament scholar, who is compelled to adopt a rather crude conception of revelation, precisely because he is a historian and has to interpret documents recording a movement of God to man and not of man to God, has nevertheless the right to demand that the Christian dogmatist should start from this particular revelation, and that the philosopher should at some point or other in his philosophy make sense of it by some other means than by obscuring the particularity of the Old Testament and by refusing to recognise that in the end the particularity of the Old Testament is only intelligible in the light of its narrowed fulfilment in Jesus, the Messiah, and of its expanded fulfilment in the Church.

JESUS CHRIST, THE LORD
BY HERMANN SASSE

V

JESUS CHRIST, THE LORD

Κύριος Ἰησοῦς. Jesus is Lord! So runs an old credal formula of the New Testament, which bears all the marks of a genuine creed and should be viewed as a preparatory step to the later Christian confessions of faith. Born of the common experience of believers, it is the response of the primitive Church to the revelation given in Christ. With this confession the primitive Church confronted alike the religions of its environment, the Judaism which treated as blasphemy the attachment to Jesus of the name *Κύριος*, and the hellenistic cults with their ' lords many.'

The origin of this confession in which for the first time belief in the Godhead of Jesus Christ was expressed is a difficult historical problem.[1] But the investigation of this problem cannot be undertaken here, since the limited space at my disposal must be devoted to a consideration of the answer to the question of what the New Testament means when it calls Jesus *Κύριος*, the Lord. Even this question cannot be treated exhaustively in all respects. I shall, therefore, confine myself to a discussion of the two most important notions which form the basis of the confession of Jesus as the Lord ; they are the notions of the *Resurrection* and of the *Exaltation* of Jesus Christ.

I

THE RISEN

' If you confess with your mouth that Jesus is Lord ; and believe from your heart that God raised him from the

---

[1] The confession of Jesus as the Lord can be traced back to the original Aramaic epoch of the primitive Church, as the formula ' Maranatha ' shows. With regard to this question and the whole problem involved in the word *Κύριος* I may refer to the report of the second conference of British and German theologians in *Theologische Blätter*, 1928, pp. 261 ff., and in *Theology*, October 1928, pp. 223 ff.

dead, ye shall be saved.'[1] These words of Paul show how inseparably the acknowledgment of Jesus as Lord is connected with the belief in His resurrection. Jesus is Lord as He who rose from the dead. For this reason the true understanding of the confession 'He is Kurios' depends upon the true understanding of the resurrection. Let us then attempt to answer the question : What does the New Testament mean by the message of the resurrection of Jesus ?

First let us inquire into the historical facts. The New Testament shows that the message of the resurrection of Jesus, or, expressed otherwise, of His rising from the dead by the Father's power, belonged from the first to the nucleus of the apostolic message but that the actual fact of the resurrection itself was not described. The apocryphal gospel of Peter first attempted to give a representation of it. In addition to the announcement of the resurrection, the New Testament contains only such reports of facts as should testify to the resurrection as an accomplished fact : these reports fall into two groups. The one group is represented by the account of the empty tomb, and can be traced back to the simple story in Mark xvi. ; no account is given as yet of an appearance of the Risen One, but a reference is made to an appearance which should take place in Galilee. The second consists of a series of brief statements and a few detailed reports of the appearance of the Risen Lord. It belongs to the great historical difficulties of the problem of the resurrection that only traces remain to us of the most important of these appearances. This is true above all of the fundamental appearance to Peter which, according to definite statements in Mark's Gospel, took place in Galilee.[2] The development of the Easter tradition has been such that though Mark's account of the empty tomb, with its legendary developments in the other Gospels, has not dislodged the various other accounts of the appearances of the Risen One, yet it has definitely relegated them to

---

[1] Rom. x. 9.

[2] The reasons which seem to show that the account of Jesus walking on the water is a reminiscence of this oldest appearance, I have collected in the *Theologische Blätter*, vol. v. 1922.

a second place. Mark's story has become the proper
Easter Gospel of the Church. Set over against these are
Paul's reports in the fifteenth chapter of the First Epistle
to the Corinthians in which is preserved an older pre-
Pauline *kerugma*. Here it is not the empty grave which
serves to testify to the resurrection, but the actual fact
of the appearances. This Pauline passage is the oldest
historical source of what actually happened at Easter.
Side by side with those of Paul stand the Evangelists'
accounts of the appearances of the Risen One. They can only
partially be identified with Paul's statements, but some—for
instance, the account of the disciples at Emmaus—can be
traced back to the earliest times. The present state of
the sources in the New Testament shows that in the first
decades of early Christianity there must have existed a
much more voluminous tradition of appearances than is
preserved to-day in the New Testament. The tradition as
we have it is only a reminiscence of a much richer tradition
from which, as a historical nucleus, the historian can still
recognise the fact that a series of experiences which could
only be explained as appearances of the Risen Christ have
been narrated by eye-witnesses. These appearances took
place in different localities (Galilee, Jerusalem and its
environment, near Damascus), at different times (to the
first apostles and Paul), before different persons (Peter,
Paul, James), and in different circles (the Eleven, the
disciples at Emmaus, and the Five Hundred). It is from
these experiences that the belief in the resurrection has
arisen. The empty tomb only became a proof of the
resurrection to a generation which, after the death of eye-
witnesses, no longer knew from personal recollection the
compelling power of these experiences, and to simple men
of the Jerusalem community, who needed a popular visible
account of the facts of Easter, and who furthermore had
to uphold apologetically before their Jewish associates the
objective certainty of their Easter faith.

The reality of the Easter experience is, then, the definite
historical fact which stands behind the belief in the resurrection. But how are these experiences to be explained?
Nothing much is gained if, following the accounts of the

New Testament, they are described as visions and then grouped under the category of visions.[1] They certainly belong, regarded psychologically, to this category : there is certainly a relationship between the Easter experiences and the visions, more particularly the so-called inaugural visions, which are related as happening to Jesus and the prophets. But even these experiences of the prophetic religion are not really explained by being considered from the psychological standpoint as visions. For the essential element in these visions is just that which distinguishes them from what, in the history of religion, is commonly known as a vision. The presupposition of the prophetic experience is the fact that there are true and false, real and unreal, visions. Psychology is not in a position to understand this distinction. From the psychologist's point of view there is no reason why the experiences of Jeremiah should be a true revelation, but the experiences of the contemporary false prophets not.[2] That within the mass of visions and similar experiences of which the history of

---

[1] Acts xxvi. 19 describes Paul's experience on the way to Damascus as ὀπτασία.

[2] Gunkel in *R.G.G.* IV. 1873 mentions once the accusation of 'lying prophecy' which was brought against the prophets of salvation in the Old Testament. He adds the remark : 'It is not becoming for us to repeat the judgment. We have rather to recognise that in outward bearing they were not to be distinguished from their opponents ; and further that they coined ideas which are inalienable from religion : we have received from them great ideas such as the creative power of Jahweh, the conversion of the heathen, and no one has spoken more beautifully of Jahweh's love for Israel.' It is remarkable that so shrewd a researcher as Gunkel could have overlooked the central problem of prophecy. Neither his outward appearance, nor his way of working and its effects, nor the creation of new religious ideas make a prophet to be a prophet, but solely that the 'Word' has been entrusted to him by God. It is of the very essence of true prophecy to distinguish itself from lying prophecy and to have an anxious fear of personal error. For that reason Amos rejected the title of 'nabi.' For that reason the great prophets of Israel . . . like Zarathustra . . . fought against the false prophets. For that reason Mohamet in his early days was afraid of being a 'kahin.' The peculiar theological problem of prophecy is to discover the boundary between true and false prophecy, between a real and a self imagined mission, between real revelation and the productions of an enthusiastic Pneumatikos, between pure and impure preaching of the 'Word' . . . for even genuine prophets may cease to be God's instruments. Compare with the theological problem of prophecy Emil Brunner's *The Mediator*, p. 194.

religion is full there should be a small section of phenomena which contains true prophecy, an actual revelation of the living God, in which the true ' Word ' of God is heard, that is not to be understood from the mere presuppositions of psychology. Revelation is a category recognised neither by the psychologist nor the historian : it belongs entirely and solely to theology.

But even among Biblical phenomena which we must classify under the category of true experiences of revelation, the Easter experiences of the disciples clearly occupy a peculiar position. They may be compared with the inaugural visions ; for in them too the Call, the Commission, plays a part. But here also a difference is to be observed. The disciples were not prophets, nor was Paul a prophet. If the terminology of the Bible, which had its origin entirely in the facts themselves, is taken seriously, it must be recognised that the apostolic office is quite distinct from the prophetic office. There had been prophets for hundreds of years[1] : the apostolic office was limited to one generation.[2] It is especially worthy of notice that, after the manifestation of Christ, prophecy indeed did not disappear from within Christianity, but its character became that of an unpretentious office of the Church. In the Epistle to the Ephesians the Church is said to be ' built on the foundation of apostles and prophets.'[3] The apostles take precedence. The elimination of prophecy from the Church as an independent factor of equal rank with that of the apostolate and its witness, is frequently regarded as the fossilisation of the Church and as the withdrawal of ' true and living religion ' behind institutional religion. But Montanism— one of the most remarkable, and, from the standpoint

[1] It is highly significant for the history of religion that the prophetic religion is to be distinguished from the ' ecstatic pneumatikos.' As opposed to the latter it recognises itself to be both new and unique (compare for instance the limits which Zarathustra, the prophets of Israel, and Mohamet made for themselves), it is limited moreover to the people of the near East and to a particular period (from Zarathustra to Mohamet).

[2] This is of course to use the term in a peculiar sense, and to apply it only to those who were commissioned by the Lord himself, and not in its wider meaning, as used, for instance, in the Didache and sometimes in the New Testament.

[3] Eph. ii. 20.

H

of the history of religion, most interesting phenomena of the early Church, and one which also sheds important light on the New Testament—is a proof of the necessity for this elimination.　The conflict between ' Office ' and ' Spirit ' is to a large extent the conflict between the apostolate and the prophecy.　The absolute character of the revelation in Christ stands or falls with the primacy of the apostolate over prophecy.　Wherever prophecy re-appears as strongly independent, it threatens the finality of Christ's revelation as having happened once for all in history, and it sets aside the witness of the apostolic office. The Church of Christ is an apostolic, not a prophetic, Church. Prophecy has a place in her only within those limits assigned to it by the apostolic office.　The Johannine Christ said of the Paraclete, the Holy Spirit, ' He shall take of mine and shall declare it unto you.' [1]　It is not a ' quenching of the Spirit ' as we are accustomed to say, not a confinement of religion within the narrow boundary of an ecclesiastical institution, not the binding of religion to history in hostility to life, but the expression of the fact that there has been a Revelation and that the ' Word ' of God is not given or served out to individuals here and there, but that the Word became Flesh.　The Holy Spirit is the Paraclete who has been given to the Church and will be eternally operative in her.　The prophetic office now receives quite a different significance : it is given to the Church.　Wherever prophecy appears and does not recognise its connection with the historical Christ, it is not the Paraclete, the Spirit of Truth, who speaks.　' Hereby shall ye know the Spirit of God : every spirit which confesses that Jesus Christ is come in the flesh, is of God : every spirit which does not confess that Jesus Christ is come in the flesh is not of God.' [2]

If this distinction has been fully understood, no attempt will be made to explain the Easter experience, which is

---

[1] John xvi. 14.　That is the doctrine of John's Gospel as we read it in the Canon.　Apparently it is concerned with an ecclesiastical correction of prophecy which had originally quite a different meaning.　Compare my attempt to explain it in *Z.N.W.* xxiv. 1925, and H. Windisch : *The Five Sayings on the Paraclete in the Gospel of John* in the volume pre-sented to Adolf Jülicher.　1927.

[2] 1 John iv. 2 f.

constitutive for the apostolic office, as being comparable with the visions of the prophetic religion. It must be something original, something absolutely unique. Whilst prophetic experiences are always those of individual persons, this experience happened simultaneously, or almost simultaneously, to a succession of men. Further, it had the same content. Those who had this experience became witnesses of the resurrection. They knew that Christ was risen from the dead. As related in Acts i. 22, it was a condition of the apostolate to have been a ' witness of the resurrection.' According to 1 Cor. xv. 7, the Lord appeared to ' all the apostles.' This was not the only condition of the apostolate, nor was every individual who had shared the Easter experience an apostle, but it was further required, for the apostolic office, that they should have been commissioned and have received their charge from the Lord. Still it may nevertheless be said that the Easter experience was the most important condition.

How then is the content of the Easter experience to be understood ? This experience is not fully understood when it is regarded as a vision of Christ. Visions of Christ, whatever they may be judged to be, were not restricted to that one time. For Paul definitely distinguishes between his experience on the way to Damascus and the ' other visions and revelations of the Lord.' [1] Thus the ordinary interpretations which would explain these Easter experiences as though the disciples had had visions of Christ in which the certainty was borne in upon them that their Master continued to live, and that they then drew the conclusion that he had risen from the dead, fall to the ground. They might well have attained to the certainty that Jesus continued to live with God without that overpowering Easter experience which shook the whole of their lives. Surely the certainty of immortality is always borne in upon men whenever a loved and honoured master has been snatched away from the circle of his disciples ? It is only necessary to recall the significance which the death of

[1] 1 Cor. xv. and Gal. i. should be compared with 2 Cor. xii. Why in the latter is there no reference to Damascus ?

Socrates had for the belief in immortality among the Western peoples. No. The disciples' experience must have had quite a different content. In these experiences the assurance cannot have contained a universal truth, but an actual fact—a fact which can only be described by the word resurrection.

What then is meant by the resurrection ? What does the New Testament understand by it ? What did Jesus mean when he spoke of the resurrection of the dead ? What did the primitive Christians understand by the word when they spoke of resurrection as though it required no explanation ? We shall find the answer if we ask the question : Where did the New Testament message of the resurrection first arouse opposition and why did it happen ? This was the case during Paul's mission to Athens and Corinth. Why did the Athenians mock at the idea of the resurrection ? Why were there men in the Christian community in Corinth who denied the resurrection ? First, it was the conception of the reconstitution of the body which, because it did not correspond with the Greek doctrine of the immortality of the soul, would excite opposition as being an unphilosophical and materialistic conception. In 1 Cor. xv. Paul took endless trouble both to vindicate the doctrine of the resurrection, in reply to the objections of the Greeks, and to show its high spirituality, in opposition to the misunderstanding of it as a purely materialistic idea. We modern people, for whose world-view (*Weltanschauung*) the conception of the resurrection is likewise somewhat incongruous, can only be very thankful that the writers of the New Testament were in this instance forced to develop more fully what seemed to them to be a self-evident conception. But it would be a mistake to suppose that it was only the question of corporeality which was a cause of offence to the Greeks. Let us recall the situation in Athens which is so graphically described for us in Acts xvii. 32. Why was Paul interrupted after mentioning that God had raised Jesus from the dead ? Is the idea of the resurrection really so unbearable to the Greeks ? Why then were the death and resurrection of Attis and Osiris not offensive to the Greek world, and why did later

Hellenism accept without any difficulty the myth and cultus of the dying and reviving deities and reconcile them with their own conception of immortality, just as the ancient Greeks had treated the Dionysiac religion ? No, it was not the idea of the resurrection which was unbearable, but the message of a resurrection which was not a myth. Here they were speaking of a resurrection which had happened, which was a historical event : that was the objection. It must be clearly understood what is meant by saying that the Christian message, in spite of all the mythological symbols which it used, was a historical message. What was insupportable for the Greek, as it is to the modern man, was that a man who had lived at a definite time and in a definite place and whose death was an established historical fact should be *the* revelation. When and where had Osiris died ? The question had no sense at all. The events which the myth relates are such as have not been reported in history ; it expresses, in modern speech, necessary truths of reason and not accidental truths of history. It must always be remembered that ancient religion knew nothing of any historical revelation.[1] The death and resurrection of Jesus as a myth, as a parable of an eternal truth, would have been tolerated by the Greeks ; but as a historical event the resurrection could not be conceived. That introduces a further point. The historical message of the ' Christian Faith ' is at once an eschatological message. With the resurrection of Jesus is associated the resurrection of the dead. In 1 Cor. xv. Paul is unmistakably expressing this relation, and it is also suggested on the Areopagus.[2] It is at this point that the division is most profound between the two world-views, the religious worlds of the Christian

---

[1] That is the real reason why the Greeks never developed a historical world-view, while the great prophetic religions of the East acknowledging a historical revelation possess at the same time a historical world-view. If Herodotus is the father of historical narrative and Thucydides is the father of historians, the historical world-view of the West is determined by the world-view of the apocalyptic and prophetic religion. The stream of thinking in terms of world history flows from Zarathustra, the prophets of Israel and the apocalyptic writers, by the New Testament and Augustine, up to the present time.

[2] Acts xvii. 31.

and the Greek.   It is at this point that we learn to understand the essential character of the resurrection.

The doctrine of the resurrection does not as yet exist where, as in so many primitive religions, a return of the dead from the grave, a reanimation of the body, is expected. The resurrection in its peculiar significance may only be recognised if the resurrection of the dead is conceived as an event happening at the end of history.   Such is the case in prophetic religion : outside Christianity it is found in Parseeism, in Judaism and in Islam.   It is characteristic of this apocalyptic hope of the resurrection that the latter is not the concern of individual men only, but of the whole of humanity.   The resurrection is a cosmic event.   It happens at the end of the world and heralds the beginning of a new creation.   Consequently death is somewhat differently estimated than by the Greeks.   It is not regarded only as the end of the individual human life but as a power which dominates the world.   To die, according to the doctrine of the resurrection, is not, as it is for the Indians and the Greeks, the transmigration of the soul from one existence to another—it is that—but it is also the horrible annihilation of man.   Regarded in this way—and this is the implication of the philosophical doctrine of immortality—death is not made easy but hard. It is taken absolutely seriously.   The dread of dying for the natural man is not to be scared away by the consolations of philosophy.   All this is due to the very different estimate of the body.   For the Greek the body is the prison, the tomb, of the soul ; for the man of the New Testament it is the temple of the Holy Spirit, God's creation and therefore His own.   The whole Biblical presentation must appear to the Greek—as to the modern man— to be childish and primitive.   It is only a question, then, whether this is an adverse criticism, or whether the primitive estimation of death and of the body is not the more correct one.   This estimation of the body is accused of being materialistic.   But the question is rather whether materialism is not to be sought on the side of those who value the body as pure matter.   To meet the reproach of materialism, Paul expressly said that so far as it is matter it cannot inherit the Kingdom of God. But it is not only matter, not only σάρξ (flesh), but something more. Fundamentally it is neither higher nor lower than the ψυχή (the soul). Body and soul can belong either to God or to the devil. The life of the soul is just as much dominated by sin as the life of the body. The antithesis of the divine and the not-divine is not identical with that of soul and body. Above both is the Πνεῦμα ἅγιον, the Spirit of God, which is to be clearly distinguished from the natural πνεῦμα of man, the ' ground of the soul ' (*Seelengrund*), as it might be called. The resurrection is the summoning of the whole man, soul and body, from death to life in the spirit. Just as man was once called into existence in the flesh in this transient world, so resurrection is a new creation.[1] Just as man's creation is indissolubly bound up with the creation of the world, and his existence is inseparably connected with the existence of the world, so man's new creation cannot be conceived apart from a new creation of the world, of a world of which it may be said ' there shall be no more death.' This world of a new heaven and a new earth corresponds to the man on whom the curse of having to die no longer rests.

These are some of the thoughts which the writers of the New Testament connected with the conception of the resurrection. Now let us return to the question of the resurrection of Jesus. It can only be understood if it is viewed in its relation to the resurrection of the dead. Paul did not emphasise this connection gratuitously. As the Risen from the dead Jesus Christ is the first-born among many brethren. If there is no resurrection of the dead, then Christ is not risen. If He is not risen, then the dead rise not. If this is so, then the significance of Christ's resurrection becomes clear : it is the beginning of a new world-epoch, the end of the old and the beginning of a new aeon, the dawn of the new world of Eternity and of the Spirit. It is only to be understood as an event at the end of history, as future become present, as the beginning of a new creation of God, as the commencement of a general

---

[1] The Jewish like the Persian apologetics established the possibility of the resurrection by referring to the miracle of creation.

resurrection of the dead. At last we grasp the force of those Easter experiences through which the disciples came to be convinced that Jesus had risen from the dead. What they experienced was the fulfilment of all prophetic and apocalyptic expectations. What are the experiences of the prophets as compared with these experiences? Did a prophet ever experience what the apostles and the primitive Church then experienced? If the resurrection is thus to be understood, then we grasp why it is not described in the New Testament, and indeed why it cannot be described. It is not representable, it is not perceivable like the creation of the world, and like the incarnation of the ' Son.' No man can behold the ' mighty works of God.' It is only in their effects that they enter in some way into our world, into our reality. Only God Himself, through His Spirit, can make us men certain of them. For this reason we are not able to describe the resurrection more in detail. The impossibility of giving more details and the necessity of bearing witness to it must be blamed for the divergent accounts in the New Testament. It is not possible to adjust the accounts of the corporeality of the Risen One as they are described, for instance, by Paul and in the Gospels. We know nothing of the empty tomb, nor the corporeality of the Risen One, nor can we relive the Easter experiences of the disciples. If we knew it all, we should still know nothing of the resurrection itself. It is a great misunderstanding, although a very old and easily conceivable one, to seek the peculiar character of Easter in these miracles. The miracle of Easter is not the fact of the Easter visions, nor the empty grave, nor the corporeality as a Thomas might see it, but the act of the living God, who awakened Jesus from the dead, which lies behind them all. In these Easter facts, the final end of history enters in some way into history ; as to how far, there is no agreement and perhaps never can be any agreement in the views expressed. When the primitive Church went out into the world with the message ' The Lord is risen,' it was not to these facts that she referred but to the act of God which lies behind them.

II

THE EXALTED

Only on the basis of the resurrection can the confession ' Jesus is Lord ' be understood. It is, however, of profound significance that the New Testament distinguishes the resurrection from the exaltation of Christ. As the Risen One, Christ would only be the firstfruit from the dead, the firstborn among many brethren. His resurrection would thus only be the beginning of the general resurrection of the dead. There would be no fundamental difference between His resurrection and ours. His ' Lordship ' would be inconceivable apart from the resurrection, but it would not be accounted for by it alone. For this reason the New Testament draws a logical distinction between the resurrection and the exaltation. In so far as both are actually inseparably connected it is a logical distinction only. It is not a case of two distinct events as the popular view recorded in Acts i. willingly conceived it. The Risen is the Exalted. Inasmuch as God raised Him from the dead He has exalted Him, He has made Him to be ' both Lord and Christ.'[1] The significance of the exaltation can be most clearly seen in the words of Psalm cx., which from a very early date was connected with Jesus : ' The Lord said to my Lord : sit thou on my right hand until I make thine enemies the footstool of thy feet.' Mark[2] and the other two synoptic Gospels following him introduce these words into the dispute between Jesus and the Pharisees. And indeed those who maintain that this conversation is not a genuine record must still admit that it goes back to the early days of the Christian community, and mirrors the first dispute between the Church and the Synagogue. Further, the words of the Psalmist are quoted in the Acts,[3] by Paul,[4] and in the Epistle to the Hebrews.[5] And the extent of its influence can be seen from the fact that the words ' Sitteth on the right hand of the almighty Father '

---

[1] Compare Acts ii. 24 ff., 36 ; v. 30 f.
[2] Mk. xii. 35 ff. ; compare Matt. xxii. 41 ff. ; Lk. xx. 41 ff.
[3] Acts ii. 34 ff.   [4] 1 Cor. xv. 25.   [5] Heb. i. 13.

became an article of the creed. The image of sitting at the right hand of God was connected with the representation of the Son of Man from the book of Daniel in the answer which Jesus gave to the High Priest's question, whether he was the Messiah : ' I am, and henceforth the Son of Man shall be seen of them sitting on the right hand of power and coming in the clouds of Heaven.' [1] From all this it is evident that even in the most primitive belief the conception of His exaltation was connected with the Messiahship of Jesus. The Crucified ascended into Heaven. As Son of Man and Judge of the world, He shares in the omnipotence of God. Here it becomes evident how the conception of the Messiah is closely related with that of the Lord. If the Crucified Jesus is seen to be the Messiah, the Son of Man must then be conceived as having ascended into Heaven. And if this exaltation is represented in the words of Psalm cx., then the title of Lord is given to Jesus. We do not know whether this Psalm caused Jesus to be described as Lord, but at any rate it facilitated the transference of the title to Him. But what is to be understood by the exaltation is clear. It signifies that Jesus after His resurrection shares in the Eternity, Omnipresence, and Omnipotence of God.

(a) *The Eternity of Christ.*—As the Exalted One, Jesus shares in the eternity of God. In the New Testament this has been most clearly expressed by transferring to Him certain formal religious phrases usually ascribed to God's eternity. He is the First and the Last, the Beginning and the End, the Alpha and the Omega. He it is who Is and Was and Is to Come, the Same yesterday, to-day and for ever.[2]

In order to understand its implications, we must briefly recall the Biblical conception of eternity. The Biblical idea of eternity has been developed in contrast to that of early Oriental astrology. In this conception, eternity is thought of as equal to the infinite sum of all intervals of time. *Aeternitas*, eternity as it is ascribed to the heavenly

[1] Mk. xiv. 62.
[2] These formulae belong to the religious language of the Hellenistic East. They may be traced back in part to very early times. The formula ' I am the First and the Last ' occurs as early as the Deutero-Isaiah and is an expression of the Divine eternity.

deities of Eastern Hellenists, is an abstraction derived from the observation of the movements of the starry heavens with their endless time. The world is eternal. If there is for it something like a beginning and an end, there is yet never an absolute beginning and an absolute end. Just as at great intervals of time the heavenly bodies return repeatedly to their original positions, so at great time-periods all Being is consummated in that all is renewed. The idea of an eternal return is the final conception of this world picture. Eternity is here the infinite sum of all aeons, it is unceasing time. Although this view recurs in isolated expressions in Biblical speech, and has even penetrated into the Bible itself in the Book of the Preacher,[1] the conception of eternity which is mainly characteristic of the Bible is an entirely different one. The religion of the Bible (and this view it shares with the Persian religion and would seem to derive from it) clearly distinguishes between the time of the world and the eternity of God.[2] In this it is opposed to the pantheism, open or concealed, which is involved in the astrological view of time and eternity which has just been sketched. Because the world and God are not identical, therefore the eternity of God is different from the time of the world. The world-time, the aeon, is not unending. It is limited by its creation and its final end. Here there is an absolute beginning and an absolute end. God's eternity extends beyond the time of the world. ' Before the mountains were made and the earth and the world were created, Thou art God, from eternity to eternity.' [3] God is the First and the Last. We see here how the ideas of the creation and the end of the world are connected with the strictest monotheism which

---

[1] Eccles. i. 10 can hardly be understood in any other sense.

[2] Compare the Persian distinction between *Zarvan akarana* and *Zarvan dareghovadata*. Plato in his discussion of the problem of time and eternity in the *Timaeus* seems to be influenced by this conception. This idea of divine eternity as something quite different from the time of the world is rejected by Aristotle.

[3] Ps. xc. 2 ; compare with Ps. cii. 25 ff. : ' Thou Lord has founded the earth from the beginning, and the heavens are the work of thy hands. They will pass away, but thou remainest. . . . But thou art the same, thy years will not cease.' It is very significant that these words have been connected with Christ in Heb. i. 10.

is opposed to every form of pantheism, be it open or concealed. All these conceptions appear contemporaneously in history and belong to the great prophetic religions.[1] According to this interpretation there is not merely a quantitative difference between the time of the world and the eternity of God, between the aeon in the sense of the world-time and the aeon in the sense of eternity. They are not related to one another like finite and infinite, but rather they differ qualitatively from one another. The antithesis of σάρξ and πνεῦμα, death and life, transient and intransient, world and God is present in the antithesis of time and eternity. They are incommensurable.[2] Eternity is not unending time but the antithesis of time, it abolishes time.[3]

It is in their relation to this Biblical idea of eternity that the New Testament statements on the eternity of Christ are to be understood. Because Jesus as the Exalted Lord shares in God's eternity, past, present, and future, the measure and boundaries of earthly time no longer exist for Him. What would be said of the eternal God is thus also valid for Him. ' Before the earth and the world were created, Thou wast, from eternity to eternity.' It has often aroused the astonishment of theologians that the conception of Christ's pre-existence should have been expressed at so early a date. It is regarded as a philosophical speculation which is really foreign to New Testament Christology. The pre-existence of Christ, however, of which the New Testament speaks has nothing to do with philosophy ; and the expression ' pre-existence ' which has been derived from philosophy ought therefore generally to be avoided, and 'eternal' or 'supra-temporal' existence substituted for it. Viewed from the standpoint of our thought and of our earthly time-bound existence, eternity is

---

[1] They are already developed in Deutero-Isaiah.

[2] ' Eternity is just as little the continuation of time as it is that from which time proceeds. Our temporality is a curved fragment of eternity ' (Emil Brunner, The Mediator, p. 520).

[3] Thus it is said in the Slavonian Book of Enoch (lxv. 6 ff.) : ' When all creatures come to an end . . . then time also will have been abolished and henceforth there will be no more years, nor months, nor days, nor hours : they will henceforth be no more reckoned, but it will be the beginning of the one aeon.' Compare Plato, Timaeus 37 D.

that which was before time was, even as it is that which will
be when time is no more. But this is only an illustration,
and not a definition of eternity. For our thought and speech
(notice only the tenses of verbs which govern all our
statements) we have only at our disposal time-concepts
which have been derived from our earthly temporal existence. The language of the Bible must use the same means.
It must speak of eternity in concepts taken from time. And
so it is that eternity is described as that which was from the
beginning, from primeval times, before the world came
into being, πρὸ τῶν αἰώνων. God, the Wisdom of God,[1]
the love of God,[2] were ' before the creation of the world,'
before the time of the world, from all eternity. ' Before
the world was founded,' the Father loved the Son.[3] ' Before
the foundation of the world was laid,' God has chosen us.[4]
The ' before ' which is contained in all these statements
implies far more than the mere temporal difference between
before and after. There is in it that which can never be
expressed in human speech, the distinction between the
eternity of God and the time of the world. The eternal,
the supra-temporal Being of Christ is the hypothesis in the
light of which the New Testament sees Christ in pre-
Christian history, but for us it is an assumption hard to
be understood. It is not so much that we must consider
how Israelitish history, the whole Old Testament, is to be
allegorically connected with Christ (indeed these allegories
as we find them in Paul and the Epistle to the Hebrews
are not meant merely as ingenious jests but are the unveiling of the deepest kernel of their history) ; but we have
also to consider the fact that the words of the Kurios in
the Old Testament are applied without apology to Jesus
Christ, and, as the words of the Lord, are placed by
the side of the Logia of the historical Jesus, and of the
words of the Exalted One as they were heard in spirit by
Paul and the Seer of Revelations. It is quite in keeping
with this method of thought that events like the death
and resurrection of Jesus are ' perpetuated ' in their own
peculiar way. It is not that Jesus was first the Crucified,
then became the Risen, and is now the Exalted ; but as

[1] Prov. viii. 23.   [2] Ps. xxv. 6.   [3] John xvii. 24.   [4] Eph. i. 4.

the Exalted is the Risen, so He is the Crucified. His death is not merely something which belongs to history, though it is indeed a historical fact. But He is now present as the Crucified, the ἐσταυρωμένος. The seeming contradiction is then at last resolved, we wait for the coming of the Lord and we know that He is present now. This apparent antinomy between the Coming One and the Present One may not be accounted for as due to placing Hellenistic mysticism side by side with Palestinian eschatology; for it was present from the beginning in the belief in the Kurios. On the contrary, here too the difference existing between 'before and after' has been dissolved, the present and the future have become one. The exalted Christ as sharing in the eternity of God stands beyond the time of the world. His eternal Being passes beyond the boundaries and the bulk of terrestrial time.

The extraordinary difficulty created by these conceptions for the modern man lies in the question : How can the eternal Being of the exalted Lord and the temporal appearance of Jesus Christ be related in thought ? Here a twofold danger threatens the theologian. Either the eternal Christ is lost in the historical Jesus, or the contrary happens. It all depends whether we recognise that in Jesus Christ time and eternity become one : eternity passes into time : God's revelation takes place in the world : God becomes man. That is the miracle of God's revelation in Christ : *Finitum capax infiniti, tempus capax aeternitatis, saeculum hoc capax futuri saeculi.* If this assumption is not admitted, then the revelation, of which the Bible speaks, has not taken place. For this revelation is bound up with events which happened in time : with the historical figures of the prophets, with the historical destiny of the Israelitish people and the ancient world in general ; with the Jesus of history who suffered ' under Pontius Pilate ' and died outside the gates of Jerusalem [1] ; with the history of the apostles. The revelation has a temporal side which cannot be thought away. But it has still another side. That which, seen from our standpoint, happened in time, seen from the standpoint of God happened in eternity. ' The

[1] Compare Heb. xiii. 12.

mighty acts of God,' the creation, the revelation through
the prophets, the incarnation of Christ, His earthly life, His
death, His resurrection and ascension, the founding of the
Church, the future coming of Christ, the judgment—
these are all events which have a twofold significance :
eternal and temporal.   Viewed from their eternal side they
are for us inconceivable : viewed from their temporal side
they are recognisable through faith as the acts of God.
For only the believer sees behind the temporal event, the
act of God which surpasses all human thought ; behind
the beginning of the world, the creation ; behind the
experience of the prophets, the Voice of God ; behind the
birth of Christ, the Incarnation of the Son ; behind the
earthly life of Jesus, the Voice and Activity of God ; behind
the death on the cross, the Reconciliation ; behind the
Easter experiences of the disciples, the Resurrection and
the Exaltation ; behind the end of the world, the Judge-
ment.   Only for faith is the history of salvation really the
history of salvation.   The believer knows that this history,
the temporal side of which he alone perceives, is the history
of God's activity and that what for us has taken place in
time, for God has happened in eternity.   Therefore for
faith there is no tormenting contradiction in Jesus Christ
belonging both to time and to eternity, but it is only the
expression of Him as true man and true God : in Him the
eternal God truly entered into history.

(b) *The Lord of the Church.*—Just as the exalted Lord
shares in the eternity of God so He shares in His omnipresence and His omnipotence.   We shall be able to say
best what has to be said in this connection if we take as
our starting-point those aspects of His Being which alone
are knowable by us.   That is the fact of the Church.   We
continue then our meditation on the exalted Lord when
we speak of Him as the Lord of the Church.   It is only
because we are acquainted with Him as the Lord of the
Church that we know His Being as Lord, His Kingship.   If,
in dogmatics, the kingly Office of Christ is discussed (in
addition to His prophetic and high-priestly offices) and the
threefold Kingship—the Kingdom of Power, the Kingdom
of Grace and the Kingdom of Glory—is distinguished

within it, it can only be from the standpoint of Grace, for this alone is an object of our experience—namely, of the experience of our faith.

The exalted Lord and His Church belong to each other. Not until the Church came into existence was He acknowledged as her Lord. It is not unimportant that the name of the Lord first appeared under the form of *maran*, ὁ κύριος ἡμῶν (our Lord). Luther's statement, in his explanation of the second article, on the personal relation of the individual to Christ, is perfectly correct, and also valid for early Christianity : ' I believe that Jesus Christ . . . is my Lord.' The personal confession of the individual ' My Lord and my God ' is an entirely primitive Christian confession.[1] Within the meaning of this confession Paul is able to describe himself as the slave of Christ. But that is by the way. In the first place, it is not δοῦλος which stands over against Jesus as κύριος, but the ἐκκλησία. Jesus is only ' my Lord' because He is ' our Lord.' We only belong to Him as members of the *Ecclesia*. The Lord and the Ecclesia belong to each other in such a way that it is impossible to think of one without at the same time thinking of the other. We cannot speak of the Lord without speaking of the Church. And the converse : as soon as I speak of the Church I speak of the Lord. They belong to each other as the Head to the Body, as the Corner Stone to the House, and as the Stem of the Vine to the Vine.

In order to understand the relationship between the exalted Lord and the Church, we will start from that remarkable saying of early Palestinian Christianity in which, though the word Church is not to be found, the identity of being existing between Christ and the Church has been classically described : ' Where two or three are gathered together in my Name, there am I in the midst of them.' [2] Here it is made clear that the presence of Christ is constitutive for the Church. Paul's letters constantly repeat the same idea. But what is to be understood by the presence of the Lord ? When we speak of Christ as being in the midst of the disciples, is it only a

---

[1] John xx. 28.   [2] Matt. xviii. 20.

symbolical expression ?   Do we mean that our imagination
graphically represents Him to us as present ? If the
scholars of Socrates or the disciples of the Buddha came
together, and spoke of their master, could they not also
say that he was in the midst of them ?   Without a doubt
the early Christians would definitely have rejected any such
comparison.   For them the presence of the Lord was something very different.   And we too conceive of His presence
very differently.

In order to understand the nature of this presence, we
remember that there is a Jewish saying which corresponds
exactly to Matt. xviii. 20.   We read Pirge Aboth III. 3 :
' Where two are sitting together and words of the Tora are
between them, the Schechinah is amidst them.'   There the
personified Spirit of God has the same position as that of
the Living Christ in the *Logion* Matt. xviii. 20.   This corresponds exactly with what we read in the New Testament of
the relation of Christ to the Holy Spirit.   The Lord who
is the Spirit is the Present One.   The experience of His
presence is a pneumatic experience—that is to say, it is
mediated through the Holy Spirit.   Only in the Holy
Spirit is it possible to confess that Jesus the Lord is also
the Living, the Present One.[1]   Here again we come up
against the enormous difficulty which a Biblical conception,
more or less taken for granted by men of the New Testament, creates for our modern thought just because it is
foreign to our world-view (*Weltanschauung*).   Just as
during the last centuries the Biblical conceptions of
the resurrection and of eternity have been almost lost to
the Christianity of the West, so in the same way the
conception of the Holy Spirit has faded away until even
theology no longer appreciates its full greatness and is only
now on its way to recapture it.

To know the effects of the Spirit and of the Spirits as
they are related in Paul's epistles, the speaking of tongues
and prophecy, visions and auditions, gifts of healing and the
capacity to work miracles and many other charismata, is
not as yet to understand what the Spirit is.   The majority
of these phenomena do not belong only to Christianity.

[1] I Cor. xii. 3.

I

They are phenomena which are to be found in all history of religion. They are derived from that ecstatic religiosity which is diffused throughout the whole earth, in which man is aware that his own powers and capacities are raised to the supernatural, for Divinity works in him. When Paul ranked precisely these primitive manifestations of ecstatic religiosity (which for a community like that of Corinth would be particularly highly treasured as signs of the possession of the Holy Spirit, and which Paul himself knew and valued in his own experience) lower than the silent influence of the Spirit of Christ, he made the same distinction as the prophets, who, although their own lives were rich in similar ecstatic experiences, yet drew a line between themselves and ecstatic seers and professional prophets. What is the significance of this division which also involves the distinction between true and false prophets ? Here a rigid boundary must be drawn between God and man, and between what is truly the work of God and what is not. Ecstatic religion discovered the conception of the *pneuma*. The *pneuma* forms a third in addition to body and soul ; it is something in man which actually belongs to another world. All psychology, unless it is satisfied with the surface analysis of the human soul, comes across this latter, the inexplicable in man, the province where events inaccessible to psychology take place. What psychology will explain such phenomena as the inspiration of the poet, the intuition of the metaphysician, the experience of the mystic, to quote those experiences by which the nature of the *pneuma* can be made clear to the modern man ? Ecstatic religion is to be distinguished from prophetic religion, whose greatest office is the separation of God from the world, of true from false religion, of the world of God from the world of demons. The criterion by which the prophets and Paul ' tried the Spirits ' has been called ' ethical religion.' If it means that the religion in question has realised the reality of sin in the presence of God, then it is correct. The prophetic religion has separated the *pneuma* from the holy *pneuma*, the Spirit from the Holy Spirit, the daemonic world from the truly divine world. With great prophecy the doctrine of the Holy Spirit, without which the whole history of the revelation of the Bible would be unintelligible, begins.[1] The answer of the pre-Christian religion of the Bible to the God-world problem is given in the doctrine of the Holy Spirit. On the one side, this doctrine stands opposed to all pantheistic and mystical religion, in which God and the world, or God and man, are either openly or secretly identified; and on the other side, to a dualism which so separates God and the world from each other that there is no longer any relation possible between them.[2] The doctrine of the Holy Spirit recognises an antithesis which is not to be transcended between God and the world, God and man, but it is aware too that God works in the world and in man. How energetically Judaism wrestled with this problem is shown in its attempts to make the doctrine of the Spirit more profoundly philosophical and yet at the same time to make it clear. The conceptions of the Word (Memra, Logos) of Wisdom, of the Schechinah of God, etc., independently of the belief in the Messiah, are a preparation for the later Christology. It is no accident that these Old Testament conceptions became later so important in the Christological discussions of the Church.[3]

It is remarkable that the significance for Jesus of the doctrine of the Holy Spirit has been so little appreciated. The fight which He waged and which He commissioned His disciples to carry on against the demons possessed a very different significance for Him from that given to it by modern commentators, for the representations which lie at the root of this side of the life and work of Jesus are strange to them. How can this conflict be understood unless there is seen behind it a consciousness so overpowering of the reality of the Holy Spirit that in comparison with it all

[1] The expression 'Holy Spirit' is, indeed, first met with in the post-exilic literature (perhaps under Persian influence). Prior to this there was the expression 'Ruach Jahweh.' It was the Ruach Jahweh which made the prophet to be a prophet (Hos. ix. 7). In this separation between the true prophets and the ecstatic nebiim of popular religion arose, too, the distinction between the true spirit of Jahweh and the Ruach.

[2] Compare the attack of Deutero-Isaiah on the Persian Dualism (xli. 4 and xliv. 6).

[3] Compare the dispute between Arius and Athanasius on the interpretation of Prov. viii. 22 f.

that 'pneumatics' have experienced, both before and since, fades away into nothing ? How is the experience at His baptism, when He received the assurance that the Holy Spirit rested upon Him, actually to be understood ? [1] How are the stories related to us of Easter and Pentecost, the Resurrection-experiences of the disciples, the beginnings of the Church in Jerusalem, and primitive Palestinian Christianity at all conceivable apart from the recognition that, behind them all, is a wholly great and new experience of the reality of the holy *pneuma* ? It was not the Hellenistic Church of the Pauline period, but the Palestinian Church, which was first a pneumatic Church. Precisely because she realised herself to be the Holy People of God of the last days, she knew she possessed the Holy Spirit. She was Israel ' after the Spirit.'

It was in the mighty pneumatic experiences of primitive Christianity (and apart from these experiences the origin of the Church would be wholly inconceivable) that the New Testament view of the Holy Spirit arose. It can be expressed in the sentence : *Ubi Christus, ibi Spiritus Sanctus : ubi Spiritus Sanctus, ibi Christus.* Christ and the Holy Spirit belong together. Faith knows no experience of the actuality of the Holy Spirit which is not at the same time also an experience of the actual presence of Christ. There is no faith in the present Christ, no confession of Jesus the Lord, which is not mediated by the Holy Spirit. From this point new light falls on the history of revelation. Where men of God have spoken, driven by the Holy Spirit, there the eternal Christ has spoken in them. For this reason the Old Testament can only be understood in the light of Christ, and the Church may well regard it as her Holy Scripture. Wherever the activity of the Holy Spirit is spoken of, there too the activity of the Christ may be talked about. If the creation of the world cannot be conceived apart from the Holy Spirit neither can it be conceived apart from the eternal Christ. That is the central reason why Christ is described in the New Testa-

---

[1] John i. 32 emphasises that the Spirit rested on Him. Compare the promise in xiv. 17, that the Holy Spirit should rest upon His disciples.

ment as sharing in the creation of the world.[1] All that is said in the New Testament about the Lord and the Spirit can only be understood from the words : Where the Lord is, there is the Holy Spirit : Where the Holy Spirit is, there is the Lord. It is, however, a false interpretation to understand these words in such a way as to identify Christ with the Spirit. True, it is possible to speak of the Lord who is the Spirit, and so to venture the words ' The Lord is the Spirit.'[2] If, however, this expression is understood in the sense of identity, then either the historical Jesus becomes a mere symbol and, in antithesis to the actuality of the Holy Spirit, loses all independent significance, or the Holy Spirit recedes into the background and becomes a mere ' power,' a *motus in rebus creatus*, ' a created motion in creatures ' ; a conception against which the Augsburg Confession rightly protests. For the Holy Spirit is the *pneuma* only if it is not regarded as a power bestowed by God, or merely as an activity of God, but as God Himself present in His activity. If we deny the reality of the Holy Spirit, as of God actually present, then the unavoidable consequence follows : Jesus Christ also ceases to be the Lord, for He is only a man equipped with divine power. The unfortunate historical attitude of modern theology which recognises only the historical Jesus of Nazareth is a necessary consequence of the impoverishment of the Biblical notion of the Holy Spirit. If the Holy Spirit is no longer true God, then Jesus Christ is also no longer God, then He is no longer the present Lord of the Church, but at the most its ' founder.' He will soon cease to be that too. The Church will then become a strange human institution which actually reflects an incomprehensible apostasy from the great Prophet of Nazareth and His teaching.

But it is the belief of the New Testament that Jesus Christ the Lord is present in His Church because He is one with the Holy Spirit—one, not in the sense of unity of person, of identity, but in the sense of unity of nature, the Homousia. He is where the Spirit is. But if this is

[1] There are still other and more accidental motives, such as the connection of the words of Ps. cii. 20 with Christ (Heb. i. 10).

[2] 2 Cor. iii. 17.

correct, it follows that what is true of the Holy Spirit is
true also of the present Lord: He is only there for us where
the Word of God is. The prophets learned through the
Word of God, which was entrusted to them, what the Holy
Spirit is. In the Word, the Word become Flesh, the fulness
of the Spirit was manifested in primitive Christianity. In
the Word of the proclaimed Gospel of Christ, and indeed in
this Word alone, the disciples of Paul and Christians of
all ages have experienced the actuality of the Holy Spirit;
all other pneumatic experiences of the Pauline communities
have nothing to do with the Holy Spirit, but were an invasion of that pneumatico-mystical religiosity from which the
apostolic Church had to be, and has been, protected. Here
is the difference between Christianity and all pneumatico-
mystical religions. We should recall here what we have
already said about the protest of modern interpretations of
religion, against the crystallisation of 'living' religion in
the Church and in the creed, against the distinction between
the apostolate and prophecy, and the conflict between
'office' and 'spirit'; the binding of the Spirit to the
Word is of the essence of Christianity as the religion of a
revelation which has occurred once only in history. Since
the Son of God became flesh we know the holy *pneuma*
only as 'the other Paraclete' which, proceeding from the
Father and the Son, is given to the Church of God and
shall abide with her for ever. The witness of this Paraclete
is inseparable from the Gospel of Jesus and is bound up
with the apostolic preaching of the Christ. Only in the
Word and the Sacrament evangelically understood, that is
to say as a Sacrament understood in the light of the Word,
can we actually receive the Holy Spirit.[1] And so Christ

---

[1] Compare *Confessio Augustana*, 5: 'Nam per verbum et sacramenta
tamquam per instrumenta donatur Spiritus Sanctus, qui fidem efficit, ubi
et quando visum est Deo,' etc. The conclusion of this article rejects definitely
('damnant,' not only 'improbant') those 'qui sentiunt Spiritum Sanc-
tum contingere sine verbo externo hominibus per ipsorum praeparationes
et opera.' The whole modern theory of religion, which regards the 'religious experience' as an original phenomenon of human life, on the
analogy of the intuition of the metaphysician and the inspiration of the
artist, is thus banished from the domain of Christianity as it is evangelically understood. The fact of this experience and its relative truth
content is not denied. It is only denied that it leads to the communion

the Lord is present with us only in the Word and in the Sacrament. But there He is actually present. There He ' whose name is the Word of God ' [1] speaks to us, calls us to repentance and to faith, forgives our sins, gives us the Holy Spirit and, in so doing, bestows upon us the knowledge of the living God.

This actual, personal presence of Christ is the secret of the Church. Her nature is only to be understood from this point of view. All the definitions of the Church which emanate from the men belonging to her, from her faith or her attributes, do not touch the deepest nature of the Church. For we Christians do not constitute the Church, but Christ the Lord alone : *Ubi Christus, ibi ecclesia.* Unless we start here we have, instead of the conception of the Church, that of a religious community, perhaps the most perfect and one which alone contains the truth, but in any case the conception of a community of individuals who are held together by the possession of a common belief. Jesus Christ is then only an object of faith, even if He be constantly proclaimed the Living One. He does not bear the Church, but the Church bears Him. But that would no longer be the Church, which is the body of Christ, as it is understood in the New Testament. The Church is present, or perhaps it would be better to say in the meaning of the New Testament : the Church comes into being there where the Lord comes to us in the Word of the Gospel. Where He is, there faith is awakened, and there is the *congregatio sanctorum et vere credentium.* [2]

For this reason the confession of Jesus as Lord is the fundamental confession of the Church. We only understand that Jesus Christ shares in the eternity, omnipresence and omnipotence of God, that He, the Crucified and the

---

with God of which the Bible speaks. It is also denied that the *pneuma* of this experience is imparted by the Holy Spirit. The forgiveness of sins will never fall to our lot in this fashion. At most, in this experience we forget our sins.

[1] Rev. xix. 13.

[2] It is very remarkable that the New Testament always speaks of the Church as something which is developing. The growing Church in Eph. ii. 21, and the Living Stones in 1 Pet. ii. 5, show the impossibility of conceiving the idea of the Church as something static.

Exalted, is actually and personally present in His Church, when we are within His Church and have experienced by faith His power over us. Outside His Church these assertions are entirely incomprehensible. We can only experience Him as Lord of His Church. We know well that the *regnum potentiae* belongs to Him; and that He is not only the Redeemer of mankind, but also the Lord of the whole creation which awaits redemption through Him. But that lies beyond our experience, and if we would say more about it we should but lose ourselves in speculations.[1] We know that the *Regnum Gloriae* belongs to Him and that His hidden Majesty shall be made manifest. But on this subject too we can say nothing more. The *Regnum Gloriae* is an object of hope and not of experience. As yet we can only know Him as the Lord of the Church. So it is that the confession of Jesus as Lord is the fundamental confession of the Christian Church. It is the confession of faith in the Living God. Whoever professes that Jesus is Lord, professes also the Father who gave to Him the Name which is above every Name, and the Holy Spirit in whom Jesus Christ is with us. Thus in the confession of the Kurios the Church gives her answer to the revelation in which the Living God reveals the fulness of His Life.

---

[1] What we may wish to say about it must be connected with the fact of the resurrection and not with the doctrine of the Sacrament which so often gives opportunity for grievous mistakes. The Sacrament ought never to be understood from its natural side but always from its connection with the Word. If the Word and the Sacrament are separated, then a twofold conception of Grace results which ends with a twofold Christ: *i.e.* the Christ who comes to us in the Word and the Christ who comes to us in the Sacrament.

RECENT TENDENCIES IN ENGLISH CHRISTOLOGY
CHRISTOLOGY
BY JOHN MARTIN CREED

VI

RECENT TENDENCIES IN ENGLISH CHRISTOLOGY

THE great Churches which issued from the Reformation of the sixteenth century took over unchanged and un-criticised the ancient doctrinal definitions of the Church on the Person of Jesus Christ, and these definitions still hold their place in official statements of doctrine. The doctrine of the Person of Jesus Christ is this : that at the Incarnation, the eternal Son of the Father, who is of one substance with the Father, took to Himself human nature, so that in the one incarnate person Jesus Christ, the two natures, Godhead and Manhood, are indissolubly joined. There was nothing formal or conventional in the acceptance of the doctrine by the leaders of the Reformation. That mighty movement had sprung from a revolt against practical abuses in the Church. If the Church and its sacramental system imperilled at any point the vital principle that man is justified by Faith and Faith alone, then system and doctrine must be recast and reformed. But the doctrine that the Son of God, for us and our salvation, had become incarnate in Jesus Christ our Lord not only did not imperil that principle, it stated the very saving truth which Faith embraced. But it was as stating saving truth, and only as stating saving truth, that the dogma held its place. *In Christo crucifixo est vera theologia et cognitio Dei.* For the speculations of ' the Sophists ' as to how Christ was both God and man Luther had a bold contempt. What mattered was that man should know that God and Christ were one. ' The Devil,' said he,[1] ' can bear it if men cling to the man Christ, and go no further.

---

[1] Quoted by W. Herrmann, *Communion with God*, E.T.[2], p. 152, from a sermon on John xiv. 23–31 (publ. summer 1543).

Yea he will also let us speak and hear the word that Christ
is truly God. But what he will not have is that a heart
shall be able to join Christ and the Father so closely, so
inseparably that it shall count His word and His Father's
to be one word, heart and will. As darkened hearts do
think and say: yes, I hear with what friendliness and
comfort Christ speaks to the troubled conscience, but who
knows how it stands between me and God in heaven?
That means that the heart has not counted God and Christ
all one, but has made for itself a Christ apart by Himself,
and a God apart from Him, and has bartered away the true
God, who wills to be found and laid hold of no where else
save in this Christ.' ' To know Christ,' said Melanchthon,
' is to know His benefits, not, as the schoolmen teach, to
contemplate His natures, and the modes of His incarnation.' [1]

Utterances such as these have become classical for
much modern theology. In the age of the Reformation
the ancient structure of theological thought was presupposed. The Reformers were men of their age, and even
if in the first ferment of the new movement there was a
determined effort to concentrate theology upon the message
of salvation and to divert it from the unprofitable speculations of a degenerate scholasticism, the effort was but
partly successful. The sacramental controversy called out
disputes upon those very problems concerning the relation
of the two natures in Christ which in the creative period
Luther and Melanchthon had thought to set aside. Ghosts
of those controversies survived the reaction of Pietism and
the criticism of the Illumination. But in the meantime
the world has changed. In an age which has learnt from
Descartes to doubt, from Kant to distinguish the spheres
of faith and knowledge, and from scholars to criticise the
very fountains of ' revealed ' knowledge, it has been timely
that we should be reminded that Christianity is not
primarily speculative, and it has been just that theologians
of the Evangelical and Reformed Churches should find their
way behind the thin rationalism of the Illumination and
the dreary epoch of Protestant scholasticism to the central
idea of the Reformation. What is of primary importance

[1] *Loci Communes*, Preface, 1st edn.

in the doctrine of Christ's divinity is not speculative solution of the difficulties, but the saving apprehension of God in Christ by Faith. ' To know Christ is to know His benefits, not to contemplate His natures and the modes of His incarnation.'

The main problems are common to us all. All the peoples and all the Churches of modern Europe are in some sense heirs of the doctrinal system of ancient Christendom, and we all live in a world which is conscious that in many respects it has moved far from its ancient moorings. What, in these circumstances, are the benefits or obligations which our inheritance imposes upon us ? And how far and in what sense are we to regard the ideas of the Reformation as a fresh beginning ? The pressure of these questions is widespread and acute, but there is much difference of opinion as to how they are to be dealt with, and even more of vagueness and uncertainty.

A German scholar has spoken of a general revivification of the doctrine of Justification by Faith as conditioning all thought on the Person of Christ in modern German theology. I do not think that any such generalisation could be made about British theology to-day. At any rate it would not be presented in this form. Emphasis differs greatly, but there is no apparent *general* tendency to find a regenerative theological principle in the theology of the Reformation era. This is not to say that the importance of the Reformation is not widely recognised and deeply felt, but the ' Protestant ' temper shows itself more generally in the assertion of the right and duty of ' private judgment,' and of the supremacy of the conscience, than in more strictly theological forms. Then again a tradition of Platonist religious philosophy, in itself not distinctively Protestant or Catholic, has been a persistent and recurrent factor in English theology. This tradition colours much recent theological writing, and in particular it is strongly upheld by one of the best known and most influential of our religious teachers, Dr. Inge. It is in keeping with this condition of our theology that the approach to the doctrine of Christ's Person is by no means universally conditioned by emphasis upon the soteriological aspect of His coming.

Christ is the divine teacher, who in life and death unveils to man the love of God. Or, again, He is the incarnate Lord, in whose Person a new divine principle has been implanted in the human race. These thoughts of Christ by no means exclude the thought of Him as reconciler, and mediator of the divine forgiveness. But the latter thought does not habitually control the doctrine.

It is not, for instance, the controlling principle in Dr. Inge's theology and Christology. Fundamentally and before all Dr. Inge is a Platonist. Religion is life in communion with the eternal world of spirit which our spirits perceive by apprehending the absolute values of Beauty, Truth, and Goodness. Even if his faith in the historic Christian religion were less firmly founded than it is, he would still be able to fall back upon this Platonic faith.[1] But, like Augustine, he knows the limitations as well as the verity of the Platonic creed. That ' the Word became flesh ' he could not learn from Plato, and it is the Incarnation which sets the keystone in the Platonic arch. To Dr. Inge, as to Coleridge, the Logos is the most congenial of the terms in the vocabulary of Christology. ' The Incarnation and the Cross are the central doctrines of Christianity. The Divine Logos, through whom the worlds were made, and who sustains them in being, is not exhausted in His Creation, but remains transcendent as well as immanent in it. In the world He manifests Himself as the source of those supreme values which we have mentioned—as vital Law in the course of nature, the directing Wisdom celebrated in the later Jewish literature, as Beauty everywhere ; and as Love. Love is a personal thing, called out by persons, and exercised by persons. We love God because He first loved us. . . . So far as I can see, nothing but a personal Incarnation, and the self-sacrifice of the Incarnate could either adequately reveal the love of God for man, or call forth the love of man to God.' Dr. Inge does not deal directly with the problem as to how we are to think of the cosmic Logos in relation to the human subject Jesus Christ. He speaks frequently of ' a personal incarnation.' ' A Divine being,' he says,

[1] ' Confessio Fidei ' in *Outspoken Essays* (2nd series), p. 53.

'chose to become incarnate.' The question whether this involves the conclusion that the Logos is Himself to be thought of as a ' Person ' or ' self ' prior to and apart from His Incarnation is not definitely raised. ' It is enough that Jesus spoke and acted as one fully possessed by the Spirit of God the Father.' ' To believe in the Divinity of Jesus Christ is to believe that in the human Jesus dwelt all the fullness of the Godhead under bodily conditions.' With the doctrine of the Incarnation stands the doctrine of the Cross. Vicarious suffering of the sinless for the sinful draws the sting of the world's sorrow and injustice. But ' the Cross, as I understand it, is not so much an atonement for the past as the opening of a gate into the future.' ' Redemption means admission to redemptive work.' There is here no failure to recognise the problem of sin and the need for redemption. Yet it would, I think, be true to say that Dr. Inge's theology neither begins nor ends with the thoughts of forgiveness and salvation. Soteriology is truly present, but it is not dominant.

In other writers too there is a pronounced tendency to interpret the Incarnation as climax and clue to a philosophy of the universe, and if this tendency often goes hand in hand with a deference to patristic theology, this is to be ascribed not merely to respect for tradition, but also to an innate affinity to that Platonic world view which lies behind much early patristic philosophy of the Incarnation. Professor Leonard Hodgson, for instance,[1] urges that ' in the Incarnation of Jesus Christ is to be found the key to the problem of creation, to that fundamental philo- sophical problem of the relation of time and eternity, as we see in the union of the two natures in Christ the central moment of history, which sheds its light on all the rest.' The real purpose of the Incarnation was to bring eternal life into the world of time. This is the dominant idea in this and in other essays in the same volume. The need of redemption from sin finds emphatic expression, but it remains a subordinate theme. The conquest of sin must

---

[1] In an Essay on the Incarnation in *Essays on the Trinity and the Incarnation*, by members of the Anglican Communion (ed. Dr. A. E. J. Rawlinson), 1928, p. 401.

be ' an integral element in the purpose and fact of the Incarnation ' because sin is ' the real obstacle to the giving of immortality to man.' But Professor Hodgson's argument may perhaps be taken to suggest that, had it not been so, the relations of time and eternity would still have called for the union of the two natures in the person of the Incarnate Son.

A recent essay on Christology by the Rev. Lionel Thornton [1] aims at showing the coherence of the orthodox doctrine of the Incarnation with an ' organic ' view of the universe, such as that expounded by A. N. Whitehead and others. The universe, it is argued, may be thought of as a graded hierarchy of organisms. At the level of Spirit the organic order is found to be related to an ' eternal order ' or to God, who is at once ground and goal of the whole. The Incarnation is the climax of the progressive incorporation of ' the eternal order ' into the organic series, and it is maintained that the organic conception of the universe makes it easier for the mind to accept the essential positions of the Nicene and post-Nicene theology and Christology. The conception of ' organism ' applied to the manhood of Christ indicates a way out of the difficulties which are raised by the orthodox doctrine of the two natures in one Person, with its corollary of the ' impersonal manhood.' The Incarnation means that ' Absolute Actuality as it exists in the Person of the Eternal Word becomes the principle of unity in a human organism.' This suggestive essay is an example of resolute refusal to acquiesce in any dichotomy between the world of religion and the world of philosophic thought.

Professor Hodgson and the Rev. Lionel Thornton are both consciously influenced by the late Baron von Hügel. They would probably both of them agree with the Baron when he writes : ' The Pauline, Augustinian, Lutheran, Calvinist, Jansenist trend, impressive though it is, will have to be explained, in part, as a good and necessary (or at least as an excusable, temporary) corrective of some contrary excess ; and, for the rest, it will have to suffer

[1] *The Incarnate Lord, an Essay concerning the doctrine of the Incarnation in its relation to organic conceptions* (Longmans), 1928.

incorporation within a larger whole, which, in appearance more commonplace, is yet in reality indefinitely richer.'[1] Both writers, I think, may be fairly claimed in support of the generalisation that the ideas of reconciliation with God and redemption from sin, though not absent, are not dominant in contemporary theology.

Yet such a generalisation at once calls for qualification, both from the side of popular religion and from the side of systematic theology.

No religious movement since the Reformation—perhaps it would be true to say no religious movement since the Lollards—has struck roots so deep in the religious life of England as the Methodist evangelical revival of the eighteenth century. This is a living memory in the consciousness of the British people, and here there reigns the thought of Christ as saviour and redeemer from the power of sin. That living memory remains. But the evangelical tradition is often hampered by a superseded Biblicism. It is sometimes unfriendly to learning and systematic thought, and it suffers accordingly.

But it is not only in popular evangelicalism that the interpretation of Christ's person is controlled by the redemptive aspect of His work. Systematic theology generally—so far as we have any—has been and still is influenced by the prevailing tendency of the last century to work mainly with the idea of Incarnation, but in the work of theologians such as Dr. Mackintosh, Dr. Forsyth, Dr. Garvie, Dr. Mozley, a certain reaction may be felt. These writers betray a manifest note of uneasiness in the present situation, and a fear that the peculiarly Christian emphasis upon the Cross may be failing to find proper expression. Unless the doctrine of the Incarnation is nailed to the Cross it tends to lose definition and to evaporate into a cosmic principle. ' We must advance,' writes Dr. Garvie, ' beyond both Latin and Greek Theology to such a conception of the Incarnation as will make the Atonement its characteristic activity, and such a conception of the Atonement as will make the Incarnation the necessary source of it. In dealing with the two doctrines separately,

[1] *Eternal Life*, p. 391.

K

as their history compels us to do, we must never allow ourselves to forget that while they are distinguishable, yet they are not separable, for the content of the work depends on the character of the person of Christ and the meaning of the work shows the worth of the person.' [1] So again Dr. Mackintosh : ' It is to the Cross we owe that profound and poignant interest which alone makes it worth while to have a Christology.' [2] The Scotist doctrine, maintained by Dorner and Westcott, that the Incarnation would have taken place quite apart from sin, Dr. Mackintosh definitely sets aside. ' Our conception of Christ, as we have seen, is relative to His redeeming work ; strike out the redeeming work, even by supposition, and the materials for a judgment disappear.' ' From the outset Christology has been controlled and inspired exclusively by a soteriological interest.' [3]

In the eighth chapter of his great work on the Person of Jesus Christ Professor Mackintosh reviews the history of Christology in the nineteenth century. Of the thirty-seven pages in this chapter, four are devoted to Britain and America. The proportion is just. In the last century Britain produced some great scholars and some great religious teachers. The powerful but erratic genius of Coleridge breathed new life into the religious thought of two generations. But there was no thoroughgoing reconstruction of theology and no succession of theological schools such as Germany produced. The problems of the age were felt and felt acutely, but they were attacked piecemeal, and in respect of our own subject the method has been rather that of adaptation and reinterpretation of the inherited system. In the Church of England, especially, the theology of the Fathers and the Councils was and is widely regarded as the classical and normative theology of the Christian Church. For example, the essay on the Incarnation by Dr. Mozley, in the recent volume *Essays Catholic and Critical*, takes the form of an interpretation and a defence of the Chalcedonian doctrine. The conciliar definition, it is urged, safeguards the belief in the proper

---

[1] *Christian Doctrine of the Godhead*, 1925, p. 121.
[2] *Person of Jesus Christ*, p. 440.　　　　[3] *Ibid.* p. 442.

Divinity of Jesus Christ. The case for its general validity has been strengthened by the relative failure of its modern rivals. Dr. Mozley accords hearty and generous recognition to the ' reduced ' Christologies of Liberal theologians. In an age of change they had their part to play and their contribution to make. But they fell short of the full doctrine of the Church which the Chalcedonian definition enshrines and preserves. The volume of essays to which Dr. Mozley contributes represents a group of ' Anglo-Catholic ' theologians. Not all Anglicans pay the same deference to conciliar definitions. Yet even where conclusions are widely different, patristic theology is generally the starting-point. Some of the most valuable English contributions to the literature of Christology have been in the form of historical studies of doctrine in the early Church. Dr. Raven's *Apollinarianism* (1923), for example—a learned account of the great heresiarch and a very just assessment of his place in the history of theology—derives an enhanced interest from the author's confession in the Preface that he himself started his study with a belief in the impersonal humanity of the Lord, and only found himself forced to abandon his position as he reviewed the history of the Apollinarian controversy. The book is thus an interesting document in contemporary English Christology.

A somewhat different point of view is represented in a recent volume of essays on Christology by Free Church writers—*The Lord of Life* (1929). Dr. Vernon Bartlett, who reviews the history of the doctrine of Christ's Person in ancient and modern times, finds the categories of the Councils inadequate and presses home the difficulties which confront any attempt to find the centre of consciousness in the divine, not in the human, nature of the Lord. Dr. Miall Edwards, who offers a systematic statement of the doctrine, interprets the Incarnation as ' the culmination of a double movement—the movement of God towards man, and the movement of man towards God.' ' The Incarnation is the full realisation of the purpose of these two personal movements, the meeting of God and man in fullest fellowship, co-operation and union.'

It is not difficult to recognise the value of the definition

of Chalcedon on the Person of Christ when it is set along-
side the interpretations which it was designed to exclude
or correct. Granted that it was desirable and necessary
that the Church should deal with the controversy by an
authoritative pronouncement, it was well that the prevailing trend of Greek theology, which threatened the
belief in the entire humanity of Jesus Christ, should receive
a check. It was well also to state the principle that in
Christ God and man were made one. But at what a price
were these advantages secured! The Christology of
Theodore and the Christology of Apollinarius are each of
them coherent ways of thinking of the Saviour's person.
The Chalcedonian definition is not coherent. Its stability
rests upon the pressure of opposing forces. If it is lifted
out of the mental and spiritual environment in which it
was shaped, and treated as a constructive statement of the
doctrine of the Lord's person, it must answer formidable
objections. The parallelism of the two natures and the
two wills, united by their common relation to the one
divine hypostasis, is a theory hard to reconcile with an
intelligible conception of personality. And the theory
finds no warrant in the Gospels. To differentiate, as Leo
does, between those occasions on which the Lord spoke
and acted in His human nature, and those on which He acted
in His divine nature, is an artificiality entirely alien to the
Gospel texts. Nor can we now work easily with the idea
that Christ had a human nature, complete yet ' impersonal.'
Whatever else Jesus of Nazareth was, He was certainly a
man.

These objections are widely recognised even by those
who, like Dr. Gore,[1] believe that the terminology of the
Councils cannot be improved upon. The historical study

---

[1] *Reconstruction of Belief* (new edn., October 1926), p. 860 ; cf. *ibid.*
p. 523. Dr. Relton (*A Study in Christology*) argues that the conception of
ἐνυπόστασία put forward by Leontius of Byzantium ' interpreted in
terms of modern thought' carries us deeper than any other theory yet
put forward. The modern interpretation which Dr. Relton proposes to
place upon the doctrine of Leontius is that the perfect manhood of Christ,
whose ὑπόστασις is in the Logos, itself pre-existed in God (p. 251).
Whatever may be the value of this particular ' modernism ' it seems clear
that it makes havoc of the orthodox doctrine that the Divine Word
' assumed ' human nature at the Incarnation.

of the Gospels has compelled a general recognition that the historical Jesus of Nazareth was humanly conditioned in His knowledge and in His entire consciousness. However the divinity of Jesus Christ is asserted, it must do justice to this plain fact. In England, as at an earlier date in Germany, it has been sought to meet this requirement by a doctrine of Kenosis. The Divine Logos by His Incarnation divested Himself of His divine attributes of omniscience and omnipotence, so that in His incarnate life the Divine Person is revealed and solely revealed through a human consciousness. This conception of the incarnate Life is a wide departure from that which prevailed in the ancient Church. Dr. Loofs has shown that no real precedent for this type of thought can be adduced from the Patristic writers. The nearest approach is to be found in the heresiarch Apollinarius. But ' to Apollinarius Christ, although consenting to all the experiences of humanity, yet keeps the consciousness of His deity throughout. He may hold His power in reserve : but it is always at His command. . . . Any belief in a more complete limitation would have seemed equivalent either to a total denial of Christ's divinity or to a view of His Incarnation similar to that of Marcellus.' [1] But however questionable may be the parentage of the idea, it is beyond question that it falls in with the thought and feeling of some great texts in the New Testament,[2] and in the hands of teachers such as Dr. Gore and Professor Mackintosh it lends itself to a powerful interpretation of the doctrine of the Incarnation. In Professor Mackintosh's exposition the emphasis falls less upon the limitations of the Lord's knowledge—a problem which is less felt as a problem now than it was a generation or two ago—but rather upon the ethical and religious value of the idea. Professor Mackintosh states four positions which he thinks may be taken as implicit in the completely Christian view of Jesus.[3] They are as follows :

(1) Christ is now divine, as being the object of faith

---

[1] Raven, *Apollinarianism*, p. 207 ; *cf.* Loofs, *Leitfaden*, p. 269, n. 4 : *ibid.*, p. 921.

[2] Phil. ii. 5–8 ; 2 Cor. viii. 9.

[3] *The Person of Jesus Christ*, p. 469.

and worship, with whom believing men have immediate, though not unmediated, fellowship.

(2) In some personal sense His Divinity is eternal, not the fruit of time, since by definition Godhead cannot have come to be *ex nihilo* ; His premundane being therefore is real, not ideal merely.

(3) His life on earth was unequivocally human. Jesus was a man, a Jew of the first century. . . . The life Divine in Him found expression through human faculty, with a self-consciousness and activity mediated by his human *milieu*.

(4) We cannot predicate of Him two consciousnesses or two wills ; the New Testament indicates nothing of the kind, nor indeed is it congruous with an intelligible psychology. The unity of His personal life is axiomatic.

Professor Mackintosh then proceeds : ' It is impossible to think these four positions together save as we proceed to infer that a real surrender of the glory and prerogatives of deity " a moral act in the heavenly sphere " must have preceded the advent of God in Christ. We are faced by a Divine self-reduction which entailed obedience, temptation, and death. So that religion has a vast stake in the *kenosis* as a fact, whatever the difficulties as to its method may be.' The difficulties have been strongly urged by Dr. Temple in his essay *Christus Veritas* (1924). Dr. Temple considers Professor Mackintosh's statement and finds the difficulties in his position ' intolerable.' ' What was happening to the rest of the universe during the period of our Lord's earthly life ? To say that the Infant Jesus was from His cradle exercising providential care over it all is certainly monstrous ; but to deny this, and yet to say that the Creative Word was so self-emptied as to have no being except in the Infant Jesus, is to assert that for a certain period the history of the world was let loose from the control of the Creative Word ' (p. 143). The theory, he feels, ' has a mythological appearance.' He therefore prefers to think that ' God the Son, who is the Word of God by whom, as agent, all things came to be, without ceasing His creative and sustaining work, added this to it that He became Flesh and dwelt as in a tabernacle among us ' (p. 140).

Yet I cannot think that Dr. Temple succeeds in carrying through his thought. In his treatment of the doctrine of God he finds the ground for distinction between Persons in the Godhead to lie in the duality of experience implied in the distinction between the Father and the Incarnate Son. ' To attribute to *a* person at once the eternal comprehension of the universe and the disappointment of Jesus Christ over Jerusalem or His cry of desolation on the Cross is to talk nonsense. It is one God ; but it is two Persons— so far as human terms have any applicability at all. Here we find the ground for that degree of distinctness in the Divine Word or self-manifestation of God in time which makes it appropriate to speak of Him as begotten of the Father rather than as merely emanating from the Father ' (p. 277). This seems to teach very clearly that the subject of the human experience of Jesus was the Eternal Son, and this is certainly the general position of the essay. But then are we not at once involved in inconsistency ? For this is nothing else than ' to attribute to *a* person the eternal comprehension of the universe '—for surely no less can be ascribed to God the Son, ' by Whom *as agent* all things came to be '—' and the disappointment of Jesus Christ over Jerusalem. . . .' Dr. Temple does not entirely overlook the objection. ' If God the Son, the Word of God, is at once the sustainer of the universe and the Babe in the Manger, does not this,' he asks, ' involve duality of Person in Him on precisely the same grounds on which it was said that there must be more than One Person in the One God ? ' To this fundamental question Dr. Temple replies that ' between the experience of the Son subject to human limitations in Jesus of Nazareth, and the Son as progressively ordering the world according to the Eternal Purpose of the Father there is not the same distinction as between the eternal and temporal modes of the divine.' And it is urged that ' we cannot expect to understand the Person of God Incarnate.' But this does not seem satisfactory. The tendency of the answer has been to weaken the distinction between the Word under human conditions, and the Word as ' sustainer of the universe,' as contrasted with the distinction between the Father and the Word.

But what kind of reason have we for supposing that ' the Person of God Incarnate,' *i.e.* Jesus Christ, thought of Himself as being also ' sustainer of the universe ' ? So far as I can see there is no evidence which indicates that He thought so, and much evidence which it is hard, if not impossible, to reconcile with the supposition that He did. Dr. Temple has given illustrations in the passage I have already quoted. Now all this may be reconciled with the belief in His personal identity with ' the sustainer of the Universe ' *on the Kenotic theory*, but, so far as I can see, on no other theory.[1] I do not wish to be understood as myself arguing for a Kenotic Christology, for I am moved by the considerations which Dr. Temple and others have urged against it. But I do not think that Dr. Temple shakes Professor Mackintosh's argument. If we take seriously both the human conditions of the life of Jesus and the theory of His personal [2] identity and continuity with the Eternal Word, then a Kenotic Christology appears to be indispensable.

It seems that there are two main ways in which Christ's Divinity may be thought of. We may emphasise the personal continuity of Jesus with the divine Logos who became Incarnate. If we do this we tend to impair the conception of Trinity in Unity and to incline towards Tritheism—a course which Dr. Tennant boldly encourages us to adopt.[3] This line of thought appears to call for a Kenotic doctrine of the Incarnation. The other line of thought is to take our start from the Divine Unity and to hold that in and through ' the Man Christ Jesus ' God reveals His Word to the world and reconciles the world to Himself.[4]

In conclusion, we shall notice an approach to our

---

[1] This is also Dr. Bethune-Baker's conclusion : ' If we are to work with the orthodox theory of the Incarnation, I am sure we can only do so by making use of the conception of *kenosis* to the full extent' (*The Way of Modernism*, p. 98).

[2] I use the word ' personal ' in its modern sense. The orthodox term ὑπόστασις of course does not correspond to ' person.' The ancient terminology has no proper equivalent for ' person ' or ' self.'

[3] *Constructive Quarterly*, June and September 1920.

[4] The two lines of approach are clearly sketched by Dr. Cave, *Doctrine of the Person of Christ*, chap. ix.

problem different from those which we have already considered. It cannot be too often recalled that in the classical
theologies of historic Christendom the divine intervention
at the Incarnation stood against the background of the
first three chapters of Genesis. For imagination and for
thought the world and man had had a definite and a known
beginning. In the writings of the Fathers the six days of
creation are a favourite subject for scriptural exegesis.
God's creation of the world and man ; man's disobedience
and fall from bliss—in these narratives the Church held
inspired accounts of the beginning of the world and of man
expressed in terms of theology. The creation was the presupposition of the Incarnation, and the Fall set the problem
which Calvary and the Resurrection had resolved. To-day
this time-honoured background of the Catholic Faith has
not only lost its hold upon men's conscious thought, but,
what is perhaps of equal consequence, it is no longer the
unspoken presupposition dominating the imagination of
plain men and women. A slow, silent and inevitable
change has passed over the common mind. The new
cosmology and the new anthropology with their vast vistas
and dim horizons have usurped the place which the Book
of Genesis once held. Where does Christian doctrine find
contact with a world view dominated by the idea of
Evolution ? Christology—the doctrine of the Redeemer's
person—had a perfectly intelligible place in the ancient
world view. What is its place and purpose now ? The
discussions are apt to seem uninteresting and unimportant,
because they have no clear relevance to our accepted
outlook on the world. Dr. Bethune-Baker is well known
as a historian of the Christian doctrine, and none knows
better than he how deeply the traditional system of doctrine
is embedded in ways of thinking and feeling which once
were natural, but now have passed imperceptibly away.
Acutely conscious of the change, he asks the question how
the Christian doctrine of the Incarnation stands related
to the evolutionary view of the world. His fundamental
answer is that the whole process of the Universe in Evolution is Incarnation. ' God is in the process, indwelling.
The whole universe is not merely the scene of His operations,

but a manifestation of Him, in all the stages of its evolution. The whole is Incarnation.'[1] In this view 'the familiar antithesis natural and supernatural disappears—the " natural " is the way in which the Divine purpose is being realised. If we picture some aspects of our experience as natural and some as supernatural, it is only a logical distinction of our own making. There is no dualism.' Advancing to the doctrine of Christ's Person, he lays down as the primary and fundamental condition of the doctrine ' the fact that the being of God and the being of Man are indissolubly interrelated.' ' The Creator is not separated from His creatures : they do not exist apart from Him. They have their origin in the will and love of God : they are the counterparts of that will and love, as necessary to the existence of God as He is to theirs.' It is indeed true that ' we cannot appeal to our Lord's own words for more than hints of such an idea.' But the same may be said of ' any of the forms the orthodox doctrine of the In- carnation has assumed.' ' What is much more to the point is that it is He and His life—His experience as Man in the world, His consciousness of Himself so far as we can read it with the new consciousness in us which He created— that suggests it.'[2] In a personal confession of faith Dr. Bethune-Baker affirms what the Godhead of Jesus means to him. In coming to know Jesus he comes to know God. Never for him does Jesus cease to be man,

---

[1] *The Way of Modernism*, p. 85. A similar point of view finds ex- pression in Dr. Matthews' essay on 'The Doctrine of Christ' in the volume of essays *The Future of Christianity* (ed. Sir J. Marchant), 1927. Thus he writes (p. 116) : ' It is probably well to restrict the meaning of the term Incarnation to the complete fulfillment in Christ, but there is a truth in the statement that all creation is an Incarnation. Nothing could maintain itself in being for a moment, but for the sustaining life of God, which, however imperfectly, finds expression in it. When once we have attained this standpoint, we are in possession of a clue to the meaning of the world-process. We can see it as the history of the growing victory of the divine life—the upward movement of the λόγος προφορικός.' But the transcendence of the Word is more strictly guarded by Dr. Matthews than it appears to be in Dr. Bethune-Baker's interpretation; cf. p. 122 : ' The Word of God fully revealed in the Person and the life of Jesus is not a part of, or an image of the Word of God, the Creator. He is the same Word " through Whom the worlds were made," and without Whom no process of evolution would exist.'
[2] *Ibid.* p. 100.

yet what he learns from Jesus is God as well as Man. ' He becomes for me merged, as it were, in God, or identical with God.' ' God stands to me for the highest values in life, and because I believe those values were actualised in the person and life of Jesus, I must use the title " God " of Him.'

The Christian Church is deeply indebted to those theologians who persistently press upon it a due recognition of the momentous change which has been brought about in the background of our thought concerning God and the world by the advent and victory of the idea of evolution in the realms both of nature and of history. If religion is to find itself in the new world, it must learn to breathe and feel and speak freely in an environment entirely different from that of the classical theologies of the past. It is, however, possible to combine a full and hearty acknow-ledgment of this debt with a certain hesitation as to whether an evolutionary Monism is the inevitable philosophy of the future, and whether such a philosophy affords the most appropriate categories in which to state the Christian faith.

The idea of evolution has arisen out of interpretations of the history of human society, and of the differentiation of species. It has been fruitfully applied to religion as to everything else which can be said to have had a history. But though religion manifests itself as a process in history, it does not necessarily follow that the idea of process is itself the best category for grasping and stating the essential nature of religion. Dr. Oman, for example, would regard the idea of process as ultimately irrelevant. He holds that the special concern of religion is ' the supernatural ' and he maintains that ' the natural ' and ' the super-natural ' are perfectly distinct and definitely distinguish-able aspects of our experience. ' Part of our experience is natural, in the sense that its values are comparative and to be judged as they serve our needs ; and part of it supernatural, in the sense that its values are absolute, to which our needs must submit.' He adds : ' We know the supernatural as it reflects itself in the sense of the holy, and has for us absolute value, directly and without further argument, and henceforth we are concerned with its existence and its relation to us, and our relation to it.'[1] In such a view as this we think in terms which not only are not those of process and evolution but even stand in some kind of antithesis to them. For while it remains true that man lives in a process, himself the creation of the past, and a temporary repository of a life which will continue after him, yet it is also true that in virtue of his capacity of recognising and responding to 'the supernatural'—that for which for him has 'absolute' truth—man rises beyond the stream of process and exercises that faith of which it has been said that 'it overcomes the world.'

The title of the subject of these essays, *Mysterium Christi*, reminds us that the Person who stands in the centre of the Christian Faith lived at a definite point in the story of a peculiar and definite people. In history Jesus takes a natural place as the last and greatest of the series of prophets of Israel. But to believers He was more than a prophet—He was the Christ of whom the prophets spake. And that is the title which has remained in closest association with His name. Which things are a parable. We do not go to the Gospels to find perfection of form or maturity of philosophic thought. Jesus did not supersede Plato or anticipate Kant. 'There is no beauty in Him that we should desire Him.' The Christian religion is not the completion of all the activities of man, though when it is accepted it must affect them all. If we claim too much for it, we hinder its true function and lose the distinctness and uniqueness of the figure of Jesus Christ. God works in many ways, and in Jesus Christ He worked to show and prove that in His eyes not all the power and beauty of the world are to be measured against the fulfilment of the law of love.

---

[1] *Science, Religion and Reality* (ed. J. Needham). Essay, 'The Sphere of Religion,' p. 297.

A MODERN APPROACH TO
CHRISTOLOGY
BY NATHANIEL MICKLEM

VII

A MODERN APPROACH TO CHRISTOLOGY

In what terms can we express to-day that significance which Christians have always seen in the Person of Jesus Christ ?

I

The ' divinity ' of Jesus Christ is the central dogma of Christianity. This ' divinity ' the old credal confessions sought to define, and, in measure, to explain. The creeds are, therefore, venerable symbols like the tattered flags that hang upon the walls of national churches; but for the present warfare of the Church in Asia, in Africa, in Europe and America the creeds, when they are understood, are about as serviceable as a battle-axe or an arquebus in the hands of a modern soldier.

Obviously the ordinary educated, or semi-educated, man of Europe or America, *a fortiori* the Easterner brought up in a different philosophical tradition, cannot attach any clear and exact meaning to such statements as that Jesus is ' of one substance with ' the Father, that in Him are ' Two Natures,' a divine and a human which co-exist without fusion, that He who once was a man on earth was also the Second Person of the Trinity, a part or aspect of the only God. Let it be admitted and emphasised that these old credal statements were designed to express and conserve values which are as vital and essential to Christianity to-day as they have ever been ; but clearly they need translation or interpretation in order to become intelligible. But what does translation involve ?

1. Any competent scholar can, of course, explain in modern terms to any sufficiently intelligent audience what is meant by the term ' substance ' in the Nicene creed ; he can explain, or at least state, in what way the two natures, the divine and the human, are said to cohere in

Jesus ; he can indicate the connection asserted in orthodoxy between the *assumptus homo* and the Triune Deity. But, when these obscure matters have been translated or expounded, the modern Christian will admit that he understands, but hardly that he believes. When, for instance, the dualistic philosophy of Hellenism has been so explained to him that he understands the assertion that Jesus is ' of one substance with ' the Father, he will welcome and accept the implication that it is God Himself whom we recognise in the man Jesus, but he may reasonably claim that in the course of a millennium and a half the world has outgrown the language and philosophical assumptions of Hellenistic dualism. When the ' Two Natures ' doctrine of the famous Chalcedonian formula has been explained to him, his dubiety will be even greater. He may be willing to accept the assurances of the learned that this formula was designed to define and safeguard the religious affirmations of its predecessor ; but he may plead that, if this was the intention of the later creed, it assuredly was not its result. For the Chalcedonian confession, formally and categorically, if not intentionally, contradicts both the Nicene confession and the surest religious intuition of the modern Christian, namely, that it is in the *man* Jesus that we apprehend God—' Jesus divinest when thou most art man.'

By the ' modern ' Christian is meant the man who is accustomed to express his ideas in the scientific and philosophical thought-forms of the twentieth century, and who, though he hopes and thinks that he is a Christian, does not regard it as a duty ' in entering the sacred domain of theology to leave behind him his customary ways of thinking.' The modern Christian, then, believes that in the human Jesus and in that holy Spirit which works in and through the Christian community God himself is to be apprehended. In so far as the ancient Trinitarian formulae intend to assert this religious conviction, they may be regarded as venerable Christian relics ; but veneration for them must be qualified by the reflection that they have become barely intelligible and are no longer literally credible, and that they have proved to be among the chief stumbling-blocks to hinder the whole Islamic world and very many

of the modern Western world from giving fair consideration
to the religious apprehension upon which, presumably, the
Trinitarian formulae were originally based.

Protestantism at the Reformation, if it had been logical
and consistent in its theology, would have rejected the
' Two Natures ' doctrine of the Chalcedonian formula
altogether.   Instead, it introduced an unimpressive modification.   It spoke of a ' personal union ' of the two natures
and a ' communication of attributes,' divine and human.
In effect, this meant that the man Jesus was endowed with
certain of the attributes of Deity, and that Deity was in
some obscure sense latent or unconscious in him.   This
involved a self-emptying or *kenosis* of God whereby He
became incarnate—a not very felicitous bye-form of the
Christian dogma of the Incarnation ; for, in place of the
Pauline suggestion that the pre-existent Christ (whatever
that may mean) ' emptied himself,' we have the doctrine
that God Almighty ' emptied himself ' and became man ;
in place of the Johannine and Early Christian conception
that the ' Word ' of God became flesh, we have the doctrine
that God Himself became flesh.   We recognise to-day the
truth of the profound religious intuition underlying the
claim that Jesus is God incarnate.   But for the modern
mind there are two grave objections to the treatment of
this dogma as anything more than a poetical conception of
reality.   In the first place, the idea that God, the Author
and Sustainer of the world, laid aside certain of his
attributes and was born as a baby, belongs to the world
of mythology, not of philosophy or imaginable fact.   In
the second place, it jeopardises a conviction alike rooted
in history and vital for religion that Jesus Christ walked
by faith and prayer, as we also are called to do.

Educated Christians to-day are wont to accept these
credal and theological statements as ' mysteries ' or symbolic representations of their deepest convictions ; but the
more clearly the exact meaning and significance of these
theological terms is explained, the more certainly must
the old statements be rejected as formally misleading
or incredible.   What is needed is not a translation of
the old formulae into intelligible modern terms, but a

L

reinterpretation in modern terms of those religious intuitions which are of the essence of Christianity as a religion.

II

It is maintained, however, by some that there is a divine inspiration or guarantee attached to the ancient formulae to which no modern interpretation could lay claim. This view, if based upon a study of the history and methods of Church Councils and of theological disputations in the third and fourth centuries, implies a somewhat bewildering conception of the operations of the holy Spirit ; it overlooks the fact, which will be elaborated later, that the traditional formulae would never have been adopted by the Church if the Church had based its theology upon what is to-day generally recognised as the Gospel. Moreover, there is no answering Le Roy's objection that ' if dogmas formulated absolute truth in adequate terms . . . they would be unintelligible to us. If they only gave an imperfect truth, relative and changing, their imposition could not be legitimate.'[1] It may well be true that, in the terms in which the problems were set, the Church in the end, or generally, came down on the right side, that the orthodox opinion was usually nearer to the real meaning of Christianity than the heresy which it repudiated ; but this does not imply that there was anything adequate, still less final, about the decisions of Church Councils, sometimes attained by far from spiritual methods and with little sense of that love and joy and peace which are said to mark the presence of the Spirit.

Others argue that we enjoy to-day no agreed philosophy or metaphysic in terms of which our theological dogmas may be expressed, and that we shall be wise, therefore, to keep to the formulae hallowed by tradition. It is true that there is to-day no universally agreed, or even provisionally accepted, philosophical system ; but this consideration is irrelevant. We need no more than intelligible current philosophical terms in which Christian thought may seek to express itself. It may well be that our philosophical language and equipment are still inadequate to express the Christian faith, but they are

[1] *Dogme et Critique* (ed. 6), p. 23.

certainly more, and not less, adequate than the philosophical terms of the third and fourth centuries. For example, the categories of ' value ' and of ' personality ' are indubitably more adequate than those of ' essence ' or of mythology.

Along these lines an important contribution to Christology is found in the chapter on ' The Structure of Dogma ' in William Morgan's *The Nature and Right of Religion*. The first thesis of the chapter is that, except when theology has been merely traditional, the current doctrine of the Person of Christ has been expressed in the current philosophical or quasi-philosophical terms of the age. Thus to the early Jewish Christians Jesus was pre-eminently the ' Son of Man ' of Daniel's vision ; to early Gentile Christianity, taught by the apostle Paul, He was first and foremost *Kyrios* or divine Lord. Then in the course of speculation and theological discussion the terms of the *Logos* philosophy were employed to express His place and significance in the drama of redemption. So through various stages the Church passed to the formulae of the historic creeds and the language of orthodoxy, wherein many to this day rest content. In the later section of the chapter, Morgan attempts to express Christology in modern terms of ' value.' This is the conclusion to which he comes. ' Jesus,' he says, ' is the supreme Pioneer in the field of religious knowledge. In the unerring clearness of his moral judgments and the intensity of his feeling for moral reality he stands in history unapproached and unapproachable. He is the incarnate conscience of mankind. . . . The second element in Jesus' significance is his faith in God. . . . The faith of Jesus in itself and apart from what was new in its content was a reality potent enough to mark an epoch in religion. . . . Again, in a degree which is altogether unique, Jesus is one with the kingdom of righteousness, truth and love which he proclaimed. . . . Jesus is the leader of mankind in the highest things, the one figure in all history whom we can follow without reserve. . . . Finally Jesus, as none other, embodies in his life those great moral realities in which God reveals himself to us and lays his hand upon us. . . . Summing up, we can say that in Jesus we find a religion we can believe, a leader we can follow—one whose faith supports ours—and the presence and working of the

living God as the God of our salvation. . . . Jesus is not
only touched with the Divine, as many are; he is all Divine.
The Divine constitutes the whole content of his human
life' (pp. 106–110).

Humanistic as is this approach to the Christological
problem, and incomplete as it may appear to many, it will
be observed that Morgan conceived himself to be asserting,
not denying, the 'divinity' of Jesus. Apart from the
significance of the language employed, which is modern,
untechnical and intelligible, two points in this presentation
deserve stress. First, the conception is based upon a
realistic study of the historical figure of Jesus and upon His
actual effect on those who through Him have found God.
Here is no *a priori* metaphysic, no mythology, no doctrinal
'mystery,' but a view based upon moral realities. Unlike
much Trinitarian and Christological speculation, we cannot
say of this view, as F. C. S. Schiller says of Hegelianism,
that it 'never anywhere gets within sight of a fact, or
within touch of reality.' Secondly, this conception is expressed in moral and religious terms. One of the most
serious charges against the Christology of the creeds is
that the 'divinity' of Christ is expressed in non-ethical,
metaphysical terms; Jesus is defined as a metaphysical
wonder, not as He who through His righteousness, His
mercy, His uttermost self-giving reveals and brings home to
men the love of God. This statement of the 'divinity' of
Christ, therefore, is not only more intelligible and real but
also more strictly religious than that of the ancient creeds.

III

The doctrine of the 'divinity' of Jesus has in the
past not been built upon a consideration of His life. Thus
it was not, in the first instance, to the teaching or the
character or the 'self-consciousness' of Jesus that the faith
of the Church was directed, but to His Resurrection. The
early missionaries, it would seem, proclaimed, first, the
heavenly Redeemer, who of His grace had descended from
heaven to share man's low estate, who had consented to
die upon the Cross, had cheated death and all the powers
of darkness by rising from the dead, and who, reascending
to His heavenly glory, had thrown open to mankind the

gates of Paradise. That this superhistorical account of
Jesus answers to the deep Christian evaluation of what His
life and death have meant for man must be admitted ;
unquestionably, however, it is mythological in form. A
myth is a tale told of the doings and sufferings of gods or
divine beings. Many are the ancient myths of such divine
beings ' in the form of God ' who have for a time come
down to earth and afterwards reascended to their proper
element ; few, if any, of these figures are so rooted in
history as the story of Jesus, and Harnack is justified in
his assertion that Christianity is not so much one myth
beside the rest as the fulfilment of myth (' der erfüllte
Mythos ') ; none the less mythology is not the language of
fact or of philosophy, but rather of poetry and imagination.
' Nor is it possible to show,' says Morgan, ' that Jesus
appears in history as a visitor from the transcendent world.
Our belief in his unique significance is the product, not of
any theoretical proof that he does not belong to the world
of time and change, but of our feeling for the eternal values
embodied and expressed in his personality and teaching '
(pp. 290 f.). The ancient creeds are speculative construc-
tions of the Christian faith ; they are not to-day, as once
they were, its basis.

Through all the centuries of orthodoxy the miraculous
birth of Jesus without a human father, His physical resurrection from the tomb, His ascent into the sky above
the clouds were taken as literal and all-important facts,
proving His divinity and authenticating His message. Upon
these pillars was erected the imposing structure of Christian
dogma. Faith in Jesus was indissolubly connected with
faith in these historical events. But modern scientific and
literary criticism has rendered precarious the old assurances.
The evidence for the Virgin Birth of Jesus is not such
as must bring conviction to the impartial historian ; our
earliest and only contemporary account of the Resurrection
appearances (1 Cor. xv. 5 ff.) makes no mention of the
empty tomb, nor is it readily supposed to-day that Jesus
returned to heaven by the expedient of travelling directly
upwards from the soil of Palestine. An element of dubiety
surrounds the ' facts ' upon which once the Christian
' myth ' and the structure of Christian dogma were un-

questioningly based.　It is idle to repine ; it is idle to refuse to see the change.

The world of the early Christian centuries was not offended by the mythological terms in which the Christian Gospel was set forth.　For better, for worse, we live in a different world.　Before the modern man will begin to believe the ' myth,' he must cross-question us about this Jesus :　Who was He ?　What did He teach ?　How much about Him is assured history, and how much pious conjecture and religious phantasy ?　This issue we cannot avoid, but it constitutes a crucial difficulty to the modern apologist.

The theory that Jesus of Nazareth never existed as a historic person is not to be taken seriously.　That He was ' crucified under Pontius Pilate ' is as certain as any other well-ascertained fact of history.　But beyond that what can be proved of Him ?　What common ground is there even among Christian scholars ?　If we consider, for instance, the reconstruction of the evangelical narratives implied by the writings of such competent scholars as Adolf von Harnack, Albert Schweitzer, Shirley Jackson Case and Rudolf Bultmann, we find such deep and fundamental differences as to raise in our minds the question whether anything can with certainty be affirmed of Jesus' life and teaching.

Some of these reconstructions, in fact, show much more knowledge and acuteness than insight, but even these have a relative justification in that the Synoptic Gospels themselves do not give us a homogeneous and credible portrait of Jesus.　This is indicated by Herrmann Schell at the beginning of his *Christus* only less decisively than by Protestant scholars such as Wrede in his famous study of the ' Messianic secret ' or Emmett and Miss Dougall in their penetrating study, *The Lord of Thought*.　Every scholar, therefore, who would reconstruct the portrait of the historical Jesus is bound either to reject some elements in the tradition as secondary, or so to ' harmonise ' all the traditions as, in fact, to explain many of them away.　So acute is the difficulty that a number of scholars, such as Loisy and Herrmann in their different ways and, more recently, Dibelius, seek to base Christianity elsewhere, beyond the reach of any possible findings of New Testament scholarship. It is generally felt by Christians, however,— a matter to which we shall revert—that to emancipate Christianity from history in this way is alike to cut the nerve of ' the Gospel ' and to deprive Christianity of a needful norm whereby its ' experiences ' may be tested. Here, then, is our dilemma : the whole Christian contention centres round the historic Figure of Jesus, yet that Figure is apprehended rather by faith than by mere historical research. Christianity stands or falls by the historic Figure of Jesus, yet the Christian conception of Jesus can never be demonstrated as the only possible interpretation of the literary evidence !

Of the lack of homogeneity in the Gospel picture two illustrations must be given. First, Jesus is sometimes represented as coming before men publicly with the claim that He is the Messiah or ' Son of Man ' ; at other times the Messiahship, and *a fortiori* the more supernatural claim, are regarded as a mystery or secret not publicly revealed till the close of the ministry or after its conclusion. The story can be retold upon either of these assumptions, but not upon both at the same time. Secondly, Jesus is represented as proclaiming the imminence of the Last Judgment, of the outbreak of the wrath of God upon all the unrepentant, of the Gehenna of fire, the wailing and gnashing of teeth, the undying, insatiable worm. Elsewhere He represents God as extending a forgivingness beyond seventy times seven to the sinner, as the One who sends His sun and rain on just and unjust, on thankful and thankless, who calls men to be perfect or merciful like Himself, as the Father who never loses His love for the Prodigal, as the Shepherd who seeks the lost sheep ' till He find.' It is possible to reconstruct the teaching of Jesus upon either of these assumptions, but not upon both at the same time. Which represents the real Jesus of history whose divinity is the centre of the Christian message ?

There is place here for two comments only.[1] First, the

---

[1] But for a relatively full discussion of the crucial issue of the eschatological teaching ascribed to Jesus see further my article in the

only New Testament writer who was certainly a contemporary of Jesus is the apostle Paul. It is doubtful whether Paul ever saw Jesus in the flesh, but he certainly knew what was said about Him and what impression He made upon His followers ; in particular, Paul was well acquainted with Peter, the outstanding apostle, and with James, the Lord's brother. Paul rarely quotes a saying of Jesus or refers to any event in His life apart from the Crucifixion, but he affords a picture of the character of Jesus at once the earliest, the clearest, and the most authentic. Again and again he indicates what will be the character of the Christian man in whom the Spirit of Jesus, or the character of Jesus, repeats itself. The portrait is indirect, but it is unmistakable. When, as in 1 Cor. xiii. or Rom. xii., Paul describes the ' fruits of the Spirit '—that is, of the Spirit of Jesus—we see clearly what Jesus Himself must have been like. Thus the portrait of Jesus as it is implied in the Pauline writings is the proper and objective norm whereby the later traditions of the Gospels may be tested. This norm rules out at once as morally impossible many of the recent ' lives ' of Jesus.

Secondly, protest against the credibility of the Gospels is often made on the ground that the only portraits of Jesus which we possess are the work of believers ; the Jesus, therefore, whom they represent is simply the imaginary or idealised Jesus of the Church's faith. It is demonstrably true that the Gospel portraits of Jesus are coloured by the theology and practice of the early Church that produced them. But not infrequently it is possible to detect and appraise the later accretion. The glosses are uniformly intended to subserve the honour and glory of the Person of Jesus, but often it is plain that the Church has misunderstood and misrepresented the teaching of the Master. A glaring instance of this is afforded by the grotesque and

Queen's Quarterly for April 1929, published by Queen's University, Kingston, Ontario. The thesis of the article is that, while Jesus adopted some of the ideas or phrases of current eschatology, His teaching was throughout *prophetic* rather than apocalyptic, and that this teaching as it is reproduced in the Synoptic Gospels has been worked over, edited and amplified in the light of the eschatological and apocalyptic expectations of the early Church.

mutually inconsistent reasons offered by Mark in the name of Jesus for the parabolic teaching (iv. 11–13). In every age, in fact, the Church has both proclaimed and misrepresented Jesus. Jesus is both revealed in the Gospel narratives and to some extent concealed behind them. If we recognise the divinity of Jesus, not in incomprehensible metaphysical attributes but in the values which He represented and embodied, it is not true that the Gospels present us with a heightened and idealised picture of Him; rather, guided by the implications of the Gospel as a whole and fortified by Paul's testimony to the Spirit of Jesus, we are sometimes able and even compelled to test the Gospel narratives and, finding them wanting, to recognise the diviner Figure who stands behind them.

That an element of subjectivity enters into this procedure is not to be denied. The Jesus whose divinity we recognise is not apprehended apart from historical inquiry nor yet upon the basis of mere historical inquiry, but by faith, which is the response of the whole personality, including the intellect, to the impact made upon it by the Person of Jesus as it is known through the Christian Scriptures and the Christian community. For to-day, as ever, Jesus is called divine, not primarily because of Church traditions of His life and teaching, but because of what, as Redeemer, He has done and does for the souls of men. To accept a metaphysical doctrine of the divinity of Jesus is entirely destitute of religious meaning or value, unless the man who accepts it has found God in and through Jesus. According to our conception or experience of redemption, then, must be our doctrine of the divinity of Jesus.

This fundamental principle amply indicates of itself why the ancient Christological formulae can no longer be accepted. That at bottom the Christian experience throughout the ages shows an underlying unity, the prayers and piety of the Church show. None the less, we have to-day a totally different conception of what it is that Christ does for us, and therefore of that wherein His divinity consists.

In particular, the theology of Athanasius, represented

by the Nicene formula, is intimately bound up with his conception of redemption, a conception widely different, for instance, from that of Augustine, and still more widely different from that of Paul. It was necessary that Jesus should be proclaimed ' of one substance with the Father,' because, under the terms of the current Hellenistic dualism, redemption was supposed to depend upon a deifying or ' divinising ' of our earthly, corruptible nature. Only by the influx of a divine substance by the divine grace could human nature be redeemed from corruptibility. The necessary supernatural power and supernatural substance were supposed to operate through the Christian sacraments. There is the most intimate connection between the Christological formulae of the early creeds on the one hand, and, on the other, the growing sacramentalism and the conception of the Church as the dispenser of sacred but tangible mysteries. It is significant that Luther used the Chalcedonian confession primarily in support of his far from Protestant sacramental doctrine. It is by no accident, then, that those who in the modern world would perpetuate the so-called ' sacramental system ' are pre-eminently attached to the ancient Christological formulae. That system in Christianity has never been divorced from the demands of the ethical life, but the conception of salvation which underlies both the Christological formulae and the sacramentarianism which goes with them is conceived not in *ethical* but in somewhat primitive *metaphysical* terms. The acceptance of a Christology grounded upon the character and religion of the historical Jesus would involve a thoroughgoing revision of sacramental doctrine.

IV

But is there for the modern Christian any genuine Christological problem at all ? Are special categories needed to express the Person and work of Jesus Christ ? Jesus was called divine in virtue of the redemption which He accomplished ; but this redemption as described in older theologies seems to many illusory or even hysterical as an experience and entirely fanciful as a hope. With the break-up of the old-fashioned orthodox theologies what is left to be explained ? Or, to put the question more constructively, what are the moral realities that remain when mythological thought-forms have been abandoned and psychology has performed its perfect work ?

The character of Jesus, as it is implied in the Pauline writings and in the Gospels as a whole, is the character which Jesus taught us to ascribe to God Himself. He is to us the revelation of God, not only in what He said, but also in what He was. Indeed, His proclamation of the infinite grace and mercy of God would seem but a dream or splendid phantasy were not grace and mercy without measure embodied in His own character and presented to us ' in flesh and blood.' He not only taught that God forgives and loves ; He made it credible. Theology has been hampered by the term the ' sinlessness ' of Jesus, for a negative cannot be proved, and absence of vice is not, of itself, perfection of virtue. But the phrase does far less than justice to the active, unstinted, triumphant love and loyalty towards God and man which Jesus showed in His life and, supremely, in His death. The Church of the classical creeds, inheriting from paganism a ready-made metaphysical conception of the divine nature, declared with passionate faith the divinity of Jesus. The modern Christian, the child of a sceptical and agnostic age, confesses that he finds in the human Jesus that which his heart recognises as divine. The wonder of the Christian revelation, which once was expressed in the phrase, Jesus is ' of one substance with the Father,' might now more naturally be expressed in the confession that the Father is of one character with Jesus.

Again, it is through Jesus that we have found God. We do not understand by this that immortality has somehow been infused into our mortal natures, nor that a debt has been paid for us, nor that ' the wrath of God ' has been appeased, but that through the Man Christ Jesus, through the records of His life, through His Spirit moving in our hearts, we have felt the touch of God—in mercy for our sins, in strength for our daily task, in the quickening of insight, in the enlarging and deepening of affection, in a peace deeper than life's discords and disasters ; we have in measure received the Spirit of Jesus whereby we cry, ' Abba, Father.'

By a true instinct the Cross has been made the symbol of Christianity. To the hopeless and the lost, to those ' tossed with tempest and not comforted,' to the scoundrel and the renegade, not less than to the respectable and pious and devoted, Christianity proclaims the pardon and the love of God, not as an idea to be intellectually assimilated but as a quickening power. To many thoughtful men it has seemed incredible that ' the Fatherhood of God ' should really involve a personal and invincible love for them as individuals. It has only become credible because Jesus Christ exhibited in flesh and blood, through human agony and on the stage of history, a love that neither life nor death nor the extremity of humiliation and betrayal could shatter or subdue. Jesus died in the first instance for His people, but with a true instinct men have seen that in principle He died for all; ' he loved me,' said Paul, ' and gave himself for me.' It is through the historic Cross pre-eminently that the love of God has been brought home to sinful and desperate men. The character, the authority, the love of Jesus, then, are to us the character, the authority, the love of God.

But this should not lead us to speak of two several natures in Jesus, a divine and a human. Every discovery made by a scientist has a double aspect : on the one hand, it is a personal achievement; on the other, it is a revelation. So every noble character that we have known has been to us in some measure a revelation alike of man and of God. In Jesus Christ this process of human achievement and divine revelation reaches its climax. Jesus on the Cross offers to God the perfect obedience of a man, and reveals and brings home to men the perfect love of God.

Is He then man or God or both or something between the two ? To call Him a god is inconsistent with monotheism ; to identify Him with God is repugnant alike to orthodoxy and common sense ; to call Him the God-man is the euthanasia of thought :

> Denn eben wo Begriffe fehlen,
> Da stellt ein Wort zur rechten Zeit sich ein !

He thought of Himself as a man[1]; He was a Jew, bringing to fulfilment, and transcending, the religion of his people. He was certainly a man, but a man with a difference, a man in whom, to use Paul's phrase, ' dwelt all the fulness of the Deity under human limitations.'

When a scientist discovers a being the like of which has never been known before, he recognises it as a living thing, but he has to invent a special name for it. The new name either expresses the emotions of the scientist or, more felicitously, some peculiarity of the creature in question. For the new and the unique we can only invent a name and frame our definition in terms of genus and differentia. Banal as the illustration may appear, we cannot have a Christology different in method from this. The statement that Jesus is ' of one substance with the Father,' or that He has two ' Natures,' a divine and a human, is a specula- tion of no validity to-day except in so far as it reveals the ' value ' which men saw in Jesus. We can discuss what Jesus reveals, and what He does, and how He saves us, but beyond this we can have no ' theory of his Person.'

Jesus was a man, not Man ; but, after all, this does not carry us far, for man is but another name for mystery. When we call Him a man, we mean only that, to the best of our knowledge, He had physical and mental powers similar to those of other men, and that He lived His life under the normal conditions and limitations of humankind. He did not seem to His contemporaries to be a strange and unintelligible Being, a visitant from another world ; they never doubted His humanity. But no one ever spoke as He did; no one ever was as He was; no one could ever do for the souls of men what He has done; His coming marks beyond all question a new era in human history. No two men are alike ; but Jesus differs from all men in a way in which they do not differ from one another. We may hope to define the differentia, though we must abandon the hope of a Christology that will explain it. The differentia, as we now suppose, lies entirely within the sphere of the spiritual and ethical, and not at all in the physical. We

[1] For a discussion of the so-called ' self-designations ' of Jesus in the Gospels see the article in the *Queen's Quarterly* for April 1929.

can no longer assert with confidence that Jesus differed from other men in the manner of His coming into the world or of departing from it, in His physical constitution or His mental powers. In this we are at variance with all traditional Christology. We are at variance not because we reject the notion of Christ's divinity and take some lower view of his Person, but through the progress of philosophical thought and historical science. Jesus differs from all men in respect of religion and morals, not in ways that are inhuman or superhuman and proper only to God ; for indeed neither His religion nor His victorious life of love and service lived in dependence upon God can with any propriety be predicated of God Himself.

There is, however, in the Person of Jesus an element that we conceive to be not only unique but absolute and final. It may be put briefly in this way : a man's character and religion are shown in his attitude to God, in his attitude to his fellow-man, and in the way he faces life with its duties, its joys, its discouragements and its disasters. In these three relationships the whole man stands revealed. Of almost all the great leaders of humanity and of countless others whose names have perished it might be said that for the most part they have trusted in God, they have been for the most part just and merciful to their neighbours and dependents, they have faced life for the most part manfully and honestly. Higher praise we could not bestow upon them. In all these relationships, to God, to man, to life, they have been *relatively* right. But the Christian judgment about Jesus is that in all these relationships He was *absolutely* right; He alone has loved God perfectly with all His heart and soul and mind and strength; He alone has lived wholly for His fellow-men ; He alone has so faced life's disasters as to triumph over them and to turn a shameful gibbet into man's glory and the symbol of his hope. He alone has been the perfect son of God, the perfect brother of man, the victor over life by faith. Herein, and herein alone, lies the claim of Christianity to be the final and absolute religion ; herein lies the uniqueness of Jesus which sets Him apart from all other sons of men. How it is possible that one man should have broken the entail of sin and spiritual darkness, we cannot tell; more important than a theory of His Person, which for ever may remain beyond our reach, is a clear understanding of what He was.

The recognition of what in fact He was, is for us obscured rather than illuminated by the language of past Christologies. If the uniqueness of Christ is manifested in the sphere of religion and of the moral life, in His personal attitude to reality, we naturally use the categories of 'personality' in which to speak of Him. The conception of 'personality,' however far we are from understanding it, has this great advantage over the thought-forms of Hellenistic dualism in that it gives us, as we suppose, a term proper both to God and to man. We are no longer shut up to the dilemma, Is He divine or human? the nature of God and the nature of man have grown more, not less, mysterious to us with the passing of the centuries; but we conceive ourselves to be 'persons' whose personality is expressed now under the conditions of time and space; and we ascribe personality also to God, though the modes of its operation and the conditions of its supramundane manifestation must remain unknown and inconceivable to us, while we live on earth as men. Jesus also is a person who like us lived under human limitations as a man; and only as we seek to express the uniqueness of Jesus as lying in the field of His character and religion and of His influence upon the souls of men in history do we keep close to moral and spiritual realities.

But Jesus Christ is more to us than merely a revelation of the right and perfect attitude to God and man and life. Not without reason has He been called Saviour and Redeemer. As following from, and firmly grounded upon, what He was in character and religion, Jesus is central to our personal religion in three ways : first, He is to us the revelation of the Father's heart and will; His voice, whether in command or comfort, is to us as the voice of God; the perpetual self-revelation of God to man through every noble character finds in Jesus its crown and complete fulfilment. Secondly, something ultimate, sufficient and complete was accomplished on the Cross, not, as we now suppose, a mysterious transaction between the First and Second Persons of the Trinity involving the Universe in its sweep, not a victory over malign demonic forces, over fallen angels and the cohorts of Satan, not the payment of an infinite debt by the medium of an infinite merit, but the exhibition on the stage of history, in blood and anguish, of a love unbreakable and all-enduring, in which men have always seen, not merely man perfectly offering himself to God, but God Himself rending the heavens, as it were, and manifesting His own love unchangeable and undimmed through rejection and betrayal, through indifference and scorn. There is a certain fitness about the legend that at the death of Christ the earth quaked, the tombs opened, and the Temple's veil was rent ; for the Cross of Christ is indeed the great Apocalypse, the revealing of God's heart. Thirdly, the life of Jesus on earth cannot be separated from His perpetual influence upon men's hearts, to illumine, to emancipate, to recreate. Through all the intervening centuries it has never been possible for Christian men to speak or think of Him as dead, and this, not in the last resort because of Church traditions about an emptied tomb, but because men have known themselves to be touched by a hand and moved by a Spirit which they have recognised as His; they can think neither of Him apart from God, nor of God but they see His face. The Christian Church, in so far as it is the company of those in whom the Spirit of Jesus is manifested, is part of ' the fact of Christ.'

The Christology of the creeds is intimately connected with the conception of the Church as a *Heilsanstalt*, a corporation supernaturally endowed and commissioned for the administration, under strictly defined conditions, of vivifying and sanctifying sacraments, the medicine of immortality, the vehicles of grace. A conception of Christ's divinity based upon a historical inquiry into what He was and what He sought to do involves a conception of the Church as a company of those who have received His Spirit and are committed to His cause.[1]

[1] This point is further elaborated with reference to the historic work of Jesus in my article on ' Jesus as Teacher and Prophet ' in *Theology*, October 1928 = *Theologische Blätter* of same date.

V

This paper in criticising earlier Christologies has put forward no new theory of His Person ; rather, it has urged that all attempts to define the ' nature ' of Jesus or His relationship to God must inevitably be fruitless. We are mysteries to ourselves. We cannot define our own nature nor our metaphysical relationship to God, much less, then, His. But the upshot of the discussion is not wholly negative. It will be no small gain, alike for the easing of troubled minds and for the furtherance of the Gospel among men, if the Church will no longer be bound to conceptions that are mythological and to a terminology that has never been anything but pagan, and will express the significance of Jesus in terms of moral reality. Our doctrine of Christ must be, not an antiquated theory of His metaphysical relation to the Godhead, but a proclamation of His character, and what He stood for, of what He has been to the souls of men, a revelation of God, of duty and of life, the shadow of a great rock in a weary land, a power of God unto salvation. These are not questionable theories about Him to be accepted by the mind, but moral realities to be discovered and experienced in life.

Finally, it is not to be expected or even desired that Christendom should be united for all time or even at any one time in the profession of one theology, one set form of doctrine ; yet Christians, differing in intellectual approach and accent, are united in the confession that Jesus is the Christ. As the Cross is the best symbol of Christianity, so the name ' Christ ' is the best symbol and expression of the Church's faith in Jesus :

(a) It is almost the only title, except the more ambiguous ' Lord,' of which we can say that it has been used in the Christian Church *semper, ubique, et ab omnibus* ; it belongs, therefore, to œcumenical Christianity.

(b) Christ is the translation of a Jewish term and therein marks the historic place of Jesus in the religion from which He came. He was Messiah. True, He was not the kind of Messiah whom the majority of His people expected or desired, but when we say Jesus is Christ, with the emphasis

M

upon the proper name, the sense in which we use the term is thereby sufficiently defined.

(c) While Christ (or Messiah) is properly a Jewish term and marks the place of Jesus in the story of Hebrew religion, yet the idea, if not the name, belongs to universal religious history. In the Saosyant of Zoroastrianism, in the Imam of Islam, in Krishna and other avataras of Hinduism, in the Buddha as man's refuge, in the incarnation-myths of the Graeco-Roman world, in the widespread conception of the *Urmensch* or archetypal Man we find variant expressions of an almost universal craving for a ' Christ.' The dreams and longings of all ages and religions can gather round that name, each enriching its significance. While, therefore, the term is Jewish, the concept is universal.

(d) It is an expression of the uniqueness of Jesus ; there can be but one Christ.

(e) It is a name full of ethical content ; it is given to Jesus as the fulfiller of the noblest visions of the Old Testament that one should arise, one upon whom God's holy Spirit should be poured forth.

(f) It is a term of authority, a royal name.

(g) The Christ rules in the name and in the Spirit of God, whose vicegerent He is. The name expresses, therefore, the function of Jesus as the Revealer, as ' the express image of the character ' of God.

(h) Not least, the Christ is a victorious title. In the West the ' finished work ' of Christ has usually been connected with His death ; His victory lies ahead. Thus has the triumphant note of early Christianity been largely lost. In the thought of the early Church sin indeed was man's own fault, and he must pay the just penalty for his guilt ; yet man in the present evil age was subjected to the dominion, or at least the heavy oppression, of demonic powers of evil and of death which exercised their baleful influence within the sphere of ' the flesh.' The powers of darkness loomed dismally over him ; he might struggle against them, but how could he prevail ? If he found himself liberated from the oppression of fear and the bonds of sin, then assuredly the demonic powers must have been overcome, the strong one must have been vanquished by a mightier than he. It was inevitable, therefore, that, when men realised in experience that Jesus was not dead but living and present still in the Spirit, and that fear and sin were being banished from their hearts, they should ascribe to Jesus not merely an individual victory in their own case but a cosmic victory over the angels and ' the spiritual hosts of wickedness in the heavenly places.' This sense of a triumph won, a victory already achieved, has always been treasured in the Eastern Church. It has been rediscovered in Protestantism in the glad proclamation of Jesus as the Saviour who ' breaks the power of cancelled sin ; he sets the prisoner free.' Christ is a term of victory.

(i) Finally, the name Christ, while it is capable of an infinite content, is scarcely open to misunderstanding nor to reasonable criticism. The term has acquired a universal intelligibility. When we speak of Jesus as the Christ, men understand, not that we are explaining Him or expounding a theory about Him, but rather that we are expressing a personal attitude towards Him. This attitude is prior to any Christology and more durable than any ; it is upon this attitude, and not upon a theory, that the Church is built.

This paper, then, offers no new theory of the Person of Christ, but indicates a new approach to the old problem. The framers and sponsors of the creeds, setting forth with a ready-made philosophical conception of God according to which omnipotence and omniscience and even im- passibility are pre-eminent among the divine attributes, must attempt to show that Jesus of Nazareth was in some way identical with, and simultaneously distinct from, the God of this philosophical theory. This method of reasoning leads to mythology, not the naïve poetry of simple religious faith and insight, but an imaginative theosophy, which, at least since the days of Kant, is inevitably obsolescent. The new way of approach is different. Men start, not with clean-cut ideas of the Godhead (for to-day science and philosophy provide them with none), but from their own sense of the sacred or divine, that is, from a consideration of whatever they recognise as of infinite worth or as im- posing upon them an absolute obligation. Religious men

admit that through the beauties and sublimities of Nature
and of art, through the inexorable demands of truth and
of conscience, through human affection and the sanctities
of home and of loyalty, through the story of human goodness and devotion they are aware of the voice and presence
of God Himself. It is in response to these divine instiga-
tions, which come to us in life and through history, that
we are religiously in touch with God. But in this case we
are not ignorant of the nature of God, so far as it concerns
personal religion, and along this path we come to a religious,
as opposed to a merely metaphysical, conception of the
divinity of Christ. This dogma should be regarded as a
profession of faith, not a proposition in metaphysics. When
men worship power or size, success or pleasure, they do
not believe in the divinity of Jesus in any religious sense.
Wherever before mercy, pity, sacrifice, patience, gentleness,
love, men bow their heads as before that which is sacred,
there they reverence and believe in those qualities in virtue
of which Jesus is called divine. The divinity of Jesus
Christ must remain central to the thought of Christianity,
because only in terms of His life and character can we
apprehend and define the Nature of the God in whom we
trust.

CHRISTOLOGY AND
SOTERIOLOGY
BY JOHN KENNETH MOZLEY

VIII

CHRISTOLOGY AND SOTERIOLOGY

I

ONE of the earliest symbols associated with Christianity was that of the fish. In the five letters composing the Greek word ἰχθύς was given the content of primitive belief in that Person who was at once foundation-stone and head of the Christian Ecclesia. He was Ἰησοῦς Χριστὸς Θεοῦ Υἱὸς Σωτήρ.

The word σωτήρ possesses considerable interest. In paganism it was applied to the healing god, Asklepios, to the Egyptian deities Serapis and Isis, to royal princes, Ptolemies and Seleucids, and, finally, to the Roman Emperor. Thus, it is a Hellenistic religious term, and its use as a title of Jesus would be facilitated in certain circles by this fact. But that it was from the side of Hellenistic religion that it found its way into the New Testament is an unnecessary and improbable hypothesis. There is a far more natural and immediate connection with the Old Testament, where one of the constantly recurring thoughts is that of the need of salvation and of that need as satisfied by God who saves. Neither in the Old Testament nor in the New is the title ' Saviour ' frequently used of God ; σωτηρία and σώζειν are found far more often as descriptive of what He gives and what He does. Over the development of ideas in the Old Testament of what is involved in salvation we need not delay ; what does need emphasising is the association of salvation with Javeh ; ' Saviours ' might be raised up for Israel, but the one true and abiding Saviour was Israel's God.

The assurances and promises of the Old Testament lived on. The New Testament is, through and through, a literature of σωτηρία both prospective and present. Not less than in the Old Testament is salvation the gift of God, but the gift is also given through and by Jesus, whose name recalls one of the former ' saviours ' of God's people, while the salvation which He brings is something which far transcends in character those temporal, physical deliverances wrought by Joshua. He is to save His people from their sins (Matt. i. 21) ; in His name alone is there salvation (Acts iv. 12) ; He is the captain of salvation (Heb. ii. 10), the author of eternal salvation (Heb. v. 9). So to Him, as to God, could be given the title σωτήρ. This can be used with specific reference, as when it is said of Christ that He is the saviour of the body (Eph. v. 23) ; it can be used in an eschatological context as in Phil. iii. 20 of the Christian expectation of the Saviour from heaven, and in Titus ii. 13 of the glorious epiphany of our great God and Saviour Jesus Christ [1]; but it can also be used in the widest sense, as when the witness of those who possess the gift of the Spirit is said to be that ' the Father sent the Son to be the Saviour of the world ' (1 John iv. 14, cf. John iv. 42).

The last word of the Ichthys formula derives, then, directly from the New Testament and, more remotely, from the Old Testament. But we may further note that the soteriological significance of the formula is not confined to the last word. On the contrary, both from the linguistic and from the historical point of view, the words ' Jesus Christ, Son of God ' are expressive of soteriology. The Messianic hope, whatever its exact content and with whatever variations in the idea of the Messiah, whether we draw upon the Old Testament or upon apocryphal and apocalyptical writings, was a hope of salvation.[2] This background of belief would have led to the recognition of Jesus as Saviour, if He were the Messiah. But we have to take into account the effect of the character of the life and ministry of Jesus. To put the matter as briefly as possible, we may say that His ministry developed from an abiding, though veiled, background of Messianic self-

---

[1] Cf. on this view A. E. J. Rawlinson, *The New Testament Doctrine of the Christ*, p. 172.

[2] Cf. Jer. xxxiii. 14–16; Zech. ix. 9–10.

consciousness and ended in a manner utterly out of keeping with every form of the Messianic idea except that which He Himself created. It was not only the chief priests who thought that His claim, which was, finally, not veiled, to be the Messiah, was decisively refuted by the fact that, as He hung upon the Cross, ' he saved others, himself he cannot save.' That was to be the σκάνδαλον over which believers in Jesus as the Messiah would have to pass. Now, while it is quite true that apart from the Resurrection the σκάνδαλον would have remained, it would be quite untrue to say that it was first by the Resurrection that the σκάνδαλον was transcended. That happened when Jesus thought of Himself as the Messiah and also as the Servant of Javeh, and spoke of the Son of Man in terms of suffering and death, which as obviously were applicable to one whose vocation was that of the Servant as it was obviously not applicable to the Messiah, except through a new creative synthesis of thought which should pass into one of experience. But, given this new synthesis, the work of Jesus could not fail to be estimated by the Christian community as it looked back upon the life, death, and resurrection of Jesus as, pre-eminently, the work of a Saviour. A suffering Messiah was, necessarily, a saving Messiah. So far as our knowledge takes us, we must hold that it was St. Paul who worked out the theology of the σκάνδαλον, but the way was prepared for him by that earliest theology of Jesus as ὁ χριστός and also as παῖς θεοῦ to which witness is borne in the opening chapters of Acts.[1]

Similarly, the confession of Jesus as the Son of God pointed in the direction of soteriology. The technicalities as to the relation of the idea of the Messiah with the idea of Son of God cease to be relevant for us when we are dealing with a Christianity which has passed outside its primitive Jewish environment. On non-Jewish soil the title ' Son of God ' was used of the reigning Emperor and could be applied to famous men in virtue of a supposed

[1] *Cf.* Acts iii. 13, 18 ; iv. 27. Even if Professor Burkitt is correct in his argument in *Christian Beginnings*, pp. 39 ff., that the Christology does not proceed from the earliest Christian circle, it must be assigned, as he says, to ' a very early stage of Greek-speaking Christianity.'

divine parent, though the title was, apparently, not in common use.[1] If Jesus had been preached as Son of God because of His mighty works a bridge might have been made across which Greeks and others could have passed to the confession of Him—if the history had been different and had not included the Cross. But the preaching of a crucified Son of God was, in itself, foolishness to the Greek mind. So St. Paul found it to be at Corinth, and there and elsewhere and for long after the contemptuous adjectives used in his triumphant rhetoric by Tertullian were, doubtless, applied with full conviction to the conception of a Son of God who had been crucified and buried : it was *pudendum, ineptum, impossibile*. For here was history and not myth. But if, after all, the history could be understood in a different way, and the adjectives changed into their opposites, that was because of the soteriological value attached to the notion of the death of the Son of God. Hellenistic ideas of dying divinities may have helped at this point ; but the Christian missionary preaching did not derive its message from Hellenistic religion ; the true source was the history of Jesus and His Messianic standing, and, behind that, the Old Testament.[2]

The whole of the Ichthys formula is soteriological, if we judge it, as we should do, by the way it came into existence and by what is implicit as well as explicit in it. So, it is simply true to the New Testament which is the history of the coming of salvation through Jesus and of Jesus as Saviour. All such disjunctions as would separate Jesus as Prophet, Teacher, even as Christ from Jesus as Saviour, are foreign to the New Testament. Neither the Gospels nor the Acts nor the Epistles give us any sanction for this kind of distinction. The dramatic character of St. Mark's Gospel is manifested through the

---

[1] See A. D. Nock's remarks in *Essays on the Trinity and the Incarnation*, p. 97.

[2] A. D. Nock's judgment, resting on wide knowledge, is (*op. cit.* p. 94) : ' A general atonement by a Redeemer is not Hellenistic. Attis, Adonis, Osiris, die, are mourned for, and return to life. Yet it is nowhere said that *Soteria* comes by their death. *Soteria* of a sort may come from their return to life, or from the assurance that they will do so in due season.'

soteriological motive which comes to full expression as determining the historical movement from Caesarea Philippi onwards. If the first and third Gospels are not so obviously soteriological, that is largely due to the incorporation of large blocks of sayings of Jesus. And in His general teaching, which was given to the multitudes and not to the disciples only, Jesus dwelt neither on soteriology nor on His Messiahship ; the veiling of the mystery of the latter involved the veiling of the mystery of the former. And we react untruly from the old liberal view of Jesus as the supreme moral teacher, the expounder of man's true character and behaviour in relation to God and to man, if we forget that Jesus was such a teacher, that what He taught concerning the Fatherhood and the providence of God was good news ; it has lived on as an inspiring power in human life and has made its appeal to not a few who have found themselves unable to pass on to what has been for the central Christian tradition the heart of the Gospel. The Church has seen that disclosed in the Passion and Resurrection narratives, and in the apostolic commentaries upon Jesus crucified and risen. The whole of the New Testament is written from within this tradition.

The right approach to the Christology of the New Testament is through its soteriology. The fundamental distinction between Christ and men is that between the Saviour and the saved. At this point the unity of the New Testament comes into view. In the Christology there are different strains. But the upward movement and the unfolding of the meaning of the Person of Jesus has as its constant background the apprehension of Jesus as the Redeemer. There is in the New Testament no speculative Christology divorced from the Gospel of the Saviour and of the salvation He brings. If, when we think of the furthest outreach of St. Paul's Christological thought in Colossians and Ephesians, we use the phrase ' the cosmic Christ,' we ought to remember that St. Paul arrives at the notion represented by the phrase, not by the speculative thought of the incompleteness of the universe and its grades apart from Christ, but by the soteriological certainty of the all-comprehending efficacy of Christ's redeeming and reconciling work. If, when we read the prologue to the Fourth Gospel, we feel that here in short compass the secret of life and of its rational character is revealed to us through the doctrine of the divine reason which is the rational principle of all life and has been incarnate in a historic Person, we must not forget that for the author of that Gospel what was wrong with the world into which the divine Reason came was not intellectual immaturity but moral and spiritual blindness. He was no less concerned with the drama of sin and salvation from sin than was St. Paul. In the apparently contrary affirmations as to the world and its salvation which from time to time appear in his writings we may note both the tension of his thought and its supreme concern. The whole world lies in the evil one and should be an object of abhorrence to believers, and yet the testimony of the believers is that the Father sent the Son to be the Saviour of the world.

It is this preoccupation with the doctrine of salvation which is decisive as to the real character of New Testament Christology. The Old Testament was the Bible of the early Christians, and one of the assurances to be found in it was that Javeh brought salvation, while with the assurance went the warning that none but He could do so. The more closely the association of Jesus with God in the salvation of men was realised, the more certain became the ascription to Him of true divinity. The soteriology of the primitive Gospel and an adoptionist Christology could not live together. Whenever the soteriological motive appeared, Jesus could be thought of only as coming to the world from the side of God. Granted an essential separation between God and the world, Jesus stood with God over against the world. It is quite impossible to represent this as part of an otiose and outworn metaphysic which we can leave behind while preserving all the religious values of the New Testament. There are, finally, no religious values in the New Testament except those which in one way or another express or are derived from the value of Jesus as Saviour. The centre of orthodoxy is to be found there, and it was from that centre that Christianity developed itself as a metaphysical theology and a philosophy of religion. A Christianity which stands in no true relation to that centre is a Christianity of provincialisms and false or, at least, one-sided developments. Such is the case with Socinianism and with all attempts to present Jesus as the greatest instance of prophetic, God-inspired personality. A religion may, doubtless, be built up on the basis of such attempts—and a religion with many fine sides to it ; what it will not be able to do is to incorporate the characteristic religious values of the New Testament and to continue the central religious tradition of Christianity. This, as it is manifested in individual experiences and in corporate worship, is the expression of a doctrine of Christ's Person which starts from and embodies the conviction that Jesus comes from God to save.

What this salvation means, and how, in the New Testament, the central fact of salvation finds its own centre in the Cross, are questions which lie outside the scope of this essay. They are dealt with elsewhere in this volume. But this may be said at this point : it was inevitable that Christian thought concerning the salvation which Jesus had brought should concentrate on His Cross. The only way to remove the scandal of the Cross was to accept it utterly. The one effective answer to Jewish or pagan taunts as to the indignity or the folly of the Cross was to proclaim the Cross as the tree of salvation. This was not an afterthought, a mere controversial rejoinder. The assurance of the necessity of the Cross for the Messiah goes back beyond His and its commentators and interpreters to the Messiah. But it may have been in the course of controversy that the strength of the religious appeal of the Cross was realised, that Christian believers understood that here was a paradox of divine action which so far from needing defence was itself a weapon fit and ready to win a whole war. ' The Church of God which he purchased with his own blood ' ; ' the Son of God who loved me and gave himself for me '—those who had such sentences at their disposal might well feel sure that they could not be on the losing side : God's way of salvation might be a strange way, but it certainly was the way of such love as surpassed all that man had ever hoped he might receive from

God. The Cross was the supreme example of God's love ;
but the Cross, thus illuminated, in its turn illuminated the
Crucified. It was as the incarnate Son that He revealed
the Father's love ; and not otherwise.

II

The development of Christological thought in its main
lines and chief representatives has been true to the New
Testament pattern—that is, the dominating influences
have been soteriological. It is this more than anything
else which has interposed an effective barrier to attempts
to exhibit Christianity as one type of religious philosophy
or as no more than a lofty ethical code. Christianity in
its doctrinal content, and, as part of that content,
Christology, have offered much material for the speculative
mind of the philosopher. Such speculations have covered
a wide range : within the field of Christian doctrine, in the
more precise sense, they link up with the doctrine of God
in its Trinitarian character, with the doctrine of the Church
and the Sacraments and with eschatology ; more widely,
they concern the relevance of Christ to the life of nature
and of man. And it would be quite wrong to suggest that
the New Testament provided no grounding for such speculations and developments. Ephesians, Colossians, and the
Johannine writings would afford sufficient material for a
reply. But any speculative Christology which merely
includes the Cross, or which develops itself without any
inner relation to the Cross—any Christology which presents
Christ as the natural, even if supernatural, climax of the
graded character of reality, is not true to New Testament
type. Any Christology which has made little of the thought
of Christ as Saviour has started with a fatal weakness which
no merits it might otherwise possess could either conceal or
overcome. A Christology which expresses itself in terms
that borrow little from the notions of Christ as Redeemer,
Mediator, Bringer of Salvation, lacks both deep enough
roots and sufficient power to grow and to endure. External
circumstances might at times suggest a swaying battle, but
there was no inner power in Arianism to gain the victory.

The School of Antioch had its very definite merits, and its general point of view was one much needed for the sake of balance and proportion ; but it was too lacking in soteriological interest for its Christology to become dominant. For those who wished for the completest breach with the whole Roman system Socinus was more radical than Luther or Calvin. But Socinus' attack upon the doctrine of Christ's atoning work, and, passing on from that, upon His Godhead, was so far out of touch with Christian devotion to Christ as to have no hope of commending itself as the true presentation of the Christian religion. And when the eighteenth-century movement which we know as the Illumination ' dispensed with Christology because first it had virtually dispensed with faith in Christ as Saviour,' [1] it ensured the discovery of its religious inadequacy as truly as its shallowness in other respects laid it bare to the criticisms of Kant. And if Kant has had far less influence in the sphere of Christian dogmatics than in the sphere of philosophy of religion, that cannot but be connected with his subordinating of the Person of Jesus as an element in temporal history to the eternal idea of the Son of God. But if this were a true and Christian distinction we *ought* to sing

> *How sweet the name of Logos sounds*
> *in the believer's ear.*

But the comment somewhere made by Dr. Rendel Harris that we do not say Logos but do say Jesus is never likely to become out of date through a change of practice. There have, as is well known, been many different forms of the doctrine of salvation through Christ, and it is quite truly pointed out that there is no one Catholic soteriology to match one Catholic Christology. But from this fact no more erroneous conclusion could be drawn than that the doctrine of salvation through Christ has been, inherently, of secondary importance. The conception of Christ as Saviour has again and again appeared in close connection with the particular moral and spiritual interests of successive ages in such a way as to show the entire adequacy

---

[1] Mackintosh, *The Person of Jesus Christ*, p. 249.

of Christ for whatever needed to be done to gain for man the blessings of freedom from the grip of evil, the forgiveness of his sins, and fellowship with God. The doctrine of the Saviourhood of Christ has never had its strength in the dialectics of the schools but in the needs of the human heart. That is true of the so-called Patristic doctrine of the ransom of the Devil, of the Anselmic doctrine of satisfaction, of the Protestant doctrine of penal substitution. Christ could meet whatever demands had to be met— the rights, such as they might be, of Satan, the claims of God's honour, the law of retribution. It is not necessary to examine here how far we can be at one with former generations in their different views of what was necessary for the salvation of man. Suppose we have reacted against one or all as far as Abelard and Rashdall did. Yet for Abelard and Rashdall Christ was Saviour in that He did for man what man most needed, what man gave no sign of being able to do for himself. Here, too, soteriology involves a Christology which transcends all notions of a merely human Jesus. Rashdall's own words may be quoted : ' the character of Jesus Christ might well inspire the desire to imitate, and move to sorrow for the sins which He hated, even if He were looked upon merely as a great teacher ; and for those who think of all great teachers as sent by God, it would also excite to the love of God. But undoubtedly the full significance of the doctrine of the atonement can only be appreciated if we can find some real meaning in the idea of a unique or supreme incarnation of the Divine Logos in Jesus Christ.' [1]

The special emphasis on soteriology is sometimes regarded as a prerogative of Protestant theology, whereby the Reformers recaptured the religious note of the New Testament. It is only with reservations that this view can be approved. With regard to the application of the saving work of Christ to the individual, the Reformers certainly broke away from current teaching. And the denial of the sacrificial, and therefore of the directly soteriological, relevance of the Eucharist led to a concentration upon the Cross as the place whereby and the

---

[1] *The idea of atonement in Christian theology*, p. 447.

method by which Christ made Himself known in what
Harnack calls His ' office ' and His ' benefactions.' [1]   But
that does not mean that the belief in Christ as Saviour
was left comparatively unemphasised in the Patristic or the
mediaeval period.   The great theologians, at least, never
fell into this error ; and if it be said that the character of
the religion of an age is not to be estimated in accordance
with the pronouncements of theologians, we may point to
the position of the Mass in mediaeval religion.   For
whatever errors had gathered round the idea of the Mass,
and especially as to its sacrificial character, the witness
of the Mass was to Christ the Saviour.   The liturgy
was a finger pointing to the Crucified, more persistent,
more full of meaning than the pointing hand of John the
Baptist in Grünewald's painting of the Crucifixion.[2]
Forsyth, whose Eucharistic doctrine was neither Patristic
nor mediaeval, saw this clearly.   To think of Christ in the
Eucharist ' as food rather than Redeemer ' seemed to him
more Anglican than Catholic, ' for it is not the view at the
central point of Catholicism—the Mass with its Agnus
Dei ' ; of the Mass he wrote that ' it keeps the rite in the
closest connection with the sacrifice of Christ and the virtue
of His Cross.' [3]

If we let the names of those who have deeply influenced
Christian thought pass before us, the same testimony is
borne, even though these have often expressed themselves
in very different ways, and represent very different attitudes
towards the philosophy of the Christian religion.   But no
one of them has failed to press the relation between Christ's
Person and His work.   Athanasius, thinking of evil in
terms of corruption and death, sees in the coming of Christ
the revelation of that divine Life which, as it works within
human nature, becomes the source of salvation.[4]   At a
much later date in the Letter *ad Adelphium* he states his

---

[1] *History of Dogma*, vii. 198.
[2] For Barth's use of this picture see his book *The Word of God and
the Word of Man*, pp. 65, 75.
[3] *The Church and the Sacraments*, pp. 239, 275.
[4] *De. inc. verb.* 44.   That Athanasius is specially concerned with the
corruption of the body does not invalidate the substance, whatever be
the case with the form, of his argument.

N

argument for the Godhead of Christ in words which sum
up the nature of his prolonged controversy with the Arians :
' What help can creatures derive from a creature that itself
needs salvation ?   But since the Word being Creator has
Himself made the creatures, therefore also at the consummation of the ages He put on the creature, that He as
Creator might once more consecrate it, and be able to
recover it.   But a creature could never be saved by a
creature, any more than the creatures were created by a
creature, if the Word was not creator.'   Anselm's *Cur Deus
Homo ?*, written with different presuppositions from those
which we note in the *De Incarnatione* of Athanasius, is, no
less than the earlier treatise, a classic statement of the
inner correspondence between the doctrine of salvation,
objectively treated, and the doctrine of the Redeemer's
Person.   And though the orthodox Christology in its
affirmation of Christ's Godhead is assumed from the
beginning, the logical dependence of the Christology upon
the soteriology is clear enough when we pay attention to
the presuppositions which form the background of Anselm's
thought—namely, that for the human race to have utterly
perished in sin would have meant the frustration of God's
purpose for man [1] ; that the redemption of man could not
have been effected except by God Himself [2] ; and that
man who by sin has dishonoured God must himself make
satisfaction to God.[3]   The particular relevance of the death
of Christ in Anselm's doctrine of redemption is bound up
with Anselm's argument that, whereas Christ as man owed
to God the perfect obedience of His life, He did not, since
He was sinless, owe Him His death : hence the reward
due to Christ for this voluntary and meritorious surrender
of life could be assigned to men.[4]   There is no doctrine of
salvation which has been more severely and, up to a point,
justly criticised than this of Anselm's ; yet in none is the
New Testament perspective, for which the work of man's
redemption is in the fullest sense divine work, more faithfully maintained.   In Aquinas the logical rigour of Anselm's
scheme is modified in respect of the earlier theologian's

[1] Book I, c. 4.   [2] C. 5.   [3] Cc. 15–24.
[4] Book II, cc. 10–11, 19.

insistence on the necessity for the particular method of redemption which has been used.   But the Angelic Doctor's teaching that it is *convenientius* to hold that if man had not sinned God would not have been incarnate [1] is a powerful dissuasive against the development of Christologies uncontrolled by the religious standpoint of the New Testament, always a danger where speculative or mythical interests are strong.[2] The Reformation theologians, as a whole, showed no desire to break with the Catholic Christology.   But its value for them was not so much that it gave the right ideas about Christ as that it safeguarded the essential evangelical reliance on Christ as Saviour.   The well-known sentence of Melanchthon, ' this is the knowledge of Christ, namely the knowledge of His benefits, not the contemplation of His natures and the modes of His incarnation,' shows where the stress was first laid.   The tension between law and Gospel, sin and grace, wrath and mercy, of which Luther was so deeply conscious, was one resolved only through the forgiveness of sins which Christ brought.   There was manifested the Godhead of Christ.   In their formal doctrines, whether of Christ's Person or of His work, there is nothing in the Reformers' teaching which deserves to be called original, except Luther's notion of the ubiquity of Christ's human nature, which need not now detain us.   But the *fiducia miseri-cordiae* to which Loofs [3] refers as being in Luther's view the whole subjective side of Christianity involved the most assured consequences as to the Godhead of Christ, in whom that mercy had been revealed.   Luther could, indeed, speak as though there were no theology which was not Christology, which would have meant, logically, the whole of theological knowledge being contained in and growing out of the knowledge of Christ as Redeemer.

Protestant theology, both Lutheran and Reformed, passed into a new scholasticism, and the first decisive theological break with that scholasticism came with Schleiermacher.   But the more this is emphasised the more

---

[1] *Summa theologica*, III. qu. 1, art 3.

[2] *Cf.* Hagenbach, *History of Doctrines*, i. 272–274.

[3] *Leitfaden*, p. 723.

noteworthy becomes Schleiermacher's very definite and
clear description of the essential character of Christianity,
as ' distinct from all other religions by regarding all its
religious impulses as dependent upon the redemption
effected by Jesus of Nazareth, and also in that this
redemption is considered as perfected and complete. . . .
Other religions express the need of redemption ; Christianity
presents its actualization ; in others the redemption is
derivative and dependent on doctrines or forms ; in
Christianity redemption is the central point and rests on
the person of its Founder.' [1] This judgment becomes more
precise when Schleiermacher expounds his doctrine of Christ.
The *person* and the *activity* of Christ are inseparable ; ' each
finds in the other its full expression. It is in respect of
His work that we treat Him as Redeemer.' He is the sole
author of that ' *conscious blessed relation to God*,' which all
other men may possess through Him ; and ' this is to
ascribe an exclusive and absolute dignity to his person.' [2]
With the manner in which the Creeds and dogmatic
formulae presented the doctrine of Christ's Person and
Protestant orthodoxy conceived of His work, Schleiermacher
was greatly dissatisfied ; and it may reasonably be argued
that he separated himself not only from the form but also
from the substance of that teaching. His own doctrine of
Christ was centred in the conviction of ' the absolute power
of the God-consciousness in him, as an original possession ' [3] ;
while, as to Christ's work, His whole act in redemption
' consists in the implanting of the governing God-consciousness, in the propagation of the creative divine activity, as
a new principle of life in the whole of human nature.' [4]
Schleiermacher admitted no vicarious satisfaction in Christ's
sufferings ; yet these had redemptive value ; for ' in His
suffering unto death there is manifested to us an absolutely
self-denying love, and thus is presented in perfect clearness
the manner in which God was in Christ to reconcile the
world to Himself.' [5]

---

[1] From the ' Condensed presentation ' of Schleiermacher's work *The
Christian Faith*, by Dr. Cross in his book *The Theology of Schleiermacher*,
pp. 135–136.

[2] Pp. 200–201. [3] P. 208. [4] P. 215. [5] P. 222.

Schleiermacher's influence was very great, and tended towards a sharper contrast between Protestantism and Catholic orthodoxy. But he leaves us in no doubt that for him the special religious values of Christianity were to be found in Christ's Person and work. He carries on the great tradition, while reinterpreting and restating it. Nor does Ritschl, critical though he often is of Schleiermacher, take a different road at this point. On the contrary, he prepares for his own discursion of the doctrine of Christ's Person by appreciative references to the expositions of that doctrine made by Bernard and by Luther. No one has shown more admirably than Bernard, ' within the limits of the dogma of the two natures,' how Christ in carrying out His redemption displayed His Godhead. His activities, ' having as their aim redemption and the revelation of love, are more than human activities ; at bottom, they are Divine.' Luther is in agreement with this when in his larger Catechism he teaches that ' it is as my Redeemer that Christ is my Lord.' Ritschl's comment upon those expositions is that ' the theological solution of the problem of Christ's Divinity must therefore be based upon an analysis of what He has done for the salvation of mankind in the form of His community.' [1] When Ritschl comes to say what this is he shows himself to be out of sympathy with the older dogmatic, even more than had been the case with Schleiermacher. But, with stress laid, not on the Redeemer who has made perfect satisfaction or accepted the punishment due to others for their sins, but on the Redeemer who has founded the divine Kingdom and mediated the forgiveness of sins, Ritschl upholds the conception of Christ's Divinity as one which ' can be rightly appraised by theology only when Christ is conceived as the living Head of the community of God's Kingdom. For we must bring Christ into relation to His people, before we are in a position to recognise that in His own order He is unique.' [2] The whole thought works itself out under the influence of very different categories from those which we recognise in the Chalcedonian formula or in the Eastern, Latin, or Reformation soteriology, but the close

[1] *Justification and Reconciliation*, pp. 416–417.   [2] Pp. 465.

correspondence between the doctrine of the work and that of the Person is maintained.

A theologian more different from Ritschl than was R. C. Moberly it would be difficult to imagine. With all his criticisms of Lutheran orthodoxy Ritschl was, unmistakably, a great Lutheran theologian. Moberly was as unmistakably Anglican. And from within Anglicanism, during the present century, there has appeared no book more influential than *Atonement and Personality*. It is a great book, not because of its particular theory, that of Christ's vicarious penitence, but as giving an insight into a *summa theologica*, not fully worked out, but with its foundations well and truly laid in one coherent doctrine of Christ's Person and work. In Moberly's pages we pass behind Luther and Anselm to Athanasius and Irenaeus. It is not so much that the soteriology involves a Christology as that the Christology *is* soteriology. What Christ does as Redeemer He can do only in virtue of what Moberly calls His inclusive humanity, and as to that he says ' if Christ's Humanity were not the Humanity of Deity, it could not stand in the wide, inclusive, consummating relations in which it stands in fact, to the humanity of all other men.' [1] Of the perfect penitence of the sinless Christ wherein Moberly saw ' the true atoning sacrifice for sin ' he writes ' only He, who knew in Himself the measure of the holiness of God could realize also, in the human nature which He had made His own, the full depth of the alienation of sin from God, the real character of the penal averting of God's face.' [2] Moberly's whole scheme is controlled by the conviction that what Christ does *for* man, *in* man, *as* man, He does and can do only because He is personally God. That is true also of Christ's presence in His Spirit.

Of the recurrence of Greek Patristic soteriology, so apparent in the work of Moberly, there was no trace in Forsyth. Notions of humanity in the abstract and of its incorporation in Christ were quite alien to him. His soteriology is, broadly speaking, that of the Reformers, purged of much that involved or suggested both theological

[1] P. 90.   [2] P. 130.

and ethical untruth.   Christology which had been worked out through the categories of a metaphysic of substance was deeply suspect with him as in peril of becoming more theosophic than evangelical.   He was critical of the Chalcedonian Definition.   All this suggests Ritschl.   But if Forsyth stood with Ritschl in much of his criticism of the forms of Catholic orthodoxy, he left him when the issue was a theology not critical but positive.   He needed more of a background and foundation than Ritschl would allow in respect of the typical Gospel blessing of the forgiveness of sins ;   the Ritschlian soteriology and Christology were not adequate to what the Church, beginning with the Apostles, had found in Christ, and what Christ had revealed concerning Himself.   Especially did Forsyth go deeply into the meaning of the absoluteness of Christ, that Christ was not *a* revelation but *the* revelation.   If Christianity was the absolute religion, wherein did that absoluteness consist ? Forsyth replied ' in an experience of Christ as the absolute conscience, *i.e.* as the judge of all, and as the Redeemer, *i.e.* the saving health of all—in a word, as the God of all. . . . He does for us the ultimate thing of the soul, its one thing needful.   He gives it its own eternal place and com-munion with an absolutely holy God. . . . To be in living, loving, holy communion with the living, loving, holy God for ever is the soul's perfect consummation and final bliss. And that is Christ's gift.' [1]   Such was the character of the religion, rather, of the life which Christ had made accessible for men ;   it has come by ' one compressed channel,' which is ' the Cross and its redemption.'   With the way in which Forsyth expressed the doctrine of the Cross we cannot deal. But it is clear that only the most exalted Christology could be equal to the demands involved in Forsyth's general notion of salvation through Christ.   The whole of that truly great book on which I am now drawing, and especially its closing chapters, is devoted to that theme.   Forsyth is one of the few great theologians who have refused to think about Christ in terms of the Two Natures' formula and yet have preserved the full value of the orthodox Christology. And it was so in his case because he was consistently loyal

[1] *The Person and Place of Jesus Christ*, p. 251.

to the standard which he set up when he wrote that ' the principle from which we must set out to understand the person of Christ is the soteriological principle.' [1] His Christology, worked out with great subtlety and power by means of the two complementary conceptions of the Kenosis or self-emptying and the Plerosis or self-fulfilment of Christ, was an exposition of the central conviction that ' the coming of Christ in the long course of history is the coming of God the Redeemer.' [2]

There is still one more name which must be called to bear its witness to this classic tradition of the unity of Christology and soteriology. Germany has a way of producing theologians who evoke passionate enthusiasm and equally passionate dissent ; and not till the conflicting passions have subsided is a true judgment of value possible. These are early days for any estimate of the theology of Karl Barth likely to stand the test of time, especially as Barth may still have much to say. But this is quite clear : Barth's doctrine of Christ is first of all a doctrine of Christ the Redeemer. What Christ has done has been to bring man to God by bringing God to man (the way *up* from man to God is for Barth altogether dependent on the way *down* from God to man), effecting reconciliation and bringing into existence the new man and the new world. Barth's ' dialectical ' method and his aversion from any appeal to human experience make it very difficult to present his thought in his own words in such a way as to make his meaning clear. But if we bear in mind the sharpness of the contrast which he draws between the transcendent God (*deus absconditus*) and weak, creaturely, sinful man, and, along with that, his conception of the life of Jesus as ' the place of atonement determined from eternity in the counsel of God, and now, in time, in the sight of men, brought within history,' we realise that in Barth's Christology Jesus must be one who comes from God to humanity, not the one who best represents humanity's aspiring efforts Godwards. More precisely, it is in His Cross that the place of atonement is reached. Barth quotes a saying, ' Blood is the basal colour in the portrait of the Redeemer,' and his

[1] *The Person and Place of Jesus Christ*, p. 332.　　[2] P. 343.

own judgment is that ' it is in His blood that Jesus shows Himself as the Christ, shows Himself as the first and last word of the trustworthiness of God to the human race, as the revelation of the impossible possibility of our salvation, as the light from the uncreated light, as the proclaimer of the Kingdom of God.' [1] However individualistic and often obscure Barth may be, he has, unquestionably, his place within that tradition which has been the constant inspiration of great Christian theology.

III

For the future of Christianity the issue lies between two fundamentally different conceptions of the nature of Christian religion. On the one hand, it may be regarded as the highest stage yet reached in religious evolution. When this road is taken, the tendency will be to minimise the contrast between the divine and the human, to see in Christ the highest revelation of the divine in man, and to substitute for the idea of redemption that of improvement. This would mean a radical departure from the substance of the historic Christian doctrine of God (it is hard to see how the Trinitarian conception could survive) and of the Person and work of Christ. Reality would tend to be viewed more and more as evolutionary process inclusive of God as well as of man. The distinction between Christianity and other religions would become wholly one of degree, inasmuch as all faiths and cults would be regarded as so many varying manifestations of the religious spirit in man ; no place would be left for the notion of a final or absolute religion. It is difficult to see how any place would be left for theology as in any respect an independent science. On the other hand, there is the road which prolongs the traditional account which Christianity has given of itself. Those who take it will see the relation between the divine and the human first of all in terms of differences, to be overcome only by the free and gracious activity of God. This activity, redemptive and recreative,

---

[1] In Barth's *Der Römerbrief*, on Rom. iii. 25–26.

will be seen at work, not in isolation, not without a preparation prophetic of its own coming, but, in its 'original
impulse, as a movement from God towards the world,
both new and unrepeatable and constitutive of a new
beginning in the life of the world.   Those who choose this
road will welcome all the light which, as it spreads outwards
from other sciences, helps to illuminate the task of theology ;
but the sanctions of theology they will find in its own
subject-matter, which is not revealed in, and cannot be
extracted from, the findings of other sciences.

This issue will not become plain in the quite near future.
Fresh attempts at mediation may appear.   But, finally,
real decisions have to be made.   It is not as though the
issue were one to which Christian worship, piety, and ethic
could be indifferent.   A Christianity of mysticism, charity,
and sacramental or non-sacramental cultus, existing without a doctrine of Christ's Person or work, is an absurdity
to imagine.   It has groundings neither in history nor in
reason.   If it came into existence it would be no more
than Unitarianism or, if the doctrine of God had been
merged in the doctrine of man, a revived Positivism.
Liberal Christianity, in its finest examples, has certainly
meant more than that, and a Christianity developed under
the thoroughgoing control of evolutionary conceptions
would, wherever its representatives wished to preserve
contact with the New Testament and the tradition of the
Church, still apply to Jesus the titles Son of God and
Saviour.   But to preserve a more than verbal contact
would be quite another matter.   Christianity as religion, no
less than as theology, has been expressed in dependence
upon the absolute value of the Person of Jesus Christ.   The
finality of Christianity *is* the finality of His Person.   But
faith in Him as final is not feasible if we think of Him in
terms of the upward movement of man, not of the down-
ward movement of God.   If it be urged that these two
movements are one, or, at least, correlative, we shall reply
that, unless theism is to be merged in pantheism, or incarnation regarded as no more than an extension of divine
immanence, it makes all the difference both in Christology
itself and in its outcomes whether the one movement or

the other is chosen as the primary truth and primary principle of interpretation.

The attacks made upon the Patristic Christology are often ill-judged. That Christology is not a speculative addition to the New Testament, nor does it commit the Church to a metaphysic supposed to be long since anti-quated. In point of fact, the Two Natures' formula, against which so much criticism has been directed, is no more than the expression of the belief that Christ is both God and man. It is a question of the substance of faith, not of its form. But it might not unfairly be said that the Nicene test-word ὁμοούσιος and the Two Natures' formula do not adequately clarify the issue for to-day. For where there is a tendency to think of God and man as ὁμοούσιοι, there it will not be found difficult to acknowledge Christ as of one substance with the Father and as both divine and human. To such conclusions the Logos-doctrine, taken by itself, would prove no hindrance, for the idea of the Logos can be used as a link between God and man through its suggestion of a unity existing by virtue of the common principle of rationality. The Apologists of the second century who made so much of the Logos-doctrine serve as a warning; for, while they did valuable work, they were in danger of losing the genuinely religious note of Christianity in a philosophy of religion. The fact that the use of the idea of the Logos to interpret Christ coincides with certain religious and metaphysical tendencies of the present age, and has a special value as a unifying method of thought, must not conceal from us the danger resident in its employment as the dominant Christological notion. New Testament Christology is not a gradually ascending process reaching its highest peak in the identification of Christ with the Logos. The grandeur of the way in which St. John claims the contemporary Logos-doctrine for Christianity (it is another question how far he was in the debt of that doctrine) is deeply impressive. But if we ask what Christ means to God, there is greater wealth of meaning in the description of Him as the Son, while if it is of His relation to man that we inquire, we must turn to the word Saviour. Only in this way can we keep the

New Testament proportion. That proportion needs to be remembered if we use such a phrase as ' the cosmic Christ.' The prologue to St. John's Gospel, St. Paul's Epistle to the Colossians, and the Epistle to the Hebrews present Christ as the Creator ; the world depends on Him for its being and life. But more is made in the New Testament of that other function of His, whereby He is the restorer of the world, or the creator, in Barth's words, of ' the new world.' For any adequate estimate of the value of Christ's Person this stress is as necessary to-day as it was in the first century. When we speak of what Christ has meant and means to believers, when we call in as witnesses the great hymns about Christ, it is the Christ who makes the second creation by redeeming the first who is presented to us. A fuller realisation of this constantly present redemption-motif in the Christology of the New Testament, which swells up at times, as in the Apocalypse and at the end of the eighth chapter of the Epistle to the Romans, into a paean of exulting joy, praise, and adoration, would preserve us from the danger of sub-Christian thinking at point after point within the complex of Christian theology. What the Swedish theologian, Dr. Aulen, has called the attempt to fit Christianity ' into the framework of a monistic-evolutionary theory of life ' [1] would be held in check, since faith in the reality of divine forgiveness, which is the subjective element in the doctrine of redemption through Christ, has no proper relation to that theory as involved in it or consequent upon it. The new vision of God for which we hear the demand in Church circles in England to-day would be advanced by a more spiritual understanding of God's transcendence and immanence. The value of these terms would be made more plain by their close association with God's holiness and God's love as these are revealed not solely but pre-eminently in Christ and His Cross. In our attempts at an exposition of the doctrine of the Trinity we should not be content to put into the foreground a contrast between an ' essential ' and an ' economic ' Trinity, but should think more of the divine persons in relation to the divine work of redemption, thus following

[1] *Theology*, vol. xvii. No. 100 (Oct. 1928), p. 219.

out the suggestions of such New Testament passages as
2 Cor. xiii. 14; Gal. iv. 4–7; 1 Pet. i. 2; 1 John iv. 13–14.
Much of the vagueness and uncertainty which attach to the
doctrine of the Holy Spirit would disappear, as the Spirit
was discerned, not as a force or influence active in the
world's life hardly distinguishable from a semi-physical
élan vital, not as the memory or perpetuation of ' Jesus
according to the flesh,' but as sent forth by the crucified
and risen Saviour to make the fruits of Calvary accessible
to men, so that He is the source and sustainer of the
Church's evangelising and teaching work. The idea of
the Church as the extension of the Incarnation would be
controlled, as it needs to be, by the recollection of the Cross
as the one place where the line uniting Christ and the Church
was tied into a true nuptial knot (Eph. ii. 25). The
theology of the Sacraments would be deepened, as these
were regarded less in their relation to the old creation and
more in their relation to the new, more closely linked with
the redemptive value of Christ's death and with man's
forgiveness and new standing in the sight of God, which is
what St. Paul means by justification. There is a peril, at
times, of overpressing the connection between ' natural '
Sacramentalism and the Sacraments of the Gospel. There
is a correspondence in so far as in each case there is a
mediation of spiritual reality by outward things ; but
there is also the same sort of distinction which exists
between God's general providence and the revelation of
His saving love in Christ. Finally, the true spring of
Christian devotion is to be found in dependence upon
Christ, as the Redeemer of each and all, and in membership
of His redeemed body the Church. It is from this source
that the freshest, clearest, and most abundant streams of
Christian piety have flowed. True Christian mysticism is
Christ-mysticism. St. Paul spoke not for himself alone,
but for a great company of witnesses, of every tribe and
tongue and people and nation, when, in words of eternal
import wrung from him by the exigencies of a great but
far-off controversy, he cried: ' I have been crucified with
Christ ; yet I live ; and yet no longer I, but Christ liveth
in me : and that life which I now live in the flesh I live

in faith, the faith which is in the Son of God, who loved me, and gave Himself up for me.'

Now, as of old time, in the Ichthys-theology lies the open mystery of the power of the Church's life, and the substance of the good news which the Church brings to the world.

THE CROSS OF CHRIST
BY PAUL ALTHAUS

THE CROSS OF CHRIST

The Problem.—The task of the theology of the Cross is to present to the understanding the ' Foolishness of the Cross ' as the ' Wisdom of God '—that is to say, it seeks to understand the Cross. Theological speculation is then in every respect *a posteriori*. That does not merely mean, what is of course admitted, that the theology of the Cross has as its foundation and starting-point the reality of the Cross, which as an event could not have been postulated ; but rather that the reality of the Cross provides the standard by which alone it can be apprehended. It is true that theological formulas, for instance those of the New Testament, were mostly prior to and independent of the actuality of the Cross, but through its actuality they were all changed, determined, purified and renewed. Before the Cross all equally must repent, not men alone but also their ideas. For the Cross shines out in its own light alone as the Wisdom of God.

I

THE THEOLOGY OF THE CROSS IN THE NEW TESTAMENT AND LUTHER

(a) *Its Origin.*—The theology of the Cross was born on Easter Day. It was only because of Easter and in the light of Easter that the awful end of Jesus became the Cross. The facts of His death and of the new life to which Jesus Christ bears witness together state the problem of the Cross and point towards its solution. He who died as a condemned criminal on Golgotha uttering the cry of the forsaken of God proved Himself the Living One, the Forgiving, the Elect; the Living One was none other than the Crucified—it is this identity which both necessitates and determines a theology of the Cross. Into the light of this identity (*i.e.* of the executed criminal as Himself the Living One, the Master) are to be brought the hints which the historical Jesus gave, before He died, as to the significance of His death, and in this light the references in the Old Testament to the Suffering Servant and His Sacrifice are illumined. The theology of the Cross was thus moulded under the direction of the Holy Spirit.

(b) *The Multiplicity of the Symbols.*—The meaning of the Cross is expressed by many and varied concepts and symbols drawn from the Old Testament and Hellenistic ideas, religious worship and law. Their profusion and variety are of theological importance : the successive change of concepts through which the significance of the Cross has been expressed demonstrates the insufficiency of any one concept to exhaust its mystery, and shows at the same time the *symbolic* nature of *every* theory. No theory can fathom the thoughts of God: each remains in the realm of the figurative and the analogical, and is therefore a paralogism. In its unsystematized manifoldness the New Testament stands far above many self-consistent dogmatic theories of the Cross which live in *one* idea, *one* symbol, and consequently necessarily forget its *symbolic* character. Because, however, the New Testament *uses* all these ideas to interpret the secret of the Cross, there falls on each of the spheres of life from which the ideas and similes are taken a gleam of their relation with their ultimate meaning. For example, when the work of Christ is presented in the language of sacrifice, sacrificial worship attains through it to the dignity of prophecy, of an anticipatory shadow of the Substance (Heb. x. i), of a reality, which, in the external and the inadequate, yet bears witness to the real problem of life in the eyes of God. Christ the Crucified is the end and Judge of all sacrificial worship, but at the same time its fulfilment. Light and dignity are shed not only on prototypes in the Old Testament, but equally on its analogies in the history of religion—on the Mystery Religions, for example, the concepts of which were used by Paul to express the fruits of the Cross (Rom. vi.). In the light of the Cross they lose, but at the same time receive, their value.

(c) *The Characteristic Features.*—With all its variety of conceptual forms the New Testament displays certain general characteristics which are present in them all. It is important for our dogmatic study that they should be borne in mind. Three are of primary importance : (1) God is clearly set forth as the subject of the work of reconciliation—the differentiation from heathenism is sharp and clear—God is not reconciled but He consummates the reconciliation ; and yet the way of the Cross is necessary for Him also. God gives His Son, but the Son is active towards God, for He consummates uniquely the worship of God. Christ reveals the Father in that He is man's representative before God. (2) The Cross is both the *reconciliation* and the *renewal* of mankind. Christ died *for all*, but believers have also died *with Him* and have experienced the power of His death. The Christ who died *for* them and lives, lives *in* them also as the living Spirit. (3) The fact of the Cross is both *perfectum* and *praesens* : it is a past and yet a present event. God *has* reconciled the world unto Himself, but the reconciliation has only healing virtue for man when he obeys the call, ' Be ye reconciled to God ' (2 Cor. v. 20). The reconciliation of the world is at once consummated and yet not consummated. The final judgment given on Golgotha only has reality for each man when the word from the Cross, the proclamation of that which was predetermined by God, is heard by each calling him to a personal decision. The Cross is no mechanical-magical transformation of the world and of men's situation, produced by the magic forces of nature, nor is it an historical fact which determines man without having called him to make a decision for himself— but the Cross is history in the sense of *perfectum praesens*, the Word, the Revelation.

Luther's Importance for the Theology of the Cross.— Among the teachers of the Church no one has preserved more carefully than Luther the depth and variety of the New Testament doctrine of the Cross. His significance is usually found almost exclusively in his re-emphasis of Paul's doctrine of justification : it is said, for the rest, that he accepted without alteration the dogmas of the

Church as developed by the Fathers and in the Middle Ages—that is, in so far as he did not feel obliged to reject them as unchristian. Still, as a reformer in the province of Christology, in the doctrine of Christ's Work and Person, Luther is important. In the doctrine of Christ's *Person* he certainly accepted the heritage of the primitive Church, but he restated it because for him the divinity of Christ gained a new and powerful reality from the doctrine of justification, ' the Father's heart and will in Christ.' In the doctrine of Christ's *Work* Luther certainly remained within the tradition laid down by Anselm. He preserved the greatness of Anselm's theory but, in redirecting it from the narrowness of the Satisfaction theory to the rich profusion of the Bible, he far surpassed it. It is significant that he felt the word ' satisfaction ' (*Genugtuung*) to be too weak and insignificant : ' Even if it is desirable to retain the word satisfaction and to mean by it that Christ has done enough for our sins, it is still too weak and too small to express the grace of Christ and it does not sufficiently appreciate the sufferings of Christ, to which greater honour must be rendered ; for He not only made satisfaction for our sins but also freed us from Death, the Devil and the power of Hell, and thus confirmed to us an eternal Kingdom of Grace and Forgiveness for all remaining sins.'

There are three significant features in Luther's interpretation of the Cross. (1) In Luther, as distinct from Anselm, the work of Christ is not directed only to the aversion of the impending wrath of God, but Christ intervenes in an existing state of wrath, experiences the punishment of God, and wrestles in His suffering with the despots who, because of God's wrath, have obtained power over mankind. It was because Luther understood the Cross of Christ to be a decisive *fight* (see Col. ii. 15) that from the outset he broke down the narrowness of the Satisfaction theory and its conception of equivalence. (2) Luther, like the New Testament, brings the Cross into the closest relation with the Resurrection. He has given us no definite hymn on the Passion. His hymn on the Cross is his most powerful Easter anthem : ' Christ lay in the bonds of death.' He passes far beyond the mediaeval conception of the Suffering Christ : his Christ is the Mighty One, the Victor. Suffering is itself the victory over the enemy and the converse : a triumph such as this is only possible in suffering. It is characteristic of Luther that he can describe Christ's ' Descent into Hell ' as both the profoundest depth of Christ's suffering and as its highest triumph : for it is all the same. (3) Luther further revived the New Testament theology of the Cross in that he regarded Christ's substitution *for* us and Christ's power *in* us as an indivisible unity. Christ not only suffers for us but He draws us into His suffering.[1]

Luther and Orthodoxy.—Like many other attempts in the modern history of the Atonement, our reflections will endeavour to find some connection with Luther.[2] We learn too, of course, from the early Protestant orthodoxy which, subsequent to Luther, sought to apprehend the meaning of the Cross in a stern Satisfaction theory. But the acceptance of Luther's interpretation of the New Testament will mean standing aloof from orthodoxy while maintaining its valuable heritage. Our own effort to interpret the meaning of the Cross cannot be accomplished without a critical analysis, on certain important points, of orthodox views.

II

THE PROBLEM OF FORGIVENESS

The Starting-Point : the Problem of Forgiveness.—Our understanding of the Cross of Christ begins, like that of the New Testament, with the declaration of the testified fact that God in Christ forgives us.

Ever since the first Easter and Pentecost, messengers have gone throughout the world knowing themselves to be commissioned to preach, in the name of Jesus Christ, God's forgiveness. The question then arises here : What is meant by saying that God forgives in Christ, for Christ's sake ? What are the presuppositions implied in saying that

---

[1] Compare more particularly the *Sermon on the Contemplation of the Holy Sufferings of Christ,* 1519.

[2] See J. C. K. v. Hofman ; H. Mandel.

forgiveness may be preached in the name of Jesus ? This question includes the more general problem of all forgiveness : How can forgiveness as from God be valid ? Who dares to forgive ?

This question directs attention to a real problem. For He who forgives is the Holy God. God is Holy : that is to say, He hates, condemns and punishes sin, and cannot admit the sinner into fellowship with Him. God forgives : that is to say, He admits the rebel with all his guilt into fellowship with Him ; He promises life to one who chooses and deserves death. How are both these two possible ? To God, as the Gospel proclaims Him, belongs unapproachable holiness which must reject the sinner, but according to the same Gospel He is proclaimed as Boundless Mercy which sits at table with the sinner. God's wrath against wickedness and the wicked is a necessity of His Holy Nature. . . . If God can forgive, what then becomes of His holiness and His wrath ? So long as God is God He cannot deny in Himself His holiness and His wrath. Forgiveness cannot mean that God's holiness and His wrath have been negated. If then forgiveness is possible it must be a sanctified forgiveness, a forgiveness in which the Divine holiness and wrath are hallowed. Who therefore may forgive in holiness, *i.e.* forgive in the name of God ?

The modern world, in many ways, no longer understands the seriousness of this question. It imagines it can play off the ' simplicity ' of the Father's forgiveness in the parable of the Prodigal Son against the Pauline theology of the Cross . . . as though Luke xv. proclaimed a universal truth and was not rather a commentary on Jesus' own unprecedented and all authoritative action. The question then remains : Who is it who dares to eat with sinners and to proclaim in parables the unconditional forgiveness of God through Himself ? Adolf v. Harnack in his keen criticism pointed out the ' horrible thought that God surpasses man in having the appalling prerogative that He cannot forgive sin because He loves, but He must always demand payment.' The old Lutheran dogmatic theologian, Hollaz, has in advance adequately dealt with this criticism. The forgiveness of God and of men are

two distinct things. We ought to forgive one another
without further ado, for we are all sinners together. But
God is Lord and Judge. We are conscious of the problem
of forgiveness as soon as we occupy some public office, and
are not merely in private relations to one another. The
father, because he has a public duty to his child, cannot
forgive without further ado as we who are on an equality
ought to forgive mutual offences. He ought to act towards
his child in the place of God—that is, he realises the force
of the question : Who is he who can forgive, forgive in
holiness ? The ' simplicity ' of forgiveness may not then
be pleaded as against the attempt to understand the
necessity of Christ's Cross in its relation to the Divine
forgiveness. But conversely, the problem involved in all
forgiving, one which every earnest man faintly perceives,
becomes clear and momentous, and helps us, in the presence
of the Cross, to interpret its mystery. The Cross both sets
and solves the problem of all forgiveness in the name of God.

The problem of forgiveness is not to be resolved into
the question : How can the sinner who dreads God and
does not believe in His grace find the fact of forgiveness
to be credible ? Any one who seeks to devise a theology
of the cross, conscious of this question only, must see
everything from the one standpoint. The Cross becomes
an overpowering proclamation of the love of God which,
face to face with sin, and suffering intensely under it, asserts
itself to be boundless love and thus awakens in us an un-
shakeable trust. This conception is certainly not false.
But, if it seeks to be the whole, it detracts from the deeper
significance of the question of forgiveness and consequently
the deeper significance of the Cross. The problem of
forgiveness is not merely the *subjective* one : How may
forgiveness be rendered credible and salutary for men ?
But over and beyond this is its *objective* significance : How
does forgiveness *come to be* at all ? The subjectivity with
which Ritschl and his school have treated the problem of
forgiveness has appeared to many as the true evangelical
significance of Christ's Cross, because they have only
recognised the possibility of two alternatives : either the
Cross of Jesus so reacts on God that it first wins for us His

readiness to forgive . . . which is an unscriptural and heathenish conception . . . or the death of Jesus works only on men, altering their relationship, leading them to forgiveness and faith, and so making forgiveness a possibility. But this alternative is mistaken. *God* is active in the history of Jesus, He wills to forgive. He is not the offended heathen deity who must first be appeased. But this is not to say that the necessity of the Cross is merely anthropological and psychological. It is a necessity due to the relationship between God and mankind. Sin has not only determined the attitude of men but also the relation between God and men. Man's attitude is only a part of the relationship; the whole relationship is determined by the wrath of God. That men are unable to repent or to believe is not merely due to their weakness and guilt, but equally to the action of the wrath of God. It is His punishment for sin. We are thus led from attitude to relation. The problem of forgiveness does not lie in the former alone, but also in the latter.

This brings us back to our decisive question : On what grounds may Jesus Christ ratify the forgiveness of God ? How far is His forgiveness sanctified forgiveness ?

The Fundamental Idea involved in the Solution of the Problem.—The answer can follow along the lines laid down by the fundamental ideas of the early Protestant doctrine of Christ's Cross. The following expresses it summarily : *Jesus Christ may complete the forgiveness of God because it is He who went to the Cross and was crucified.* Here is implied the twofold distinction recognised by the orthodoxy under the terms *obedientia activa* and *passiva.* Jesus Christ can forgive sin because by obedience he has sanctified the *will* of God, against which mankind is revolting. Jesus Christ can forgive sin because bearing the *wrath* of God, which rests on mankind on account of their rebellion, He sanctified it in His obedience. God forgives only through the Righteous One, and God forgives only through Him who suffers unto the death of the sinner. This is then the significance of Christ's Cross as it is seen in the light of the reality of this same Cross.

Before we develop this idea further it might be emphasised

that our answer could be expressed simply as : The power of Jesus to forgive sin lies in the fact that He is the ' Son.' For to be the Son among sinners means to be among them as the Righteous One, and at the same time as the Suffering Son, and as suffering, not only because of them, but also with them. And the converse : He who is righteous in a world of sin and sanctifies the Will of God and the wrath of God without flaw or breach can only be the Son. The Cross establishes forgiveness only as the Cross of the ' Son.' The Son as one who voluntarily endured the Cross bears witness to Himself as the ' Son.'

III

OBEDIENTIA ACTIVA

Obedientia Activa in Early Protestant Dogmatics.—In the act of forgiveness, God's holiness first stands fully revealed by the fact that He only can forgive in the name of God who has offered perfect obedience to Him.

We shall develop this conception as we analyse its argument side by side with that of the early Protestant dogmatics. The early doctrine taught that Jesus Christ perfectly accomplished the Law, which had no obligation for Him, and that this fulfilment represents a merit which is transferred to us, reckoned to our account as though accomplished by us. Through Christ's work God's claim against us is cancelled. It is against this conception that the rationalistic criticism of the Socinian type has been directed ; their principal ideas were taken over by Ritschl and the theology of his school. There can be no doubt that this criticism ignores the deepest significance of the old ideas, the validity of which we shall try to establish. With regard to the form in which the doctrine is expressed, in large measure the objection is justified. It is open to attack not only from the standpoint of the natural moral consciousness, which would hardly be a sufficient court of appeal, but also from that of the New Testament.

Criticism.—As distinct from the older, the new dogmatics are unanimous in emphasising that Jesus is said to have fulfilled the Law not primarily for our sakes but for His own—that is, for the sake of His own personal relationship with God. The old doctrine, starting as it does from the conception of pre-existence, rightly connects the submission of Jesus to the Law with the Kenosis of the Son of God which was prompted by love for us. That the Son of God, through human decisions and submission, must learn obedience on earth and fulfil the eternal will of the Father who is His Life and His Blessedness, is indeed a part of that Kenosis which was for our sakes. If, however, we contemplate the matter from within the Kenosis, then we must admit that He who became man was not free from the law of God, but as man must in truth submit to it for God's sake and not primarily for man's sake. Jesus obeys the Father and offers His will to Him because He is the Son and loves the Father. Consequently it is incorrect to teach, as the old dogmatics did, that Christ's obedience was vicarious in the sense that it might be reckoned to us. Here the old Lutheran theology trangresses against the fundamental idea of the nature of obedience as Luther expressed it. Obedience is not a concrete act where another can deputise, but it exists only in the expression of the personal free whole-hearted action of the debtor. God does not desire anybody's obedience, He desires mine. For this reason my disobedience cannot be made good by anything else in the world, neither would my own future obedience, which already belongs to God, ever be able to atone for past failure; for a failure which is past cannot be recalled, and the awful purity of God appears in the irrevocable nature of time. Nor can it be retrieved by the obedience of another, for clearly that which I have failed to do can only be made good by my own obedience. This doctrine did not stand at the same high level as the Reformers' ethical judgments which have been and indeed still are the peculiar characteristic of evangelical ethics as compared with those of the Roman Catholic. The same is true of the expression *meritum* or merit which is quite thoughtlessly employed in reference to Christ's work, although the criticism of the Reformers had completely demolished the notion of merit. From the Lutheran point of view the term ' merit ' is impossible as an ethical concept, and yet in our classical liturgical prayers we constantly find an appeal to ' the precious merit of Jesus Christ.' When the Fathers speak of the fulfilment of the Law and of Christ's merit as being transferred, these expressions are, from the reformers' point of view, impossible and offensive, but they may have reference to the absolutely unique unconditional meta-ethical substitution of Jesus Christ for us which is beyond and above all Christian analogies ; but if so it is a reference to the meta-ethical in the very unsuitable form of an ethical concept! But although we may appreciate the expressive form of the old doctrine, which we must discuss again later, we must nevertheless reject it; for great numbers of people to-day it is an invincible obstacle to their understanding of the Cross. Because they cannot reconcile themselves to Anselm's doctrine and to that of the seventeenth century, they are alienated from the theology of the Cross as it is found both in the New Testament and in Luther. The one hides the other. To-day, then, we have the important task of expressing both the Scriptural and the Reformers' interpretation of the old doctrine in the language of our own generation.

Obedience and Forgiveness.—The vicarious character of the obedience of Jesus does not consist in the transferability of His obedience to us ; but it is because He rendered perfect obedience that He alone can bring the Divine forgiveness to us. Because in His obedience He was wholly God's, He can be wholly ours. And in so far as He is a mediator He obeyed for us. For our predecessors the idea of the Representative obscures that of forgiveness, and here the criticism of the Socinians was not wrong. On the contrary, the doctrine of forgiveness must be foremost and must condition the doctrine of substitution. The distinction cuts deeply. In their theory our fathers desired to express and to preserve in all its uniqueness the divine wonder of forgiveness in Christ, and their ethically obnoxious idea has the enduring significance that it emphatically reminds us of the ethical incomprehensibleness and obnoxiousness of God's unconditional forgiveness in Christ. The objection felt to the old Lutheran formula is to some degree the objection felt by humanity and ethics to the scandal of forgiveness. But the worst is that the Lutheran Fathers represent in the form of a theory, which purports to be complete in itself and ethically satisfactory, one which actually shatters every ethical conclusion. They never disclose the ultimate inadequateness of every theory, nor is there any trace of a critical self-transcendence of the theory as an insufficient representation of the mystery. The old theory recognises guilt and witnesses to the impossibility of man's making compensation. But they have not a sufficiently radical understanding of guilt and of God's holiness : they do not *perceive the absolute impossibility of compensation* in itself. They assert the equivalence between our debt to God and restitution through Christ. If dogmatics would once admit that we have here only a childish effort at an explanation and one which a deeper understanding must leave behind, all would be well. But this is exactly what is lacking. The effect of the emphasis on equivalence has been to rationalise the mystery of forgiveness, which means that it does not sufficiently stress the incalculable *wonder of forgiveness* which simply faces us. Reconciliation and forgiveness belong together, but not equivalence and forgiveness. The conception of substitution must be separated absolutely from that of equivalence. The emphasis placed on equivalence over-looks the fact that an atoning adjustment is impossible in the face of the seriousness of the demands of God's holiness, which drives home the fact that all my yesterdays are mine and those of other men are theirs. The Fathers were anxious to treat the problem of the holiness of God and of forgiveness seriously, but they failed to think it out radically enough. Otherwise they would not have conceived it as a tenable idea that there was a verifiable *temperamentum justitiae et misericordiae*, a settlement between righteousness and mercy in Christ's obedience. Theology may well ponder over the presuppositions of Christ's forgiveness, and when it has grasped that His obedience is the condition of His power to forgive, then it may call Him the ' Reconciler.' But there is no question of a ' settlement ' which we could think conceivable. We perceive only the truly inconceivable, that God has abandoned His right to drive us from Him and to destroy us, and that He does so only in Christ : in Christ we are free from guilt, in Christ who is obedience. Here a connection is indeed made between our freedom and His obedience on account of which we can speak of ' atonement.' But this reconciliation can only be called equivalent in so far as it pleases God to complete in obedience the wonder ; . . . and it remains a wonder in the face of reconciliation, of forgiveness. It is precisely *this equivalence* which could not and would not be reckoned in a theory of transmission.

But in saying this we are not abandoning in any way the attempt to understand the ' necessity ' of the cross, the ἔδει, ἔπρεπεν and ὤφειλεν of the New Testament. It is not simply the alternative of the theory of equivalence or of the Scotian theory, conceived arbitrarily as ' *acco͵tio* ' through God, when He might equally well have chosen some other means of bringing salvation. We must seek, too, to recognise in the Cross a *necessity* grounded in the holiness of God. It is mere prejudice that would equate this necessity with a settlement or a compensation. No alleged idea of equivalence is the standard for what God must have accomplished in the Cross of Christ ; but what God actually did accomplish then is the standard by which to determine the significance of equivalence in the theology of the Cross. The doctrine of the Cross of Christ must seriously consider that it is *a posteriori*, and also that its categories are derived primarily from the actuality of the Cross. The conception of equivalence as it was developed in the old theory introduces an unauthorised *a priori* element into the meaning of the Cross.

The Knowledge of the Perfect Obedience of Jesus.—Jesus rendered perfect obedience to the Father. The perfection of His obedience is not indeed to be proved by historical methods. The sinlessness of Jesus is no historical fact, even though in this respect the Gospel picture of Jesus must cause the historian to pause. Its interest is not to present the historical picture of the man Jesus under the category of an ' ethical judgment,' and then to pronounce it morally perfect, as A. Ritschl wished to do. The perfection of Jesus cannot be apprehended prior to faith in Him, but

only in and with faith in Him—that is, when the witness of
the whole New Testament has won it from us. We might
say that from the time when God, at Easter, acknowledges
the Crucified we are convinced of the perfect obedience of
the Son. Only from this standpoint dare we, and ought
we, to understand the concrete events of the life of Jesus
presented by the evangelists as manifestations of His un-
broken fellowship with God, His perfect service to God.
That is ' history in the light of faith.'

The Death of Jesus as Divine Worship.—Throughout His
whole life Jesus offered to His Father the obedience of
reconciliation. But His death stands out with unique
significance. It is more than the confirmation, at its
severest test, of a life's long obedience, more than the ' com-
pendium' of His life. These terms do not do justice to
the strong emphasis in the New Testament on the *blood*
of Christ. This has certainly arisen from the analogy of
sacrifice. But its basis is wider than this, it is the fact
itself. *All* obedience is the forsaking of one's own life, and
thus means dying. But actual dying is again without a
parallel. It is to give all, to sacrifice all : to surrender life
before death, is still an element in life itself. But in death
it is not a portion of living in the element of life which is
surrendered, but life as such is surrendered to complete
darkness. Then it is first possible to know what God is—
namely, He who gives all but has also the right to take all,
absolutely everything. It is in dying that it is first possible
to decide whether a man does fulfil the first commandment ; whether he risks all in his trust in God, even when
God takes all, including life itself. Therefore perfect
obedience first exists in the ' blood of Christ.'

IV

OBEDIENTIA PASSIVA

*The Wrath of God is Sanctified through the Sufferings of
Jesus.*—Furthermore, forgiveness vindicates the holiness of
God because only He can forgive sins in the name of God who

suffered and bore the entire wrath of God and thereby sanctified it. Our analysis of the early Protestant theology leads us to a preliminary expression of our own view. How far did Jesus as the Crucified sanctify God's wrath against man?

(a) *The Suffering because of the World.*—First then : Jesus endured the antagonism between God and the world both in His earthly destiny and in His soul. His suffering was in some sense two-fold : with the world and because of the world. It runs through His entire life. From the beginning it bore the ' form of the Cross.' But it reaches its climax on the Cross itself.

The Son of God who is completely obedient to the Father must necessarily suffer in our world. Because He submitted Himself to God as no one else has done, He felt the world's opposition to God as no one else can do. In this antagonism to Jesus is manifested the world's antagonism to God. His suffering and His death are the uncovering of the world's sin, but they are also the revelation of the Divine wrath. For it is as wrath that God compels the antagonism of the world to *this* act, that it shall lay hands on the Son—not merely the crowd, the fickle multitude, but men of high degree, the Pharisee, the theologian, and the priest, as custodians of the divine law and the sacred tradition. It is wrath that leads God to expose, through the sufferings of Christ, the religiosity and morality of men. It is wrath that forces the Son, because He is the Son, to experience the outburst of universal and ever-present sin. Jesus sanctifies the Divine wrath, when He does not refuse to enter into this awful antagonism between God and the world ; when He permits it to become actual and to emerge from obscurity in His words and His deeds, in the unrelenting sternness of His claims and His unshakable loyalty to God ; when He willingly endures, as His sacrifice, the misapprehension of the people and of His disciples even unto the death on Golgotha.

And as the world's opposition to God was objectively revealed in His destiny, so Jesus suffered it too in His own soul. It has become usual in some sections of German theology to-day to be indifferent as to the ' soul of Jesus.' It is said that theologically we are not concerned with the 'personality' of Jesus, that we know Him no longer after the flesh. As protests against the liberal evaluations of Jesus, such interpretations are easily understood. But it may well happen that under the name of 'personality' that may be set aside which is indispensable for faith in Christ. The Christological attempts of the dialectical theology show a decided tendency towards Docetic errors. 'The Word became flesh' surely means that the personality of God entered into the personality of the man Jesus. The acceptance of the belief in the resurrection and pre-existence cannot mean that we have no concern with the visible human conduct and spiritual experience of Jesus. True, it is only of importance to us because Jesus has risen from the dead and is the Son of God. But just because of this it *is* important for us. Indeed the spiritual sufferings of Jeremiah have theological and not merely historico-psychological interest for us ; by meditating on his 'confessions' we may discover what it really means to be called by God to be His messenger in this world. Theology must and can become deeply absorbed in how Jesus the Son bore in Himself the sins of the world. We ought to read the Gospels from this standpoint : How did the Son of God suffer in spirit under men and for men ? But this point of view cannot be developed here in detail. Anyone who follows it up will discover that the life of Jesus from its very beginning stands under the sign of the Cross. Jesus sanctifies the wrath of God in that He is Himself both angry and suffering from His anger. His anger is the anger of the scorned messenger of God, and the anger of rejected love is vicarious suffering. Here then is the point : He suffers as no one else because He lives as no one else can live, that the Father's Name may be sanctified, His Kingdom come, His Will be done. This uniqueness of Jesus' spiritual suffering under a world which is in rebellion against God naturally does not permit of being empirically demonstrated, in any abstract fashion, from the Gospels. We see the suffering breaking through in many soul-shattering words, but His uniqueness can only be known by those who through faith have learnt to see in him the Son of God.

(b) *The Suffering with the World under the Hand of God.*—Further, Jesus did not only suffer as under mankind, but also *with* them *under* the hand of God. As a consequence and punishment of human sin, God's wrath rested on mankind in a twofold sense. First, there is ' the silent imposition of wrath ' which all must bear even though they do not know its reason and its significance : the destruction of our life through death, through conflict in the kingdom of sin, through the veiling of God in a world of sin and death. Secondly, there is the actual experience of the declared imposition of the wrath of God, of His holy condemnation at the tribunal of the conscience to which He leads men by His word. Jesus sanctified the wrath of God because, in this double form, He bore it as the punishment of the sins of mankind. He became true man, in the whole depth of their suffering under the hand of God. He can forgive because He took upon Himself the load of humanity in complete solidarity with mankind. He sanctified the wrath in order that He might overcome it. He overcame it in that He sanctified it.

Here indeed other questions arise. That Jesus endured the silence of the Divine wrath is both evident and understandable. He bore the world of sin as a trial of faith and love required of Him by God. He experienced the power of the world of sin and death to divide man from God ; and as the Son, enjoying a unique proximity and fellowship with the Father, He experienced a condition of hardship which it is beyond our power to comprehend. He endured this imposition of wrath, which is immanent in the world, even to the experience of being forsaken of God. What to all of us is a punishment for our sins, God made the hardest trial of all for Him. This wrath was not His, but the world's. But Jesus entered into it.

Here we come to the problem : can He, however, have died the death of the sinner and have experienced God's holy rejection as we must experience it in the *desperatio* of the judgment of our conscience ? He only can feel the real wrath of God in this sense who is conscious of sin because he knows sin. Dare we think of Jesus as suffering from a *consciousness of guilt* in His relation to God ?

P

Clearly, only then would He have died our death. For death is always the price of sin, and Jesus, as representing the world of sin, had to taste the nature of this wrath in the temptation, through his awful death, of being forsaken of God. But the question now is : whether the despair of Jesus may be regarded as that of the sinner who knows that God may justly destroy him as a rebel ?

Our answer to this question must always be tentative. If we remember that it is the *Holy One* who suffered there and who knew no sin, then there must necessarily be a cleavage between His suffering and ours at the hand of God. If we remind ourselves that it is Love that suffers there, then the cleavage vanishes. How are we, who as sinners cannot know what perfect love is, to understand what complete solidarity may be achieved by perfect love ? Then too we may not forget, what belongs essentially to His ' sinlessness,' that His was not the enjoyment of a peaceful consciousness inwardly isolated from others. We may say with Martin Kähler, ' If our Saviour was man, through his choice and his work he was merely " man," then he was not ashamed to be our brother,' then the unique cannot remain alone, He cannot cover himself with the *toga of His sinlessness* as an individual person *in abstract ethics*. He must take upon Himself consciously and personally the whole liability. From this point we can dimly perceive his love leading Him into the suffering of mankind under God, even to the completest identification with our consciousness of guilt.

Obedientia Passiva in the Early Protestant Dogmatic Theology. — So far we have approached this question hesitatingly and tentatively. In this respect our presentation differs from that of the early Protestant dogmatic theology. But there are other important differences. We must now enter upon a discussion of these.

According to early dogmatic theology Christ completely paid the penalty which mankind had deserved on account of sin, including the punishment which awaits man in hell : this latter, Christ did not suffer extensively, as to its duration, but intensively, in its inner essence (*quoad earum vim, pondus ac substantiam*).

Here the objection must be raised that an important side of the sufferings of Jesus, the enduring of wrath as suffering under the world, is not sufficiently emphasised ; nor is the fact that Jesus bore the sin of the world in the sense that it brought Him, in accordance with the Will of God, into an inner as well as an outer distress. The early dogmatic theology concentrates all the more earnestly on the immediate sufferings of Jesus under God. But are we able to follow it in this respect ? If it taught that Jesus bore our punishment, then it must be carefully stated what is meant by punishment. The punishment which now rests on mankind must be distinguished from that which awaits him in the future. If it is approached from Luther's standpoint, then it can be said of the latter, namely hell, that it cannot be laid upon Jesus, since hell is the immanent law of sin which has so worked itself out that man can do nothing more than, in horrible loneliness, seek himself, in his rebellion against God . . . and yet he must live near to God. This punishment is not an addition from without, as it would easily appear to be from the older theology, but the fulfilment of the inner curse of sin. The ' eternal punishment ' is the eternal sin. If the meaning of hell is to be rightly expressed, then it is senseless to teach that Jesus has borne the punishment of hell. That can only be taught if the punishment of hell is conceived as a reprisal from without, instead of the destruction of life from within. It is only so far possible to agree with Luther as to say that Christ suffered hell in that He was tempted, in His death, to *desperatio*, to a despairing revolt against God which is damnation. But in that He overcame this temptation He had no further connection with hell.

Christ's Cross and Satan.—In the doctrine of Christ we have no wish to omit all reference to hell. The New Testament, the Greek Fathers and Luther understood the work of Christ as also a fight against Satan. In the Greek theology there is indeed a danger that the wrath of God may be overlooked because of the emphasis laid on the power of Satan. Anselm's greatness is that he has replaced in the centre the relation of Christ's work to God. The Cross for him is not the destruction of Satan's power but the *satisfactio* (*Genugtuung*) of God. Luther united, so to say, the conception of the Greek Fathers and of Anselm into a synthesis such as it had not known since the New Testament. In his theology the conceptions of the wrath of God and of Satan are treated equally seriously. They belong together. The wrath of God uses Satan as its instrument. The ground of Satan's power is to be found in the wrath of God. Thus Luther sometimes relates the work of Christ to God alone ; all the instruments of the Divine wrath sink into insignificance over against the actuality of the wrath of God itself. At other times Luther describes (and this occurs not only in his sermons but also, for example, in his commentary on the Epistle to the Galatians) Christ's work as a fight with the instruments of the Divine wrath, with Satan, with the personified powers of Death, Sin, Law, and Hell. Thus Luther's doctrine is at once theocentric in its teaching of reconciliation and concrete-realistic in its doctrine of redemption. It is the relation of Christ's work to Satan that gives the doctrine of redemption its cosmic breadth. It is not a question of ' God and the Soul,' but of the whole world, of the situation created by the wrath of God as a reality affecting the whole cosmos : it is not merely an experience of the conscience, but it is related to the ' Prince of this world ' and his over-throw. The theology of to-day must stress this point. If the reality of the daemonic and diabolic is to be felt by us, more than by earlier generations, then the Gospel must be proclaimed more emphatically as a release from the power of Satan. And yet (as we shall learn from Luther) the relation to Satan is always included within the relation to God. Satan could not be taken seriously if God's wrath did not work through him, and he is deprived of power when the Divine wrath is appeased. For this reason Christ's work must always be essentially a doctrine of reconciliation, a doctrine of forgiveness : for where there is forgiveness of sins there is also freedom from the power of Satan. The reference to Satan is not added, so to speak, as a second thought to the theocentric refer-ence of Christ's work (as reconciliation). Any particular reference to it has only value so far as through it we are reminded of the cosmic-realistic element contained in the Divine wrath.

Poena Vicaria ?—Meanwhile let us return to the old Protestant doctrine of the suffering of punishment. The impossible statement, Christ suffered the punishment of hell, is essential to the old doctrine because it is determined by the idea of equivalence. This conception is as much to be rejected here in its reference to the suffering of Jesus as in its reference to His obedience. Punishment can no more be transferred to another than can the obedience due from another. If this is valid universally, then it follows that, in so far as punishment is abandonment to sin and its deceit, it is an immanent consequence of sin. Punishment in this sense cannot be removed from sin and the sinner. The sufferings of Jesus do not signify the rendering of a settlement of debts which were due from man, but Jesus entered into the misery of man's actual punishment from a sense of solidarity with him, in order that there shall never be a complete, eschatological punishment. It is expiation when God sends the One through whom He will forgive to share with complete solidarity the sufferings of the human race as conditioned by the Divine wrath. But propitiation is not equivalence in the sense of the old Protestant theory. When we ask, therefore, what may be the profundity of Jesus' suffering of death, it is not the place to postulate consequences of the idea of an equivalence between our deserving punishment and His punishment. We know that in Christ we are free from the wrath to come, and we can divine that He is able to give us this freedom from wrath only because He has entered on behalf of mankind into God's present judgment of wrath. That is enough.

V

SATISFACTIO VICARIA

Substitution, Exclusive and Inclusive.—In summing up, the question arises : In what sense were the obedience of Jesus and the sufferings of Jesus on ' our behalf ' ? What is the meaning of substitution for forgiveness ?

The answer to this question has already been stated implicitly ; it remains now to develop its implications more fully. We must consider the chief possibilities of the doctrine of substitution. We can distinguish between an exclusive and an inclusive substitution.

Exclusive substitution has its place primarily in the province of natural life. Its cause is to be traced to the inequalities of life, of gifts and of powers ; and its completion is found in society, either in a rational division of labour or in the service of free love. In both instances the one may step into the place of the other in such a way that the task or duty, which originally fell upon all, is now undertaken by the representatives. The representatives undertake a duty in order to relieve others. It is in this sense that the miners work underground for us. The purport of substitution in this case is to be found in the fact, that the represented thus do not need to do the work undertaken by the representative. Although such representation has, normally, personal and moral presuppositions which are both presupposed in, and are the foundation of, the community, yet, considered in and for itself, it has a material and impersonal content.

The inclusive substitution has its place predominantly in the province of *personal* life : the transition from the one to the other is always fluid—there is no exclusive substitution that does not contain an inclusive moment. The personal is the sphere of the non-transferable. Here, then, substitution cannot mean relieving another of his burden, but rather helping him to bear it : it is not depriving another of an activity of life, but leading him into a fuller enjoyment of it. The mother suffering deep spiritual pain for her lost son only desires to win him to repentance through her pain. The substitute watching over the danger and distress of his people desires to lead them to a share in that watch. The significance of substitution here is clearly not that of gain through the relief resulting from the stronger undertaking an act for the weaker, but rather giving those thus represented the active fruitful power which characterises the representative. It is so far possible to speak of an exclusive moment as existing within inclusive substitution as to say that the representative stands in a position which could not possibly be occupied by the one he represents. It is only through the representative's conduct that the other is drawn into it : he could never attain it alone. So the representative's act is 'ideally' unique and solitary, and in this sense exclusive.

Substitution and Forgiveness.—What then is the relation of substitution to forgiveness ? Are the obedience and suffering of Jesus substitutive in an exclusive or in an inclusive sense ? The answer seems clear. For it concerns the province of the personal life. ' I sanctify myself for them that they also may be sanctified in the truth ' (John xvii. 19). That is inclusive substitution. The ' for them ' finds its completion in the ' that they also.' It would seem then that substitution as applied to Christ's work must be understood as purely inclusive. But in coming to that conclusion we have not adequately considered that the question is concerned with the substitution of the *one who forgives*. The significance given to substitution here is not *immediate*, as in the case of inclusive substitution when those represented are drawn into the other's attitude. But the import of this substitution is the full authority of forgiveness. Forgiveness means granting unconditional fellowship independent of and apart from any other action. Forgiveness assumes a relationship prior to all action : it creates a new state of affairs between God and man prior to and independent of any action on the part of man. Substitution is to be termed exclusive because it derives its significance from its complete authority to found a relationship which is independent of all action. Substitution is to be termed inclusive in so far as the relationship is the foundation of a new attitude and in so far as the new situation, thus created and freed from all conditions, empowers, liberates and compels new activity. We must follow these two lines of thought successively.

The Creed expresses in exclusive phrases the unconditional character of the fellowship granted through forgiveness. Because Christ rendered obedience, therefore God's fellowship with me is not conditioned by my obedience, it is available for me even in my disobedience. Because Christ endured completely the conflict between God and man, and bore the sin, therefore God's fellowship with us does not depend on the depth and perfection of our repentance : we may come before God in all our imperfect penitence. Christ's obedience is thus valued as the obedience of all mankind, and Christ's passion as man's judgment (Christ *for* us). Such is the language of faith which glories in forgiveness granted without conditions. It is the greatness of the orthodox doctrine that it can use such language. It is the boldness of the certainty of salvation which speaks here. The fulfilment of the law is not the condition of fellowship with God ; in this sense the believer in Christ is free from the law. Whenever this certainty is decisively emphasised it will find strong expression in thoroughly antinomistic phrases. From this standpoint the questionable phrases of orthodoxy are to be understood in their *expressive* [1] character. The certainty of the faith that in Christ we are free from the claims of the law and from eternal punishment is expressed in the following sentences : ' Christ fulfilled the law instead of us and suffered the punishment of hell instead of us.'

But the *unconditional* fellowship of God with us must nevertheless be a *sanctifying* fellowship. It is in truth the fellowship *of God* with us. The new relationship may and ought to be lived in a new attitude. In this respect substitution can only be expressed in *inclusive* terms. Jesus Christ obeyed the Father *in order that* through Him all the disobedient should also obey. Christ suffered *in order that* they might all be led from a false security and apathy to a judgment of repentance. Christ in His surrender to God died the death of the sinner, *in order that* in our surrender to him all death might become divine worship. In this case it cannot be said that his obedience *is* an act of mankind, but that it *will become* an act of mankind. His suffering *will be* man's passion, not through the imitation of Christ, but, as Luther said, Because Christ is alive, therefore His Cross is become a ' sacrament ' in us (Christ *in*

---

[1] Dr. Althaus points out that the adjective he uses is in German a technical term derived from modern art.

us). The living Christ draws His own, those who believe in Him, into the obedience, passion and death of His Cross.

Christ for us and Christ in us.—It is along these two lines of reflection that Christ's substitution first finds full expression. The exclusive and inclusive aspects belong together and ought not to be separated from one another, though there may be considerable tension between them. The doctrine of Christ's work has always languished when only one aspect of the truth has been emphasised. Orthodoxy is mistaken in describing Jesus' substitution as *purely* exclusive, while Mysticism and the mystico-ethical redemptive doctrine of Schleiermacher and his disciples are mistaken in interpreting it as *purely* inclusive. The *one* witnesses to what Jesus has done for us without saying in the same breath what He does in us. But the *other* submerges the Christ for us in the Christ in us.

Orthodoxy has thus fallen from the height attained by Luther and the New Testament. The development of the doctrine of Christ's Cross is identical with that of the doctrine of justification. For Luther justification was both to pronounce righteous and to make righteous *in one*. Melanchthon understood justification in a purely forensic and no longer an effective sense. The reason being that he did not wish to destroy the certainty of salvation by connecting the question of renewal with that of justification. To mention in the one breath, almost in one word, both justification and renewal seemed to endanger the unconditional character of justification, the true jewel of the reformation, and the certain basis of salvation. For this reason under Melanchthon's influence the doctrine of renewal was fully detached from that of justification. The doctrine was certainly to be taught but in a quite different connection from that of justification. The same happened to the doctrine of Christ's work. Christ in us found expression in the doctrine of the ' unio mystica,' but that was indeed far removed from the doctrine of Christ's Cross. This separation is not unimportant. The conception of an unconditional fellowship with God must deteriorate unless it is proved *in the same breath* to be sanctifying fellowship. The doctrine of an unconditional fellowship with God if taken alone can be misused as a cloak for wickedness. The mystics describe the humour of the man in the street as caused by the doctrine of the Cross : ' now I can booze at his expense.' If the one-sided emphasis of orthodoxy on the exclusive aspect of the doctrine of substitution appeared to imperil the sternness of the ethical : on the other side the ethical interests of the doctrine of renewal led to the rejection, by Schleiermacher for example, of the exclusive conception and, consequently, the acceptance of a purely inclusive doctrine of Christ's Cross. In the one case the doctrine of justification is taught without being vitally related to that of renewal ; and in the other case the doctrine of renewal is taught without a real understanding of justification. Schleiermacher and Orthodoxy show, only from opposite sides, that Luther's idea of justification which is also that of the New Testament, as the unity of forgiveness and renewal, of the exclusive and inclusive character of Christ's work, has been lost. It is the task of modern theology to regain this unity.

Our faith in the Crucified is *at once* faith in His power to forgive and in His power to sanctify. Christ can only sanctify in forgiving. And He forgives in order to sanctify. *In forgiveness the fellowship which is granted sanctifies just because it is unconditional* : for man's sin consists in his desiring to live to himself, and faith in forgiveness is a radical break with this original sin ; by his faith in forgiveness man renders for the first time due honour to God and fulfils, as Luther said, the first commandment. It is precisely when he no longer attempts to bring his own fulfilment of the law before God that for the first time he fulfils the law—namely, the first commandment—and in fulfilling it he fulfils all the rest. The converse is also true, it is only *in Christ that God's fellowship with us can be unconditionally granted, for by it we are sanctified for God.*

Expressed otherwise : only through *faith* in Christ *pro nobis* is Christ *in nobis* ; but equally : His *pro nobis* is not to be distinguished from His availability as *efficacissimus in nobis* (Luther).

But a misunderstanding which might arise from the parallelism of the last sentences must here be avoided.

The mutual interrelation between *pro nobis* and *in nobis*, justification and renewal, is in no sense a strict correlation, so that it might be said : that just as forgiveness or justification is the (real) ground of renewal, so renewal may be described as the (ideal) ground of forgiveness, or justification. For forgiveness is indeed indissolubly connected with renewal, whose foundation it is. It may be said that apart from the idea of renewal there is no forgiveness, for the purpose of forgiveness is the fellowship of man with God, and God is Holy. Forgiveness and renewal constitute then *one* Will, *one* Act. But forgiveness is not based on renewal in the sense that the pronouncement of forgiveness might, to that extent, be morally conceivable as an analytical judgment of regenerated man, standing already ideally in the presence of God. This method of basing forgiveness on renewal fails to consider the fact that forgiveness, by admitting man into the presence of God, has wiped out the past. God does not look at what man is and He does not look at what man has been. If we believe that God does not look upon the actual present being of man and as a consequence that in prolepsis God already sees man as he *will have become (Geworden-sein)* in the future, then we forget that man's being in every passing moment is continuously before God as *that which has been, (Gewesen-sein)*. No *having become (Geworden-sein)* can obliterate from before God *what has been (Gewesen-sein)*. That which we have been always continues to exist in our being, and even though it is no longer active, yet it is there as guilt. No ' what we have become ' can take away our guilt. What we have become cannot therefore be taken as a reason for the forgiveness of guilt. Every such doctrine of justification is really refusing to take seriously the true character of our life in time before God. The serious character of time for theology is, that it is concerned not only with our actual being before God but also with that which we have been. For He meets me not only nor primarily in that image of myself into which I ought *to grow*, but He meets me before and simultaneously with the claim of every hour, the claim which I ought to *fulfil* precisely in that hour. The unfulfilled demands of each passing hour are before God. No future can efface the daily 'present,' but this 'present' remains also in the future as an unrepealed past event before God. How then could man's future righteousness be the cause in any way of his present justification before God? The conception of a divine prolepsis, if introduced here, detracts from the seriousness of time and of its accompanying conception of guilt. *It is not only the conception of a proleptic, divine analytical judgment that has to be abandoned but also the conception of an analytical judgment of justification in general.* For the essence of an analytical judgment is that it is concerned only with the *being* of man and does not take into consideration what he has been. Thus the very concept of an analytical judgment as such destroys the real gravity of the idea of guilt. For God does not look only on what a man is, but also on what he has been. Therefore if in eternity He should declare a man to be righteous who *has become* righteous, it would follow that the judgment of justification in its totality could never be analytical, for what a man has been belongs to his being, and is indeed not annulled by what he has become. Thus eschatological justification is synthetic.

Propter Christum.—Justification or forgiveness in Christ retains the character of the incredibly wonderful. It cannot in any way be ethically rationalised. It is non-ethical, indeed anti-ethical. For it frees man from what he cannot and indeed ought not to free himself, and from what he may not and dare not think himself to be freed, from what accompanies him in his every moment—namely what he has been. He can only believe it as he looks upon Christ who offers him forgiveness as the Crucified, as the One who by His obedience and by His suffering has completely vindicated the Father. Faith knows forgiveness *propter Christum* as a fact, and it would not be justifiable to interpret this *propter Christum* as applying to the Christ who, working in us, renews us. Certainly, God only forgives us in Christ who at the same time is our Regenerator, and He forgives us in order that this regeneration may take place. But that interpretation of *propter Christum* fails to consider the relation of forgiveness to that which we have been. To reflect on this aspect is to recognise that *propter Christum* must be interpreted in its exclusive sense, as our old Lutheran Fathers understood it. It is not that God forgives us because Christ is mighty *in us*, but God forgives us because Christ is there *for us*. We have noted already that *propter Christum* so understood may not be interpreted in the sense of an ethically conceivable judicial settlement. That Christ's being and His having been should hide, from before God, our being and our having been is God's thought of love for us ; it is incomprehensible, and is only grasped by him whose faith has been born out of fear and trembling. *Propter Christum* taken in our sense does not substitute for the ethical construction based on Christ in us another based on Christ for us. But faith in *propter Christum* in its true sense means precisely the end of every unduly clarified doctrine of reconciliation. No theory, then, must consider the *propter Christum* of the Church doctrine and the *propter regenerationem per Christum* as two parallel ways of accounting for forgiveness. On the contrary, *propter Christum* genuinely understood belongs to a totally different dimension. It seeks to ' establish ' an *entirely different interpretation* from the former theory. In fact, it stands for no theory, for any such must always meet the demand for a consistent and judicial judgment ; but it only suggests to men that forgiveness is determined by God *in Christo*, not arbitrarily, but in the deep wisdom of His holy love ; for this reason it is *propter Christum*. It is a wisdom which our thought can follow in some measure but which we cannot verify by a theory of equivalence. Every equivalence theory can only have value as being a symbol of that which is not an *arbitrary* act of God but an activity of His *wisdom*. But it is the wisdom of God in *miracle* and *freedom*, and to it Christian doctrine can only bear witness by a critical overcoming of every trace of the rigidity and of the exaggerated clearness of dogmatic conceptions engendered by an equivalence theory.

CORPUS CHRISTI
BY ALFRED EDWARD JOHN RAWLINSON

X

CORPUS CHRISTI

I

THE word *corpus* in Latin, apart from its primary and original meaning of ' body ' (especially a human or animal ' body '), can by a recognised extension of meaning denote also a community, guild, corporation, or political ' body,' a ' body corporate.' The word is freely so used in good classical authors ; and we, inheriting the metaphor, readily speak of a ' body politic,' a ' public body,' a ' body ' of men, of police, or of troops. So familiar, indeed, is this usage that we speak with equal facility of those who belong to such aggregates as ' members ' (*i.e.* ' limbs ') of the ' bodies ' in question ; and, in so doing, we almost forget that we are using a metaphor.

Behind the Latin phrase *corpus Christi*, however, there lurks the corresponding Greek New Testament phrase σῶμα Χριστοῦ, the implications of which St. Paul (who employs it) develops in ways that have ever since been familiar—' Ye are Christ's body, and limbs thereof severally ' (ὑμεῖς δέ ἐστε σῶμα Χριστοῦ, καὶ μέλη ἐκ μέρους).[1] The teaching based by St. Paul upon this fundamental conception in the passage from which I have quoted [2] need not here be elaborated. When once the Christian Church had been described as a ' body,' it was not unnatural to speak of Christians individually as ' members ' or ' limbs ' of that body. It is the initial description of the Church as a ' body ' which requires explanation. There appear to be no pre-Christian analogies. The word σῶμα in Greek denotes ' mass,' ' bulk,' ' carcase,' or ' body.' It could be used, in contrast with σκία (' shadow ') to denote the ' reality '—

---

[1] I Cor. xii. 27.   [2] See the whole passage (I Cor. xii. 12–27).

St. Paul so uses it in Col. ii. 17. But the word does not appear in pre-Christian Greek usage to denote the idea of a ' society,' a ' body corporate,' with ' members.' St. Paul's use of the phrase σῶμα Χριστοῦ appears quite extraordinary. From whence, we may ask, was it derived ?

II

St. Paul's Epistles are, of course, only occasional letters. Even when we have sorted them out and arranged them in more or less probable chronological order, it is a mistake to read them in sequence as though they formed a continuous treatise, or even to assume that their chronological sequence affords, of necessity, any secure clue to the development, chronological or logical, of the thought of their writer. An idea which, so far as documentation in literature goes, appears for the first time in a particular passage in one of the extant epistles need not be new as an idea in St. Paul's mind. It may, for all that we know to the contrary, have been a familiar commonplace of his regular teaching, despite the fact that no mention of it had hitherto chanced to occur in the course of such portions of the Apostle's correspondence as have been handed down to us. But the converse case is quite possible also. A particular passage in one of the extant Epistles may conceivably serve to throw light upon what would otherwise have been the obscure origin of one of the Apostle's familiar conceptions, despite the fact that the idea involved had been mentioned before.

Now, in St. Paul's First Epistle to the Corinthians the idea of the body and its ' members ' or ' limbs ' is already taken for granted as a familiar conception. ' Know ye not that your bodies are limbs ' (' members ') ' of Christ ? ' [1] St. Paul is rebuking the practice of fornication, and he appeals, as to a familiar commonplace (unless, indeed, we are to regard the introductory words, ' Know ye not ? ' as being merely a rhetorical trick of style), to the idea that Christians are ' limbs '—that their very bodies are ' limbs ' —of the body of Christ. The description, therefore, of

[1] 1 Cor. vi. 15.

Christians as together constituting the 'body' of Christ is presumably earlier than 1 Corinthians. It is none the less possible that in a passage or passages which occur at a later stage in the same Epistle we may find the clue which we seek; and the suggestion which I would make is that the origins of the idea are, in effect, sacramental. St. Paul connects membership in the 'body' with Baptism; those who are baptised in Christ's name are incorporated thereby into the one Body, and are made to drink of the one Spirit (1 Cor. xii. 13). That is an intelligible thought, so soon as the idea of the Church as itself constituting the Lord's 'Body' is in being. That the Church itself may be rightly described as the Lord's 'Body' is an idea which I believe to have been suggested by the language used with regard to the Eucharist. Between the use of the phrase 'Body of Christ' as a description of the Church and the use of the same phrase as a description of the sacramental 'loaf' of the Eucharist it is permissible to suspect a connection; and the rite, surely, precedes the doctrine.

III

'We, that are many, are one loaf, one body,' writes St. Paul, 'for we all partake of the one loaf' (1 Cor. x. 17). The idea that the unity of the loaf, broken for sharing in common, typifies or represents or expresses the unity which should hold together the Church is found also in the early sub-Apostolic document known as the *Didache*, the relevant words of which run :

'We give thanks to Thee, our Father, for the life and the knowledge which Thou hast made known to us through Jesus Thy Servant. To Thee be the glory for ever. As this that is broken was once scattered over the mountains and being brought together became one, so may Thy Church be brought together from the ends of the earth to Thy kingdom.' [1]

The *Didache* links together the idea of the one Church with the idea of the one loaf that is broken, but does not use the term 'body.' The *Didache*, unlike St. Paul, does

[1] *Didache*, ix.

not mention the Last Supper, nor does it quote the words
'This is my body' or 'This is my blood.' It would be
rash to conclude that the tradition of the Last Supper was
unknown to its compiler or author, whoever he may have
been. A good deal depends upon whether those Christians
who were expected to make use of its liturgical forms were
intended to read them with, or without, the Last Supper in
mind.

St. Paul refers both to the Last Supper and to the words
of the Lord Jesus, which he gives in the form :

'The Lord Jesus in the night in which He was betrayed
took bread : and when He had given thanks, He brake it,
and said, This is my body, which is (broken) for you : this
do in remembrance of me. In like manner also the cup,
after supper, saying, This cup is the new covenant in my
blood : this do, as oft as ye drink it, in remembrance of
me.' [1]

At an earlier point in the Epistle St. Paul had written :
'The cup of blessing which we bless, is it not a κοινωνία'
(a 'sharing '), 'of the blood of Christ ? The loaf which
we break, is it not a κοινωνία' (a 'sharing ') 'of the body
of Christ ? ' [2] Then follow the words quoted already :
'Because there is one loaf, we, that are many, are one
body' (or, 'because we, that are many, are one loaf, one
body '), 'for we all partake of the one loaf.' [3]

The use of the phrase 'one body' (which is not found
in the Didache) side by side with the phrase 'one loaf' as
a description of the Church in St. Paul is to be connected,
surely, with the fact that in St. Paul (though not in the
Didache) the eucharistic 'loaf' is itself so described, and
that St. Paul believed it to have been so described by the
Lord Jesus Himself.

IV

St. Paul's further teaching with regard to the Eucharist
may be here briefly considered. The passage concerned
with κοινωνία occurs in the context of a warning against

[1] I Cor. xi. 23–25. The word 'broken' (κλώμενον) perhaps did
not form part of St. Paul's original text.
[2] I Cor. x. 16.   [3] I Cor. x. 17.

participation in non-Christian cults, and more particularly,
as it would appear, against participation in sacrificial meals.
Just as in Judaism those who eat of the sacrifices have
fellowship with the altar,[1] so to partake of what is offered
in sacrifice to pagan divinities (who, in St. Paul's view, are
' demons,' and not God) is to have fellowship with the
' demons.' God is jealous ; and to be partaker of the
' cup ' and of the ' table ' of the Lord is not compatible
with being also and equally partaker of the ' cup ' and of
the ' table ' of ' demons.' [2] The phrase ' table of the Lord '
(here used for the Eucharist) denotes in Mal. i. 7, 12, the
Jewish altar of shewbread at Jerusalem. St. Paul need
not have derived it from that source—his language here
may be oppositional, directed in pointed antithesis against
analogous phrases in the religious terminology of heathenism.[3] What precisely St. Paul meant by his phrase about
' having fellowship with ' or ' becoming partakers of ' the
' demons ' (κοινωνοὺς τῶν δαιμονίων γίνεσθαι) is obscure.
He could not, of course, speak of a ' communion *in the body
and blood*' of the ' demons ' : the probability is that he is,
for the sake of his argument, assimilating the terminology
of his description of pagan sacrificial ' participation ' to the
Christian terminology, so far as it was at all possible to do
so without ignoring the differences.[4] It should be borne
in mind that St. Paul's allusion is in any case not to the
' Mysteries,' but to εἰδωλόθυτα or ' meats offered to idols '
in the ordinary sacrifices of paganism.

St. Paul, in the other passage in which he refers to it,[5]

---

[1] κοινωνοὶ τοῦ θυσιαστηρίου εἰσί (1 Cor. x. 18). The phrase appears
to be a Jewish reverential circumlocution for sacrificial communion or
fellowship with God.

[2] 1 Cor. x. 18–22.

[3] *Cf.* the well-known invitations δειπνῆσαι εἰς κλείνην τοῦ κυρίου
Σαράπιδος (*Oxyrhynchus Papyri*, Nos. 110 and 523). These examples
are, of course, of Egyptian *provenance*, and date from the second century
A.D. Whether analogous terminology was in use in connection with any
pagan cult in St. Paul's age and neighbourhood is not definitely known.

[4] See A. D. Nock in *Essays on the Trinity and the Incarnation* (ed.
Rawlinson), p. 134. I agree with Mr. Nock in rejecting Lietzmann's
theory based on the reference to Porphyry in Euseb., *Praep. Evang.*,
iv. 23.

[5] 1 Cor. xi. 23 *sqq.* The so-called ' words of institution ' have been
quoted above. I proceed here to discuss the meaning of *vv.* 26 *sqq.*

interprets the Eucharist as a ' proclamation ' or setting forth of the Lord's death, with the eschatological reference ' till He come.' To partake of the Eucharist in an unworthy way or in an unworthy spirit (ἀναξίως) is to be ' guilty ' in respect of the body and blood of the Lord. What St. Paul means by this statement is explained by what follows—' he that eateth and drinketh eateth and drinketh judgment ' (or ' condemnation ') ' to himself, if he discern not the body ' (μὴ διακρίνων τὸ σῶμα) ; and by ' not discerning the body ' St. Paul apparently means ' not discriminating ' the eucharistic loaf, which in a sacramental or ' spiritual ' sense is the Lord's ' body,' from common bread. How unmistakably ' superstitious ' is St. Paul's view of the Eucharist may be inferred from the fact that he regards cases of sickness and death which have occurred at Corinth as being the direct divine penalty of the profane use of the sacrament.[1] That the ' loaf ' and ' cup ' of the Eucharist are for St. Paul ' spiritual ' (i.e. supernatural) food and drink is to be inferred, further, from the fact that he can utilise for the purposes of a sacramental analogy not only the ' baptism ' of the Israelites ' unto Moses in the cloud and in the sea,' but also the ' spiritual ' (i.e. supernatural) food and drink which in Hebrew legend were supposed to have sustained the ' fathers ' in the original wilderness wanderings.[2] At the same time, it is clear that the sacraments do not work magically. With the majority of the Israelites God ' was not well pleased ' ; and these things happened unto them ' by way of example ' (τυπικῶς)—let the Corinthians take warning ![3]

V

At this point I revert once more to the consideration of St. Paul's use of the phrase ' body of Christ ' as applied to the Church. Whatever its origin (and I have argued that the idea was in the mind of St. Paul a corollary of what to him was involved in the Eucharist), the conception

---

[1] ' For this cause many among you are weak and sickly, and not a few sleep ' (1 Cor. xi. 30).
[2] 1 Cor. x. 1–4.   [3] 1 Cor. x. 5–11.

of the Church as the Messiah's ' Body ' is, as we have seen, quite extraordinary. It is not an at all obvious or (according to Greek ideas) an at all natural metaphor; and we must dismiss, I think, from our minds the familiar associations of the word ' corporate ' in modern speech. We must attempt, by a deliberate effort, to make real to our minds the extreme violence of the metaphor involved in the description of the Church as a ' body,' a σῶμα. The phrase would in Greek suggest primarily the ideas not of social organisation or corporate life, but of corporeality ; visible, concrete reality ; unity (as it were) of a ' bodily ' kind.

The unity, in other words, of the Church is for St. Paul not simply a ' spiritual ' unity : it is at the same time a ' bodily ' unity. The phrase ' the unity of the spirit,' for example, in the sense in which it is used in the Epistle to the Ephesians,[1] does not mean ' unity of spirit ' in the modern sense, as a conception which might stand in conceivable contrast with ' unity of body ' : it means ' the oneness of the Spirit,' considered not as in contrast with the oneness of the Body, but as its complement. There is one Body, and correspondingly there is one Spirit. The unity of the Church is for St. Paul not ' spiritual ' as contrasted with ' bodily ' ; it is ' bodily.'

VI

And it is ' bodily,' because sacramental. ' In one Spirit,' writes St. Paul, ' were ye all baptized into one body.'[2] The one Baptism, which (among other things) mediated the gift of the Spirit, is for St. Paul the effectual means, as it were, of incorporation into the one Body.

[1] Eph. iv. 3. The petition in the ' Collect or Prayer for all Conditions of men ' in the Anglican Prayer Book ' that all who profess and call themselves Christians may be led into the way of truth, and hold the faith *in unity of spirit* ' involves both a misinterpretation and a misquotation of the passage in Ephesians, which speaks not of ' unity of spirit,' but of ' *the* unity of *the* Spirit ' (τὴν ἑνότητα τοῦ Πνεύματος), as a corollary of the unity of the Body. For our present purposes the question of the authorship (Pauline or sub-Pauline) of the Epistle to the Ephesians is not important.

[2] 1 Cor. xii. 13.

The fundamental idea underlying the conception of the Church in the New Testament is that of Israel, the People of God. The Church is the new, the true, the redeemed Israel, the ' remnant according to the election of grace,' [1] into which, by the mercy of God, believing Gentiles also have now been admitted. The bearing of the Messiahship of Jesus upon this conception is obvious—it is through the Messiah that the Church is redeemed : it is through Him, and by relation to Him, that the new Israel is constituted. There had been a moment at which the true Israel—the Messianic ' remnant '—had been reduced to one single Person : the Messiah Himself. ' Ye shall be scattered ' (so says our Lord to the disciples in the Fourth Gospel) ' and shall leave me alone.' [2] It is not otherwise in the earliest Gospel, that of St. Mark—' All ye shall be offended : for it is written, I will smite the shepherd, and the sheep shall be scattered abroad.' [3] The Lord Jesus before Caiaphas, as before Pilate, stands absolutely alone as the true seed of Abraham. At a later stage He, the Remnant, returns from the exile of death : it is only by being gathered to Him, in the new Israel, that anyone else can inherit the promises.[4]

And men are ' gathered ' to Him, in the new Israel, by Baptism. As the Israelites of old had, in St. Paul's phrase, been ' baptized unto ' (or ' into ') Moses,[5] so men now were ' baptized ' unto (or ' into ') Christ. The fact that such baptism was upon the basis of ' faith ' of course goes without saying. No one would be ' baptized unto Christ ' without faith in Him—that was obvious enough. In the earliest beginnings of Christianity none but believers in Christ were baptized in His name—the problem of Infant Baptism had not yet arisen ; and conversely, all who believed were baptized—the problem of Quakerism had not arisen either ! It is permissible to take for granted,

[1] Rom. xi. 5.   [2] John xvi. 32.   [3] Mk. xiv. 27.
[4] I owe this conception, and much else in this essay, to Dr. T. A. Lacey's book, *The One Body and the One Spirit* (see esp. pp. 51 *sqq.*). Dr. Lacey refers also to St. Paul's argument in Gal. iii. 16, remarking that though we may think St. Paul's exegesis intolerable, we may yet acknowledge the truth of his conclusion.
[5] 1 Cor. x. 2.

therefore, the universality of Baptism. It was by means of this rite that men became members of the new Israel, by being ' aggregated ' to Christ.

The Christians of New Testament times did not forget that the Messiah Himself, Jesus, on whom their salvation depended, the Lord who in His own Person summed up the New Israel, had (' for the fulfilling of all righteousness,' as they expressed it) [1] Himself been baptized—with the Baptism of John. That the Christ was a sinner they did not believe ; that He had been baptized in the Jordan by John was an historical fact. It had been the will of God that the Messiah should submit to this Baptism—it was part of the fulfilling of God's righteous purpose for Israel. It was a typical, a Messianic, a representative act. The new Messianic Israel must be a people purified, made clean, and made new.

The Baptism of John was, in itself, ineffective. It is described in the Gospels as having been ' a baptism of repentance unto remission of sins ' [2] ; but it lacked the gift of the Spirit. John had himself looked forward to One coming after him—a Mightier than he. [3] When the Mightier One came—when the Messiah Himself was baptized—then that which was lacking was added. As the Gospels express it, the heavens were opened, the Spirit descended. [4] The Messiah, as ' the firstborn ' (in St. Paul's phrase) ' among many brethren,' [5] stands forth as God's Son. In a real sense the true, the redeemed Israel, the ' firstborn ' of God, [6] is, in the person of Jesus, already in being ; even though there is a ' baptism ' still for the Messiah to be baptized with—a baptism, this time, of blood. [7]

When from the realms of death Jesus came back victorious, there was from henceforth a Baptism proclaimed in His Name. Was it directly enjoined by the Saviour ? The later Church thought so. [8] Was it a continuation of John's Baptism ? It resembled John's Baptism, in so far as it was a baptism ' unto the remission

---

[1] Matt. iii. 15.   [2] Mk. i. 4.   [3] Mk. i. 7.
[4] Mk. i. 10.   [5] Rom. viii. 29.   [6] Exod. iv. 22.
[7] Lk. xii. 50.   [8] Matt. xxviii. 19.

of sins,' presupposing 'repentance.' Unlike John's
Baptism, however (and in this resembling the Baptism of
Jesus Himself), it involved the gift of the Spirit.[1] There
was a further point, in which it differed from both : it was
a baptism 'in,' 'into,' or 'unto' the Name of the Lord
Jesus. It linked believers to Him. His was the Name of
Power, the 'fair' or 'good' Name (τὸ καλὸν ὄνομα), which
was 'invoked over' Christians (τὸ ἐπικληθὲν ἐφ' ὑμᾶς)[2]
in Baptism. It is necessary, if we are to understand the
New Testament doctrine of Baptism, to allow full weight
to the force of contemporary ideas with regard to the power
of the Name.[3] Because His Name was called over them,
believers were 'gathered,' 'aggregated' to Jesus by this
Baptism ; they belonged to Him, they were made one with
Him, they were held to share His experience ; with Him
they were 'buried' in Baptism, being 'baptized unto His
death '—they were from henceforth dead to their old sinful
past ; and with Him they were risen, 'raised from the
dead,' to walk henceforth in that 'newness of life,' that
new life of the Spirit, which meant sonship to God.[4]

St. Paul's sacramentalism, in the passage from which I
have been quoting, is exceedingly strong : but it is not
derived from the 'mystery cults.' It is worked out, not
in the language of rebirth or of regeneration (which comes
into the New Testament later,[5] and which—so far as the
mere terminology goes—might conceivably have had such
an origin), but in the language (manifestly Christian, and
derived from the experience of Christ) of death, burial, and
resurrection. St. Paul uses elsewhere the Old Testament
idea of creation afresh (καινὴ κτίσις)[6]—the renewal,
restoration, or making over anew of that creation of God
which (according to Hebrew ideas) had been marred and
spoilt by the entry of sin. In the case of those who are
'in Christ '—for to be baptized 'into Christ' was to be
from henceforth 'in Christ' and to belong to God's
renewed Israel—the renewal, the eschatological 'creation

---

[1] Acts ii. 38.　　　　[2] Jas. ii. 7.
[3] See especially W. Heitmüller, *Im Namen Jesu* (Göttingen), 1903.
[4] Rom. vi. 3-4.　　　[5] John iii. 3 *sqq.*; 1 Pet. i. 3, 23.
[6] 2 Cor. v. 17; Gal. vi. 15.

afresh,' has already, as it were by way of anticipation, begun.[1]

To be ' in Christ ' and to belong to the New Israel are from henceforth the same thing. The New Israel, according to the New Testament thought, is ' in Christ ' as the Jews were in Abraham, or as mankind was in Adam. The Messiah, the Christ, is at once an individual person—Jesus of Nazareth—and He is more : He is, as the representative and (as it were) the constitutive Person of the New Israel, potentially inclusive. He includes, He is one with, the New Israel ; and the New Israel is one with, is united to, Him, as its Head. The Spirit, moreover (the characteristic gift and distinguishing mark of the New Israel), is the Spirit which was upon Him. It is He who ' pours forth ' the Spirit upon the Church [2] : and the ' Spirit ' can be described indifferently either as ' the Spirit of God ' or as ' the Spirit of Christ.' [3] The idea, and the actual phrase, ' *body* of Christ ' (I have argued), may have been suggested in the first instance by the language used with regard to the Eucharist. However suggested, it supplies exactly the idea which was wanted. ' In one Spirit,' writes St. Paul, ' were we all baptized into one Body . . . and we were all given one Spirit to drink.' [4] We are expressing St. Paul's thought with complete accuracy when we say, with a conscious realisation of what the words literally mean, that we are *incorporated* by Baptism into Christ.

VII

Union with Christ in His Body (*i.e.* in the new, visible Israel, the Church), which in Baptism is begun, is maintained and kept vital (according to the thought of St. Paul) by means of the common participation of Christians in the Eucharist, a rite which by St. Paul is interpreted, as we have seen,[5] not merely as a supernatural (or ' spiritual ')

---

[1] It should, however, be observed that in rabbinical Judaism a newly converted proselyte is sometimes described as a ' new creature.'

[2] Acts ii. 33.

[3] Rom. viii. 9.

[4] 1 Cor. xii. 13.

[5] *Supra*, p. 228 f.

food and drink,[1] but as involving also a κοινωνία of Christ's
Body and Blood (*i.e.* a spiritual participation or fellowship
with Christ in His Passion) and a ' proclamation ' or
' setting forth ' of Christ's death ' till He come.' Is
St. Paul here original ?   Or does he proclaim simply the
generally recognised Christian tradition ?   Was the Pauline
conception of the Eucharist *different* from that which
prevailed (shall we say ?) in the Church of Jerusalem, or
was it the same ?

The hypothesis that there may have prevailed in the
earliest age of the Christian Church a certain measure of
variety of Eucharistic doctrine and practice in different
localities, despite the fact that we hear no echoes of controversy with regard to this subject, cannot be simply ruled
out.   The Pauline emphasis, despite the fact that the
Eucharist appears to have been universally celebrated upon
the *first* day of the week (*i.e.* on the Sunday, and not on
the Friday), is characteristically concentrated upon the
idea of the Passion.   The Eucharist for St. Paul is to be
interpreted by reference to the words and deeds of the
Lord Jesus on the night in which He was betrayed, and
the Lord of the Eucharist is the crucified Lord—though of
course He is the crucified Lord who is to-day risen and
victorious.   (There would have been no Gospel in Calvary
if it had not been followed by Easter.)   Was St. Paul's
emphasis the original emphasis ?

The Eucharist in the Acts of the Apostles is described
simply as ' the breaking of the bread.'[2]   It appears to have
been celebrated on the first day of the week, as being the
day upon which Jesus rose from the dead.   That the risen

---

[1] That God in the Eucharist bestows upon men πνευματικὴν τροφὴν
καὶ ποτὸν καὶ ζωὴν αἰώνιον is an idea which occurs also in chap. 10 of
the *Didache*, a passage which it is difficult not to regard as having been
influenced, either directly or (more probably) indirectly, by St. Paul's
teaching in 1 Cor. x. 3, 4.   On the other hand, I see no reason to discover
in the *Didache*, any more than in St. Paul, the influence of any kind of
specifically *hellenistic* ' Mysticism.'   St. Paul finds an analogy for the
' spiritual' food and drink of the Eucharist in the Old Testament
(Exod. xvi. 14 *sqq.*; xvii. 6 ; 1 Cor. x. 3, 4) ; and the idea of ζωὴ αἰώνιος
(originally eschatological) in the *Didache* passage could have been derived
from the Gospels (*cf.* Mk. x. 17).

[2] Acts ii. 42, etc.

Lord was made known, and was recognised, in the breaking of the bread, is the suggestion of the story in the Gospel according to St. Luke of the two disciples on the road to Emmaus.[1] The Eucharistic chapters of the *Didache*, as has been already remarked, do not allude to the Last Supper. There is, further, the problem of the shorter text of St. Luke xxii. 14 *sqq.*, which omits *vv.* 19^b-20. It is a widely held view that the *textus receptus* of Luke in this passage has been contaminated under the influence of the tradition of St. Paul's words in 1 Cor. xi. 23 *sqq.* If this view be correct, the direct witness of the Synoptic tradition to the authenticity of our Lord's words ' Do this in remembrance of me ' disappears, the words in question being in any case absent from the texts both of Matthew and of Mark. Professor K. L. Schmidt would go further. He is disposed to conjecture, upon the ground of ' style-criticism,' that the *original* form of the distinctively Lucan tradition of the Last Supper narrative omitted also Lk. xxii. 17 and 19, or in other words that St. Luke had access to a form of the Last Supper tradition which omitted wholly the ' Words of Institution,' and which referred simply to the Lord's unfulfilled desire to eat that year's Passover meal with His disciples, combined with the confident looking forward to the eventual sharing together of the Messianic Feast in the Kingdom of God.[2]

Apart from this last radical view, it has been argued by Lietzmann, among others, that the Eucharist, in its original form, was not in effect derived from, or specifically connected with, the Last Supper tradition, but that this connection was first made by St. Paul.[3] The primitive ' breaking of the bread ' (so it is argued) was in its essence simply a continuation, in the unseen (though realised) presence of the risen Lord, spiritually thus re-united with His faithful disciples, of the earlier meals which, as a Jewish *Chaburah* or company of table-companions, the Twelve had shared with Jesus in Galilee. The Lord, as was natural,

---

[1] Lk. xxiv. 30, 31, 35.
[2] K. L. Schmidt in *Die Religion in Geschichte und Gegenwart*, Art. 'Abendmahl, I, A. im Neuen Testament.'
[3] H. Lietzmann, *Messe und Herrenmahl*, pp. 249 *sqq.*

had been accustomed on these occasions to break the bread
and to offer the thanksgiving over the food : and His
manner of doing so may have been characteristic.[1] Now
that He was no longer visibly present, some other person
did what the Lord used to do ; and in the little ceremony
of bread-breaking and thanksgiving to God which inaugurated the common meals of the Church, the Lord was
remembered and still was believed to be present as the
unseen Host at what may perhaps have been already
described as His ' table.' In the joyful faith that the Lord
Jesus, wherever ' two or three ' gathered together thus in
His name, was present still in the midst of them,[2] the little
company ' did eat their meat with gladness and singleness
of heart.'[3] The meal was at once a religious fellowship-
feast in the present, and an anticipation and spiritual
foretaste of the blessed re-union hereafter in the greater
fellowship-feast of the future Kingdom of God. In eager
longing and confident hope they looked forward—*Marana
tha !* (' Come, Lord ! ') was their cry. And because, in a
spiritual sense, the Lord already ' came ' and was present—
because, in a certain sense, there was already an
' Epiphany ' of the risen Lord, though unseen, in the midst
of His own—there was raised also the answering
' Hosanna ! ' to meet the Lord at His coming.

In all this there was involved, however, as yet, it is
suggested, no reference and no allusion, direct or indirect,
to the Last Supper, or to the thought of Jesus as crucified.
That was St. Paul's great innovation.

VIII

Now, it appears to me to be possible that in the theory
of eucharistic origins thus sketched out there may be an
element of truth. The summary account in the opening
chapters of the Acts of the Apostles of the earliest Apostolic
preaching of Christ in Jerusalem suggests that the emphasis
was not at first primarily laid on the Cross. What the
Apostles preached was the Resurrection,[4] regarded as an

---

[1] *Cf.* the Emmaus story (Lk. xxiv. 30 *sq.*).
[2] Matt. xviii. 20.   [3] Acts ii. 46.   [4] Acts ii. 24 *sqq.*

unmistakable and Divine vindication of the Messiahship of Jesus, in spite of that Death of shame which to Jewish minds was a σκάνδαλον.[1] It is possible, no doubt, to overstate the antithesis. St. Paul, the great preacher, *par excellence*, of the ' word of the Cross,' proclaims also the Resurrection ; and, conversely, he affirms that the conviction ' that Christ died for our sins according to the Scriptures ' was already part of that Christian tradition which he had received.[2] That the sufferings of Christ were not merely in accordance with the Divine ' counsel and foreknowledge,'[3] but that they had a redemptive and positive value is, moreover, the probable implication of that ' Servant ' Christology which appears sporadically in the first half of the Acts,[4] and which is in all probability pre-Pauline and independent of the specifically Pauline tradition.

Nevertheless, when all the necessary qualifications have been made, it appears probable that ' the word of the Cross ' was in St. Paul's preaching central, in a sense in which it may not have been equally central in the preaching of others. It was to St. Paul the very heart of the Christian message, the supreme ground of his ' glorying.'[5] The suggestion is at least an intelligible one that St. Paul may have been the first Christian teacher to lay the emphasis upon the thought that the risen Lord, with whom, in the Eucharistic rite, Christians had fellowship, was the Lord who was crucified : the first Christian teacher, it may be, to interpret the Eucharist by reference to the Lord's words and deeds at the Last Supper.

To accept the possibility of such a suggestion is by no means to impugn the historical character of the tradition of the Last Supper itself. That St. Paul had simply invented his version of the Last Supper, or (what comes to the same thing) that the narrative of 1 Cor. xi. 23 *sqq.* (devoid, in itself, of historic foundation) was revealed to St. Paul in a vision, appears to me to be frankly incredible ; nor, again, do the origins of the tradition appear to be

---

[1] 1 Cor. i. 24 ; *cf.* Gal. iii. 13.   [2] 1 Cor. xv. 3.   [3] Acts ii. 23.
[4] Acts viii. 32 *sq.* ; *cf.* also Acts iii. 13, 26 ; iv. 27, 30 (the word παῖς).
[5] Gal. vi. 14.

adequately explained, from the point of view of the historian, by the description of it (with K. L. Schmidt) as an ' aetiological cult-legend,' an ἱερὸς λόγος.[1] The reiterated words, ' Do this in remembrance of me,' ' Do this as often as ye drink it, in remembrance of me,' which (apart from the longer Lucan text) are not found in the Synoptic tradition, were perhaps not spoken by Jesus—it is at least conceivable that they may have come to be added, in the course of liturgical practice, by way of explicit authorisation for the continual observance of the rite ; and so, too, the words ' unto the remission of sins,' which are peculiar to Matt. xxvi. 28, may be held to be only an explanatory gloss. When all has been said which along these lines may rightly be said, the solid core of the tradition (the elements, for example, which are common to Mark xiv. and to St. Paul) persists as an unshakable narrative of fact, a story quite uninventable. The Lord Jesus, on the eve of the Crucifixion, actually did take bread, blessed it by the giving of thanks, and said, ' This is my body,' and proceeded, taking a cup, to say ' This is my blood of the Covenant,' or ' This is the Covenant in my blood.'[2]

St. Paul, then, did not invent the Last Supper—the story of the Lord's actions and words at that last meal on the same night in which He was betrayed was a story handed down in the Church. It is nevertheless just possible that the earliest Christians, though they preserved the tradition, did not at first see the point of it. *St. Paul did not invent the Last Supper, but it is just possible that he was indeed the first Christian to see what it meant !* His interpretation (on this hypothesis) excited no controversy, it was accepted, and in the end came to prevail generally, because it was obviously right. *The Last Supper did actually mean what St. Paul thought that it meant.*

The Pauline account of the Supper itself, and of the actions and words of the Lord Jesus, came to him, as he says, from tradition—a tradition which went back to

---

[1] K. L. Schmidt, *op. cit.*, col. 9.
[2] Lietzmann, *op. cit.*, p. 218 ; *cf.* A. D. Nock, *Essays on the Trinity and the Incarnation* (ed. Rawlinson), p. 120.

Christ.[1]   If St. Paul was, however, in actual fact the first
Christian in this connection to see clearly what the tradition
involved, he was in a position to claim that—so far as the
interpretation of Jesus' actions and words was concerned—
he had his ' tradition from the Lord ' in an even more direct
sense.   It was one of those cases in which St. Paul had ' the
mind of Christ '—and the Church could not dispute it.

IX

For—to go back to the Last Supper itself—what in
effect was the Lord Jesus actually doing, when He took
bread, and gave thanks, and said ' This is my Body,' and
when, giving thanks over the wine, He said, ' This is my
Blood ' ?   Expressed as a Jew might express it, He was,
in some strange fashion, superseding the ' covenant '
anciently made with the fathers by a new ' covenant ' in
His own offered life : He was deliberately consecrating His
death (now foreseen to be imminent) to be a sacrifice to
God on behalf of His people.   Interpreting in advance the
significance of His coming Passion, He was in effect making
it to be, for all time, what it otherwise would not have
been, viz. : a sacrifice for the sins of the world.[2]   *It is the
Last Supper which makes Calvary sacrificial.*   It was not
the death upon Calvary *per se*, but the death upon Calvary
as the Last Supper interprets it and gives the clue to its
meaning, which constitutes our Lord's sacrifice.   The
doctrine of sacrifice (and of atonement) was not, as I
believe, read *into* the Last Supper ; it was read out of it.
It was the Last Supper which afforded the clue !

X

It is possible that the Church may not at first have
perceived these implications ; St. Paul did perceive them.
Whether the words ' Do this in remembrance of me ' were,

---

[1] ἐγὼ γὰρ παρέλαβον ἀπὸ τοῦ κυρίου, ὃ καὶ παρέδωκα ὑμῖν (1 Cor. xi. 23).
The verbs παραλαμβάνειν and παραδιδόναι are the regular words for the
' receiving ' and ' handing on ' of a tradition.   The *ultimate* source of the
tradition was in this case ' the Lord.'
[2] ' To the Jew first,' but ' also to the Gentile ' (Rom. i. 16).

R

or were not, actually spoken by Jesus does not greatly
matter.   That the Church, in continuing the observance of
a ritual meal in remembrance of Jesus, was by the Spirit
being guided to understand rightly the ultimate mind of
the Saviour, what Christian can doubt ?   But what
St. Paul emphasized was the thought of the Passion ; for if
the Sunday Eucharist was indeed a fellowship-feast with
the risen Saviour, it was to be remembered, too, that the
risen Lord was the Lord who for our sakes was crucified,
and who at the Last Supper had deliberately consecrated
Himself as a sacrifice. ' This is my Body ' . . . ' This is
my Blood.' If the Lord spoke actually those words, the
Church ought not to forget them.   St. Paul was manifestly
right in his view. ' As often as ye eat this Bread, and
drink this Cup, ye do proclaim the Lord's death, till He
come ' ; and the Eucharist, therefore, is not merely a
fellowship-feast—it is more ; it is a means whereby the
Church is identified with Christ in His sacrifice, a communion of the Lord's Body and Blood, a ritual means of
participation in all that the Lord's sacrifice means.

The ' showing ' or ' proclaiming ' of the Lord's death
in the eucharistic rite is to be understood, moreover, as
being not simply a glorifying or praising in words : it is
(to quote Friedrich Heiler) ' a dramatic setting forth and
rendering present ' of the Lord's sacrifice—a spiritual
sharing, indeed, in the Lord's offered life. ' The Pauline
passion-mysticism ' (writes Heiler) ' is not confined to the
individual experience of the Christian, but has its place
also in the cultus.' I would myself go further than this—
I would say that St. Paul's passion-mysticism has its
primary roots in the cultus. I would quote Heiler again :
' Ignatius of Antioch ' (he writes) ' gives unambiguous
testimony. . . . He sees, set up in the Eucharist, a
θυσιαστήριον, an altar of sacrifice : there takes place for
him a συμπάσχειν, a real sharing of the suffering and
dying of Christ.   It was from this cross-and-passion
mysticism, associated with the Eucharist, that Christians
drew the strength to endure cruel martyrdoms.   To die
the martyr death is nothing less than " to drink the cup of
the Lord," to become " the pure bread of Christ." Even

as the eucharistic celebration is an inward and mystical dying with Christ, so, conversely, a real dying for Christ is the celebration of an eucharistic sacrifice.' [1]

XI

The observance by Christians of the weekly Eucharist on the day of the Lord's Resurrection is the historical origin of the Christian Sunday or *dies dominica*, which has no other original sanction. The day was ' kept ' (in the words of a recent American writer) ' as a day of gladness by all Christians, whether from among the Jews or from among the Gentiles, by those who kept the Sabbath and by those who ignored it. After some centuries it was possible to celebrate it as a beneficent day of rest, like the old Sabbath in its original institution, but with no precept of obligation except the custom of remembering the Lord in the eloquent sacrament of His Body and Blood. By maintaining that " dominical precept " the Roman Church shows itself more evangelical than the " Evangelicals " who prefer to remember Moses and his law.' [2]

A ' dominical precept ' ? It will be remembered that the literal authenticity, as a saying of Jesus, of the words ' Do this in remembrance of me ' has been regarded as doubtful ; and there are those to whom, on the grounds of strict, literal history, it will appear to be more improbable than not that the Lord Jesus, on the actual occasion of the Last Supper, was deliberately and explicitly legislating with regard to the future. Nevertheless, the Christian Eucharist, as the Church knows it to-day, has arisen, as a matter of actual historical fact, out of the words and actions of Jesus on that occasion ; and the Christian Church, in the Eucharist, does what Jesus then did. The continual observance of the rite may be regarded at least as a commandment of Jesus ' after the spirit.'

The spiritual loss sustained by those portions of Christendom in which the Eucharist as at least a weekly observance—the characteristic mark of the Christian

[1] F. Heiler, *The Spirit of Worship*, pp. 33 *sq.*
[2] W. Lowrie, *Jesus according to St. Mark*, p. 162.

Sunday, and the centre and heart of the Church's worship
—has been suffered to fall into virtual desuetude is not
easily measured. Here, beyond question, the Catholic
tradition has a contribution to make towards the full riches
of the spiritual life of the reunited Church of the future—a
contribution wholly in harmony with the positive witness
of the Evangelical faith. This essay may in the meantime
be allowed to end with the quotation of some words
traditionally ascribed to St. Paul—words which may serve
to express the ultimate grounds of the writer's hope for
the eventual growing together of all Christians in unity :

> ' There is one body, and one Spirit, even as ye
> were called in one hope of your calling ;
>   ' One Lord, one faith, one baptism,
>   ' One God and Father of all.' [1]

---

[1] Eph. iv. 4–6.

THE HIDDEN GLORY OF CHRIST
AND ITS COMING REVELATION
BY HEINRICH FRICK

THE HIDDEN GLORY OF CHRIST AND ITS COMING REVELATION

I

OUR *theme* includes the consideration of everything in the earlier essays of this book which comes under the heading of Christology. We must be the last to attack a problem which becomes the more mysterious as one reflects upon it. Even in the early times of Christianity this enigma was faced, and in no generation since has it escaped consideration. Indeed Christendom has repeatedly bestirred itself to solve the riddle. Every power of the intellect, the imagination, the will, and the feeling has been summoned to remove Jesus Christ from the dangerous twilight of our inconclusive inquiries—but the attempt has not succeeded, and will never succeed ' until He comes in glory.'

We mean by this the proposition that *His glory is now hidden as far as we are concerned.*

Here we touch a dark mystery. Thus both in the language used by Christianity, to those without (in mission and apologetic), and in the spontaneous language of the interior life (in dogmatics and perhaps still more clearly in ethics), we are brought up against a great problem : that, since the days of the Apostles, Christendom speaks in an ever fresh succession of superlatives about Him, the Son of God and Mediator, the Incarnate God, who through Eternity is one Person of the Trinity, and every generation of Christians confesses that this majesty is a *hidden* majesty, certainly not only for unbelievers, but also in a special sense hidden as far as believers them-selves are concerned. It would be a mistake to think that the primary concern of Christendom has been always merely to clothe the figure of Jesus in a magnificent vesture of titles of honour. The intellectual warfare has surged round the ' hiddenness ' of Christ at least as often as round His majesty, especially at those times when that majesty has been misconstrued as honour rendered by men. As often as the attempt seemed successful in removing Him from ' hiddenness,' by pointing out this or that aspect of ' reality ' as an expression of His majesty, as a proof of His true presence, as a revelation of His glory, then the proposition has once more been reasserted as the result of embittered conflicts within Christendom : ' His majesty is a hidden majesty.'

On this twofold statement everything depends : Christ is the Lord of Glory, but His eternal nature is for the present ' hidden ' from us.

Thus the two Christological predicates of glory and ' hiddenness ' are not related throughout as the two scales of a balance which alternately rise and fall. It is not true that the greater ' hiddenness ' of the glory means a weakening of His glory. It is also not true that a more complete revelation of His glory would be an intensification and a heightening of it. It is quite otherwise. This point may be well observed in the polemic of the *Reformation* against Roman Catholic Christianity. There the two points of view stand side by side ; first, that through the Papacy the glory of Christ has been perverted into a visible glory and, secondly, that proper honour has not been paid to His glory. Indeed, these two points of view are basically one : for through our striving to make visible the hidden majesty of Christ we degrade it. In the opinion of the Reformers the truth lies in the other direction : perceptibility must be renounced, and the glory of Christ conceived as a hidden reality ; only thus does this glory transcend the relative sphere and achieve divine majesty.

The memory of this historical example should warn us henceforth from a double misunderstanding : first of all, from regarding the ' hiddenness ' of Christ as the same thing as the ' hiddenness ' of God in His ultimate eternal Being. ' Gott an sich,' the ' deus *absconditus* ' is certainly a ' hidden ' God. In this essay, however, we speak only of the God of revelation, the ' *deus revelatus* ' and

of ' hiddenness ' not outside this conception and in opposition
to it, but directly concerning the ' *deus revelatus.*' The
' hiddenness ' which we mean is thus a hiddenness of the
Mediator, of the ' deus *revelatus.*'

Herein lies the problem, to the examination of which
genuine Christology must address itself : that Christ, the
Founder and Lord of the Church, with all His power and
glory, remains hidden.

Secondly, it is clear that ' hiddenness ' in our sense of
the word does not concern the metaphysical inaccessibility
of a transcendent world. What we mean here is the
invisibility of Christ, whose presence dwells in the fellowship of believers, of whom, from whom and in whom they
have all things. The ' hiddenness ' of Christ must not be
understood as referring to a transcendent world where the
inner tension of belief is to be released.

We speak rather of a ' hiddenness ' which is so grounded
in history that it aims at a historic objective, and is not a
matter of speculative dialectic to be set in contrast to our
own experience in the time-order, but it is something of
which the beginning and fulfilment take place on this
earth, so that this ' hiddenness ' is our immediate concern.

II

We may hark back to the New Testament in order to
understand our subject thoroughly.

The foundation on which Christology rests is here above
all the ' revelation.' A secret hidden up till now is, so the
New Testament declares, revealed in Jesus Christ.[1] Hiddenness and revelation stand here over against one another : in
Christ the ' hiddenness ' has come to an end because the
revelation has appeared in Him.

But now a new difficulty arises. What does ' revelation '
mean ? What is meant by ' the Word becoming Flesh ' ?
If we consider the historic Person of Jesus of Nazareth, one
problem after another arises. His human life ran its course
in the time-world and was cut off by death like the life of

[1] Cor. ii. 1–10 ; Rom. xvi. 25, 26 ; Col. i. 26 ; Eph. iii. 9, 10.

all men. For us who have acquaintance with Him only through a mediating message, He was hidden in the kingdom of death and in the shades of the past. Then there is the further difficulty that His concrete revelation, which is historically accessible, is in the highest degree a matter for dispute. The words and deeds of Jesus, His Person, His inner life may be reckoned by us to be of high worth, yet do not stand outside the category of similar earthly experiences, but show the destiny of relative value common to all history. The historical record alone in no way proves that here in truth we have the Word of God uniquely given ; indeed, the conception of the historical Jesus gives rise to peculiar difficulties.

These difficulties are clearly expressed in the Epistle to the Hebrews. Men brought up in the Jewish faith dissented for two reasons from the conception of the Messiah as proclaimed by Christianity.

First, Christ like all heavenly beings, like God Himself, is hidden from our eyes. The fellowship may conceive the ' hiddenness ' as Christ's ' standing before the majesty of God,' yet exactly by this picture it is made clear to each one *that He is not visible to our own eyes.* The Messiahship of Jesus is hidden as a secret in God. How then can we speak of consummation and revelation, and of the superseding and completion of the old covenant by a new ?

Secondly, however, this Messiah is especially displeasing to the Jewish mind because of those features of His revelation which are not hidden, but in virtue of their historicity are placarded for all to see. In so far as Christ becomes manifest, His majesty is quite different from His messianic glory. It appears as the converse of what was hoped for : a designed distortion of the Messiahship into its opposite. For the Messiah of the Christians is seen by the eyes of the world as one who is *crucified,* which involves reflection not only on the historic crucifixion, but on His complete humanity. This humanity of Jesus contradicts throughout the expectation of the glory of the Messiah. Instead of the golden crown Jesus wears the ignominious token of evildoers—the crown of thorns.

In consequence, a twofold doubt concerning the dignity of Jesus arises. The letter to the Hebrews considers both issues, and its particular statements may be understood when they are taken together with the corresponding questions.

The first obstacle to belief may be expressed thus. When even now the glory of Christ remains hidden and the Messiahship of Christ is only a hidden Messiahship, how does the Christian hope arise of future blessedness with its certainty of peace and joy in the life of the redeemed ? What is the original and final element in Christian belief in comparison with the belief of the Jewish fathers ?

The second obstacle arises, not from comparison with older forms of thought, but from the fact itself of a historic revelation in the Person of Jesus : how can a human life which was characterised by temptation, sorrow, death, and sacrifice, which was human like our own, how can this be a revelation of God, a messianic glory, absolute authority for us ?

The Epistle to the Hebrews meets these doubts with the aid of a picture which is taken from the thought-forms of the doubters themselves. It describes Christ as the High Priest who dwells hidden within the inner sanctuary before the face of God, interceding for us by prayer and by offering His blood. The picture portrays a heavenly cultus, whose earthly counterpart was earlier the rite of the Jewish Day of Atonement, and has now become the Christian liturgy. Man has often cherished these thoughts, especially at those times when his spirit, hungering for consolation, has conjured up pictures of the origin of earthly happenings in eternal heavenly archetypes. But the Epistle to the Hebrews is not to be understood thus. For it has in mind not an eternal sphere of being separate from the world, but the beginning and end of a heavenly transaction breaking into the time-order as an earthly history, and ascribes to the present mysterious event all the marks of *genuine temporal* significance : it is an event that has happened once and for all, the purport of which cannot be reversed, determined by a beginning and an end, and characterised by definite temporal qualities (*kairoi*).

The picture of the heavenly High Priest has, like a triptych, three parts which belong to one another throughout. First, the eye rests on the rendering up of the sacrifice for all time (Golgotha) and the entrance of the High Priest into the inner sanctuary, which involves His disappearance before the eyes of the people. In this first part of the picture Jesus, so to speak, turns His back on His followers. Thereupon follows, in the second panel, the ritual act of the High Priest in the holy of holies. This present happening in the sight of God is hidden from the fellowship, and renews every day the miracle of grace. Thirdly, there follows the final picture : the High Priest comes forth again from the hidden sanctuary, the brightness of the Godhead rests on His face, and He proclaims the gracious presence of the heavenly glory, while He now turns his face towards the earth.

The whole picture is rightly understood only as a unity of the three individual pictures. Thus we may not isolate the second, which concerns the present, but must understand that the glory of Christ now hidden depends upon what once happened ' outside the walls of Jerusalem,' and is to be consummated in what is to take place at the end of the age : the appearance of His glory.

This picture, both a unity and a diversity, awakens our questionings and at the same time gives an answer to them. If we take the picture in the threefold unity, the answer which it implies is to be understood thus : the Jewish expectation of the Messiah in glory is not denied or enfeebled, but preserved in utter perfection. But the traditional idea of the coming of the Messiah is illumined by Christianity. The divine glory is unveiled in a threefold rhythm. The end—that is, the inauguration of the new age of glory, and the consequential downfall of the old age—remains undiminished in power. But the path which God pursues is now revealed : it is not the way of sudden invasion apart altogether from a mediator, but a way of pity suited to our condition. Revelation occurs only as revelation *for us*. For our sakes who must perish

before the momentary revelation of God's glory, this glory
veils itself,[1] so that we may perceive it without perishing,
to our health and not to our destruction.

Thus the Epistle to the Hebrews gives a clear answer
to both questions on which doubt has been raised. The
answer to the first problem is a *theology of the word*.
The hiddenness of Christ is not an occasion for toilsome
apologetic and artificial explaining away, but belongs
intrinsically to the mode of a revelation of God which is
solicitous for our well-being. Such a revelation comes to us
as a word of promise. It calls us to a personal decision,
to fellowship with God which is called ' faith.' It does not
override our personality, but appeals to the conscience
(Heb. iv. 2 : ' For unto us was the Gospel preached, as well
as unto them ; but the word preached did not profit them,
not being mixed with faith in them that heard it'). This
doctrine of revelation is again clearly set forth in Luther's
words : *Promissio et fides sunt correlativa ut, ubi promissio
non fuerit fides esse non possit, et ubi fides non fuerit promissio nihil sit.*[2]

Man is not overruled, but earnestly approached as a
being who is called to make a personal decision before God.
But this pursuit of man by God would not be real (but
at the best beautiful imagery) if God's encounter with
man did not involve man's complete self-discovery. The
theology of the ' Word ' consequently develops in the second
place into a *theology of atonement*. This is not the result
of the influence of foreign cults, even if the formulae of
Christian faith have been influenced by these cults, but the
inner logical consequence of the word of revelation. For
this we have a clear witness in Isaiah vi., where God's call
awakens the confession, ' I am a sinful man,' and the
sending forth of Man is made possible by an atonement.
The Epistle to the Hebrews has also answered the second
problem : What is to be said of the crucified Messiah ?

---

[1] The beginning of the reign of glory will be like a ' burglary ' (as a
thief in the night): 1 Thess. v. 2 ; 2 Pet. iii. 10 ; Rev. John iii. 3 ; xvi. 5 ;
Matt. xxiv. 43. *Cf.* Heb. x. 27, ' a fearful expectation of judgment.'

[2] *Op. Lat. Var. Arg.*, vi. 152 ; see also Luther's *Lectures on the Letter
to the Romans*, 1515–16 (ed. J. Ficker), i. 40.

The answer to this question is : ' And as it is appointed unto men once to die, but after this the judgment ; so Christ was once offered to bear the sins of many, and will appear the second time without sin unto salvation.' [1]

Now this second assertion was emphasized afresh in the time of the Reformation : the *theologia crucis* (theology of the Cross) ranged itself in battle against the *theologia gloriae* (a theology concerning God's glory). The mysteries are not for inquiry, but for adoration. The subject of theology is not *Gott an sich* but Christ as Emmanuel, ' God with us.' *Hoc est Christum cognoscere, beneficia eius cognoscere.*[2]

Thus the hiddenness of the messianic glory among men has a twofold reason : (1) only thus is revelation as ' Word ' to ' faith ' possible ; (2) only thus does the fearful thought of a revelation of God in His glory become transformed for us into a means of healing and an opportunity of salvation.

At the same time the mode of His ' hiddenness ' becomes comprehensible. It is (1) no absolute hiddenness, and therefore not to be confused with the idea of a *deus absconditus*. It is rather a veiling of the Word of promise with one object, to prevent our annihilation and to make possible our salvation.

It is (2) something provisional, not immutable, an interim between the first and second appearance of Christ. Its character is to be understood not in Platonic but in eschatological terms. The purpose is not to recall us from the flow of time to a timeless peaceful eternity, but to summon us continually by means of an appealing example to austerity and penitence as well as to hope and joy. In this sense the earliest Christians described their attitude as one of ' waiting,' [3] and declared to the world the message of salvation : He comes !

---

[1] Heb. ix. 27, 28.

[2] Melanchthon's *Loci Communes*, 1521 (ed. Plitt-Kolde, 4th edn., 1925), p. 63. See also p. 61, footnote 1 : *salubriter cogitare*, an expression used by M. Luther.

[3] Heb. ix. 28 : by ' them that look for Him ' is meant what we understand by the ' Christians ' or the ' believers.'

Titus ii. 13 : ' looking for (the fulfilment of) that blessed hope, and the glorious appearing of the great God and our Saviour Jesus Christ.' More briefly in 1 Cor. i. 7 : ' waiting for the revelation (τὴν ἀποκάλυψιν)

III

Therefore Christology must be approached from three sides :

(1) As a statement about the historical Jesus of Nazareth ;

(2) As a statement about the present invisibility of the Head of the fellowship ;

(3) As a statement about His coming again.

In recent times interest in history has resulted in the concentration of almost exclusive attention on the first subject. The greater part of this book is concerned with it. But important as it is, especially to-day, Christology cannot rest here. A discussion of Jesus of Nazareth is only ' Christological ' in so far as the second and third parts of the picture are envisaged in synthetic unity with the first part of the picture in the Epistle to the Hebrews, representing the historical event. The historical aspect of Christology may be discussed only as part of a larger *whole*.

In our essay we consider only two of the three pictures : the present hiddenness of the Messianic glory and its coming revelation. Naturally we are dependent upon the theological statements which have been made about the Jesus of history. But only in parts, and not to the extent that a new affirmation about the Jesus of history would be able to confute us ! Just as an inner unity held together the three pictures of the letter to the Hebrews, so it is with our subject and the Jesus of history. We cannot do without history. But Christology is not exhausted in its historical aspect. Indeed the historical aspect itself is part of a larger conception. The consideration of Jesus of Nazareth is a living issue to the Church only in so far as

of our Lord Jesus Christ.' Present hiddenness and coming revelation of the glory of Christ are set over against one another in Col. iii. 3 and 4 : ' your life is hid with Christ in God ; when Christ who is our life shall appear, then we shall also appear with him in glory.' One out of numerous parallel passages may be chosen, which strongly emphasizes the difference between ' not yet ' and ' one day.' 1 John iii. 2 : it has not yet appeared what we shall be. We know that when he shall appear we shall be like him. For we shall see him as he is.'

Our theme, ' the hiddenness of Christ's glory and its coming revelation,' depends upon these words of the Scripture.

He is the present Lord and the Christ who is to appear at the end of the world.

The two last-named points of view became in Church-history more important than the historic figure of Jesus. It is true that the emphasis vacillates between the past, the present and the future picture of Christ. But in the *main Christian tradition* the emphasis from the early times rests essentially on recognition of Christ as *present* Lord. The 'kingly glory' of Christ means for the present, for Catholics as for Protestants, in the first place the gracious government of the invisible present Saviour.

Only in backwaters, in times of excitement, and within schismatic groups does the gospel of the 'End' have authority. The official theology concerns itself primarily with a Christology of the exalted Lord of the Church. Indeed in so far as it is concerned with Christology, the disagreement between Catholics and Protestants lies *within* these limits. Lutherdom certainly emphasizes strongly the hiddenness of the kingly glory of Christ, and therefore celebrates Good Friday as the most typical holy day. Over against this, in the Catholic year Corpus Christi Day gives intelligible expression to the idea that in spite of the invisibility of Christ His present rule cannot remain hidden, but breaks forth clearly into the light of day. But this contrast lies within the same circle of ideas—that is, of an evaluation of the present Lordship of Christ. The Catholic and the Protestant join in discountenancing all fanaticisms, both those which conceive the coming Kingdom of Christ as a 'parousia' and those which strive to imitate slavishly the poverty of Jesus of Nazareth.

Thus the Lutheran doctrine of justification may be described as a hymn to the hidden kingly reign of Christ. For when here the new man is thought of as an inner hidden creation of the Spirit, living through faith alone, this is the human mirror of the hiddenness of Christ. As Christ Himself, so the new man remains hidden until the last day. This is a basic thought of Luther's which is rooted as deep in his philosophy of life as it is in important passages of the New Testament. We may be content with quoting Col. iii. 3 f. : ' For ye are dead, and your life is hid

with Christ in God. But when Christ, who is our life, shall
appear, then shall you also appear with him in glory.'

The decisive declaration of belief for here and now
runs : ' I believe that Jesus Christ is my Lord.' The
attention of Christology is centred on the present Lord who
is exalted and hidden. It is not our duty to pursue the
many-sided development of this fundamental conception,
but we must refer to two critical issues which present
themselves as part of our problem.

First of all, the *eschatological* character of Christology
suffers from this interpretation. The last things do not
now appear in a sufficiently serious light. They occur to
the mind only when the present life is artificially extended
into the future. Luther does this, for example, in the
second and third articles. There the ' parousia ' of Jesus
is not mentioned at all. It says only : ' that I belong
to Him, and live under His rule in His Kingdom and serve
Him in eternal righteousness, purity, and blessedness
inasmuch as He is risen from the dead, and lives and
reigns throughout eternity.' Further, that the Spirit
' will at the last day awaken me and all the dead, and
will give me eternal life together with all believers in
Christ.'

In these formulae the return of Jesus is not mentioned
at all. Of a ' coming ' of Jesus—' here below,' ' on the
earth,' ' again ' in the world—there is no mention. All that
is emphasized is how *we* come to *Him* in His Kingdom !
Eschatology consists in this, that the idea of the spiritual
man, the second Adam, is brought to its final accomplishment. To this conception, and to this conception alone,
belong the resurrection of body and soul, judgment and
eternal life.

It is not sufficiently said that eschatology truly conceived
requires a social fact (the body of Christ) and the world
as a whole (the new heaven and the new earth). Here
Col. iii. 4 is merely treated as a consoling vision of the
future, and in order to do this is emptied of all references
to the external world and confined to the individual
Christian. Certainly the author of the Epistle to the
Colossians meant more than this. The unveiling of Christ,

' your life,' at the end is the revelation of One who is already
at hand though invisible, that is, of the supporting foundation, of the cornerstone laid long ago which carries the
whole building.   The doctrine of the end is for the Epistle
to the Colossians not a discussion of how in the future the
present characteristics of our life may be traced, but a
message about the supporting basis of our life.   Christ
is our life and consequently the ' end '—the ground of
existence !   Ought this early Christian apprehension of
truth to be revised ?   Or does not the essence of the
Gospel depend directly on it, *i.e.* that emphasis must be
put on the ' end,' and this end is to be understood as a
revelation of the life now hidden, as the coming forth of
Christ, as the appearing of the ' Kingdom '—a new heaven
and *a new earth* ?

The second consideration lies in the field of *ethics.*
Lutheranism [1] has neglected the conception of Christianity
as service.   Above all as a social ethic it is prone to con-
servatism, and little prepared to allow the Gospel to count
as the source of inspiration for real social changes.
Lutheranism proves its power in the ' hiddenness ' of the
inner man.   It is especially great in times of need.   The
virtues of cross-bearing—patience, constancy, stubborn
resolution, and holy defiance of circumstance—may then be
developed.   But as soon as the pressure from without is re-
lieved, Lutheranism has no guidance to give in social ethics.
It has no hope to offer to the world as a whole.   Of course
it does not preach, like so many sects, the approaching
destruction of this world, but fits itself willingly into a given
situation.   For the attention of religion is directed to the
individual man, and especially to his conscience.

In opposition to this, the so-called ' millennium ' beliefs
have advanced their claim.   They do not offer a unified

---

[1] More than elsewhere we have here to distinguish between Luther
and Lutheranism.   The pure doctrine of faith means such a faith, that
is at the same time love, because genuine faith cannot be without love.
The character of Christian life as expressed by *service* is not an addition,
but original Christianity.   See M. Luther in *De libertate Christiana*, 1520.
Not Luther, but Lutheranism is the real object of that criticism, which—
not only from outside (by non-Lutherans), but ever again from inside
(by reference to the genuine meaning of faith)—was directed against the
Lutheran ' quietism.'

picture. All kinds of points of view, some of them even contradictory, are mingled together here. But emphasis upon the coming great event, the ' parousia ' of Jesus, is common to all. Are they thereby nearer to original Christianity than the main Christian tradition ? This would be true if the sects had a true understanding of the present hidden Kingdom of Jesus and a corresponding comprehension of Christianity. Frequently it is just here that they are lacking. From the point of view of the Lutheran ' justification by faith,' it is not difficult to point out the unsatisfactoriness of those ' sect ' opinions. This stress on the near ' parousia ' of Jesus drives one either to indifference towards the present or to nervous activity. Theologically both may come under the watchword ' sanctification.' Thereby the apocalyptic sects have the choice whether they will conceive sanctification as separation of the elect from the rest of mankind, or as activity amongst the lost. In the first case, Pharisaism and lack of love towards others ensue ; in the second, mere presumptuous morality, as though ' man were builder of the Kingdom of God ' : in either case a violation of the principle of ' justification ' by faith alone.

In this way, however, the fact of the hidden glory of Christ is misconstrued, for in the one case the kingly reign of Christ in the present is not taken seriously, and in the other His *hiddenness* is not taken account of.

Thus we come to the result that by one-sided emphasis either on the present or on the future, the other link in the Christological chain of thought is neglected.

Is there no way out of this difficulty ? If both thoughts were held firmly together as of equal value, would not the one-sidedness be avoided ?—For here and now, the lesson of justification : for the coming new earth, the expectation of the end.

In these circumstances the problem would be divided and thus made easier. Not *all* human need would be at once assuaged. Emancipation would come by degrees. The Kingdom of Christ as a present *regnum gratiae* (rule of grace) offers us even now emancipation from the one great evil of humanity, sin. Yet there still remains the other

burden of mankind, the longing for harmony between the
' inner world ' [1] of belief and the outer world, the yearning
for happiness and strength. The dream of a world in which
the powers of the Spirit are vindicated until all things are
brought under His rule remains unfulfilled. Complete
lordship including power over the external world will be
assumed by Christ at the end of time, at the beginning of
the *regnum gloriae*.

Dostoiewski has developed the conflict in his ' Great
Inquisitor ': emancipation would be complete for men when
harmony was established between a completely healthy
conscience and a perfected external world. Christ's work
of salvation, as far as it concerns the consciousness of guilt
in man, will remain incomplete as long as our concern
for daily bread continues. Herein lies the profound truth
of the three questions of the Tempter to Jesus, as Dostoiewski explains. How may Christian theology hope to
answer the question of the ' Great Inquisitor ' by the related
conceptions of a present *regnum gratiae* and a coming *regnum
gloriae*? Is this way possible ?

The customary language of theology does not at all
favour such a modification of grace and power. Neither
does it allow grace to be confined to the mere present, nor
power to the future. Power and grace belong in idea
more closely together than that division of the rule of Christ
would lead us to suppose.

It is said that grace is a conception for here and now.
That is true, but not the whole truth. For grace—present
to faith—is always a promise of the future. Grace is the
first-fruit of that which is to come, not our present complete
possession. The *regnum gratiae* aims at a new earth purified
thanks to grace ; thus its realisation lies in the future. By
grace the powers of the new earth set up a ferment in the
old world. That is the real nature of grace. The word
' grace' would become an empty shell if it were not understood as the beginning of a fulfilment which is to come.

Therefore this paradox is valid : the Kingdom of power,
which is to appear at the end, is already here, although now

[1] *Innenland*, an expression used by Karl Heim, e.g. *Das Wesen des
evangelischen Christentums*, 1925, pp. 46–58.

hidden from us. At the end only the *revelation* of glory is to be understood ; the glory itself is already here, and will be made accessible to us as grace. This expression from the New Testament, the ' first-fruits of the Spirit,' means that the powers of the Coming One are at work now.

Thus the little word ' and ' in our title is not to be taken as synthetic, but analytic. It does not join a second concept to a first, as if grace and power were to be separated from one another, but it comprehends them both in one. As in our own existence the question of conscience and of daily bread may not be separated from each other, so in Christology the hidden glory (*regnum gratiae*) and its coming revelation (*regnum gloriae*) are in their nature one and the same. Then what does ' and ' signify ? It can be answered only by a theological inter-pretation of time.

IV

The *problem of time* has of late been superficially treated in Protestant theology. Generally speaking, two trains of thought about time were considered sufficient. The one conception of time was formal and empty ; the other was determined by content, but in a merely negative sense.

The formal conception of time was generally associated in Germany with the name of Immanuel Kant. Time then, just as space, was held to be a mere form of consciousness.

Those who went beyond this view, and apprehended time as objective and determined by content, in general approached the subject in quite a negative way. They said time is *Zeitlichkeit*, *i.e.* the sphere of perishableness and moral corruption.

Both ideas require revising, and although this is not the place to carry out this criticism, its result must be kept in mind so that we may give an answer to the Christological problem. The result, however, is, it would appear, in both cases the thesis that theology must break with the conceptions of time which have held the field till now, and develop in their place an independent Christian conception of time.

We may now consider the merely *formal* conception of

time. Those who share this view treat temporal expressions in the Bible and in the teaching of the Church just as spatial expressions—namely, as mere pictures. They regard statements about the 'beginning' and 'end' as really a pictorial intuition of something the nature of which is timeless. This essence which is the real ground of their being has, we are told, as little to do with the time which we experience, as with the space in which our present life and, consequently, also our percipient minds are bound up. But is that true?

It must in any case not be forgotten that the early Christians thought always in terms of the temporal future when they spoke of the Gospel. Now we know indeed how the glowing expectation of the first Christians has become transmuted into other forms of eschatology. The main Christian tradition which came later has preferred to speak of the transcendental rather than of the earthly heaven, and has called the attention of men rather to the solemn fact of their own death than to the 'new heaven and the new earth.' It is important to make clear that in this tradition the dissolving of time-events into mere images of something timeless never completely succeeded. It was quite different with pictures of space! Reflective men have at all times detected the representational character of our oft-repeated intuitions of 'below' and 'above,' of 'on this side,' and 'on that side.' Even before Copernicus mankind had grasped that God's heaven is something different from a place in space. We may refer to a quotation of M. Luther's. It is known that he held firmly to the old pre-Copernican view of the universe—and yet very clearly understood that all spatial expressions are mere pictures. At the same time, however,—this is here decisive for us—he held firmly that time conceptions were not to be resolved into pictures. He says, for example, in the Catechism, about Christ: 'He sits on the right hand of God, whence He will come.' Now what is the meaning of 'the right hand of God'? 'This is not a special place which is or may be occupied by a body as a golden chair, but the almighty power of God, which cannot be in any one place, and yet must be everywhere. Nowhere can it be in one place, for were it ever in a specific place, it must be comprehensible by our finite understanding and confined. . . . The divine power, however, may not and cannot be thus confined and measured.' [1] The *Formula Concordiae* says with the same purport : *dextera Dei ubique est* (God's right hand is everywhere). Thus, the spatial picture serves as a representation for something, the nature of which is not spatial.

Now may *dextera Dei ubique est* be placed by the side of *dies novissima semper est* (the last day is every day) ? That is the question : if the answer must be Yes, then Time must be considered as merely representational. At all events Luther did not accept this view. The *liebe jüngste Tag* is for him not out of time, but at the end of time. As surely as the day of a man's death is in time, so surely will the return of Jesus be ' at the last day ' an event in time. The second coming, when He will come as Lord, is just as much an event as the first coming when He appeared as a servant on the earth. For Luther the time plan in eschatology is not a representation of reality, but reality in its literal interpretation.

We see that the spatial and temporal elements in eschatological language are throughout treated differently. Is this difference also binding for us ?

The answer to this question depends essentially upon whether *content* is ascribed to the conception of time. In this regard we must protest against a commonly accepted apprehension of time—namely, against the slighting of it as if time were the same as *Zeitlichkeit*, and *Zeitlichkeit* amounted to that which is not eternal, and implied even the absence of God ! Whenever from the beginning man has esteemed time as something which is without or even opposed to God, he has soon slipped from theological into philosophical thinking and has usually ended with the contrast *time—eternity*.

The ' hiddenness of Christ ' becomes thus inevitably misunderstood, as though it were a representation of the ' wholly other ' which is in the divine world as opposed to our human world. Time is then a quality of the immanent

---

[1] *W.A.* [= Weimarer Ausgabe = M. Luther's works ed. at Weimar], vol. 45, p. 634.

world; the transcendental world is beyond time. As a matter of fact, in this way all existence is moulded in the form of a spatial picture (here—there), and time sinks to a negative quality of this world which is removed from God.

In this view, however, there is nothing more left for Christology to do. For the hidden glory of Christ does not imply an inaccessible transcendental world in opposition to an accessible world here and now. The Christian conception of ' hiddenness ' is rather in the same category with such conceptions as completion, fulfilment, appearance, revelation. Hiddenness is, here, not a matter of fact which belongs to the transcendental world, but is in the womb of the future. In other words, Christology comprises and implies a quite definite interpretation of reality—namely, *a conception of the time in which we live as having positive content.* Time, being in time, acting in time, the temporal, *i.e.* change as a positive quality, belongs also to the transcendental, not merely to the immanent. Christ Himself in His hiddenness is not cut off from time, but active, living, creative, in and through time. In this way the Christology of Luther was framed. We may cite : Christ's sitting at the right hand of the Father ' must be acknowledged to be efficacious and dynamic, an act in operation unceasingly ; it must not be thought that He has gone up on high and sits above, and leaves us to manage as best we can below. On the contrary, He has gone yonder because thence He can best act and reign here. . . . When He was on earth He was too far from us, now He is near to us.'

' He has gone to heaven because He has begun a spiritual Kingdom, in which He will rule amongst us by justice and truth. . . . He has to work on earth from heaven, to rule the conscience and soul of man by the Gospel, to represent the believers and intercede for them with the Father as an eternal mediator and high priest, and He gives to believers the power and strength of the Holy Spirit.' [1]

Here the same category is applied to faith in Christ, as Luther at other times applies to faith in God : it is a *creative act* and at the same time its object is described as *for our highest good.* Both characteristics are equally

[1] *W.A.*, vol. 12, p. 662 and 546 *s* ; Kirchenpostille 21–22.

important; indeed the range of their application is conveyed in its completeness only when it is understood that here they are correlated.

In Christology an ontology is implied—that is, a dynamic ontology : in Christ God is not quiescent, but vigorously at work. This again implies a very definite character of Christology : the so-called soteriological trend of life, for everything conspires to our healing. The soteriological emphasis of the doctrine of Christ and the dynamic interpretation of the nature of reality are here only two sides of the same statement.

V

Now we have reached the point from which a widespread misinterpretation of our subject may be surveyed and, as it seems to us, a doctrine of Christ *compatible with modern knowledge and corresponding to the New Testament* may be achieved.

Now we may transcend the false belief that Christ's hidden reality is in a world beyond that of temporal existence, a kind of overworld from which by reason of our temporal form of experience we are fundamentally separated. Whoever follows this interpretation of our theme will be ruled by one tendency : to bring the glory of Christ out of its (timeless or supertemporal) hiddenness into the midst of our realm of time. Then it is asked how the invisible can be made visible.

A proposal of this nature aims at making known the representative of Christ on earth, the Christ here and now living and visible, who more or less may be said to occupy the place of the hidden one.

Here we recall that Church history for long periods has been seeking diligently with all its power to bring the glory of Christ into the light of day. This view has reached its most extreme expression in the Roman Catholic conception of the Church as the body of Christ visible on earth. Indeed, Protestantism originates from a conscious rejection of this idea, and sees even to-day in the Roman Catholic system an untrustworthy attempt to set a visible compensation in the place of the hidden glory of Christ. But

has not Protestantism itself fallen in the course of its history
into similar errors, only in another direction ?   How often
have Protestants in controversy with Rome supposed that
they, even more than Catholicism, were able to show to the
world the glory of Christ, *e.g.* through the witness of pure
' Christianity,' through superiority in Christian *theoria* and
praxis pietatis, or through the idea of Christ and the experience of Christ ?   They let the institution go, but they set
in its place spiritual religion, the visible results of the
work of Christ, and the humanly demonstrable truth and
power of Christianity.   Is that really something different
from a compensation for Christ ?   One may call an empirical
fact indeed *His* fact, but as long as it remains a matter
which man may value in the same way as other empirical
facts, whether higher or lower in the scale, Christ Himself
will be smothered by the mists of human finitude.   To
establish by argument, or to present the glory of Christ,
does not exalt, but rather degrades His rank.

In comparison with such attempts, the Christology of
the orthodox school of the sixteenth and seventeenth
centuries became more cautious and theologically thoughtful.   At the first glance the Christology of that time seems
to us to be rather grotesque.

How curious, for example, was it to ask the question :
how far Christ in His humiliation, the child at Mary's
breast, the man crucified, indeed the dead man in the grave,
could be at the same time Lord and Ruler of heaven and
earth?   Nevertheless, even such a conflict of opinion as that
between the orthodoxy of Giessen and that of Tübingen,
becomes conceivable as soon as we look at them from the
standpoint of this essay.   It was an attempt to bring
together in harmony the hidden glory of Christ and its coming
revelation.   The satisfying formula of compromise ran that
Christ even in the condition of humiliation possessed all
divine power, but freely renounced the exercise of it.

As for consolation—and indirectly also in proof
of the correctness of the thesis—partial influxes of glory
from the invisible world into the visible were observed.
His power, so it was said, was patent even in the lifetime of
Jesus, as light through rents in the curtain from time to

time becomes visible : *quando, quomodo, et ubi voluerit*, when and how and where He wanted.

For instance, orthodox interpreters treated the Transfiguration as typical, and interpreted it by the words of 2 Peter [1] : ' We have seen his glory.' According to their interpretation the faith of the apostles in Christ was founded on occasional influxes of the brightness of His glory. As though to console us for the weakness of belief which suffers because of the invisibility of Christ, from time to time a partial revelation had to be given. This commission was given to Church-history, and certain men and events were so explained. Finally, it was attempted to vindicate the life of a Christian in this way, and among other things answers to prayer were celebrated as victorious influxes of the power of Christ from His hiddenness into the visible world.

But what are the real facts ? Are partial influxes of the glory of Christ into the visible world to be supposed ? The presumption upon which all such reflections rest is always a qualitative distinction between our existence as men and another ' reality ' which henceforth we must represent to ourselves in the form of the transcendental. Our theme, however, has nothing to do with this.

The correlation between grace which is offered to us, and the hidden glory of Christ, is not so conceived in the New Testament, which speaks of two ages, of the present and of the coming age, instead of using metaphysical terms. By the coming age early Christianity meant a reality which is to encompass us in the near future here in the world of time, and which will appear in its completeness at the end of time. A ' hidden ' glory is spoken of, because the nature of this coming revelation is *known*. Sporadic, miraculous, influxes from a transcendental world are not referred to, but it is rather the glory of Christ which according to John i. and the view of early Christianity is being made known here and now as ' grace and truth.' We know the glory of God, namely in the face of Jesus Christ. Even the very late Second Epistle of Peter puts the transfiguration on the holy mount in a very clear time-synthesis : the

[1] i. 16–18.

recollection of the 'virtues' of Jesus Christ, and the anticipation of 'His' coming again.

Certainly the earlier records in the New Testament
have completely guarded the mutual relation between
Christ's glory and grace. Most of the miracles of Jesus
are miracles of healing, and it is here especially remarkable
that, in outstanding passages of the New Testament, healing
is also forgiveness of sins. The glory of Christ reveals itself
as creative grace, which is able to encompass our life in all
its aspects, even the bodily aspect. The word concerning
the body's healing is an addition, certainly not the fundamental condition, on which faith would depend. To believe
in the glory of God does not mean to drag this glory into
the light, but to recognise Him, who comes in the offering
of grace, as the one almighty Lord. It is not as though
we were to ascribe to Him a second attribute (glory) in
addition to grace, but in grace He who is always our Lord
comes near to us, quite independent of our attitude to
Him. So we arrive at the result: all we know of the hidden
glory of Christ is learned in obedience to His word of grace.

The divine power approaches us as grace, so that we may
say : 'My Lord and my God.'

Christ's glory is not hidden *an sich* (in a metaphysical
sense), but it is for us in this age so long as the form of our
experience is time. Here He approaches us as grace by
which we apprehend the unmistakable power of God
working for our salvation, divine power expressing itself
in time.

Conversely, it is equally true that the grace which has
its source in divine power will at its final consummation be
identical with glory. For in the end the rule of grace is completed by the unlimited triumph of Christ over all enemies.

Thus *grace* is the form in which His *power* reaches us
now in the given situation. Divine *power* is the spring
and the consummation of His *grace*. There is only one
single divine process, His Kingdom. The fact that we
speak of two kinds, or even of three kinds, of ' government by Christ ' is mere stammering speech about the
original miracle of the living God ceaselessly working,
who pursues His creatures in all their activities.

His hiddenness is thus not makeshift, weakness, a defeat, to which we must painfully reconcile ourselves, but rather kindness, an inexhaustible granting of grace by the Father who ceaselessly follows the prodigal son, and postpones the day when His glory, destroying everything opposed to God, will become visible. His glory is hidden to our advantage : for it is revealed in the word of grace which reaches and encompasses us.

Here we have reached the specific Christian meaning of time as expressed in the New Testament word *Kairos* and in 2 Peter [1] : ' Christ delays His coming because He has patience with us and does not will that anyone should be lost, but rather that everyone should come to repentance.'

Time is, according to this view, a medium for expressing the ' patience of our Lord,' the creative Almighty One who marvellously rules the world—in spite of sin and death— and enters into our lives in order to prepare us for the coming revelation of the glory.

VI

Our discussion issues finally in a *synthetic view*, which redeems us *theoretically and practically* from the distress of our human life.

We may again recall the words of Melanchthon in order to formulate the theoretic result : *Semper enim hoc est regnum Christi quod Spiritu suo vivificat, sive sit revelatum, sive sit tectum cruce* (By Kingdom of Christ is meant, that He gives life by His spirit, whether His reign is revealed or whether it is hidden by the cross).

Here are brought together the dynamic ontology and the soteriological Christology, the reign of God in the con-summated kingdom and the rule of grace which we now experience, the present (hidden glory) and the future (revelation). It is not the form of space by which our existence is primarily determined. For this world—both the transcendent and the immanent world—has reality in so far as it is a creature of God's, and so long as He energises it. Every moment in which we live is unique ; a conception

[1] iii. 9.

of the world in terms of space is like a transverse section through God's creative action in time. We cannot ' explain ' why He has permitted that our lot in life should be characterised by sin and death. We can only realise in obedience to the facts of reality that all being is flux and movement, not the stillness of completion, and that we ourselves are in the midst of it. For our own existence is delivered up to time, a fact which is inescapable as well as inexcusable. Every advance into the next moment of existence is a step towards death, which increases our responsibility. The message of salvation as offered by the world religions, by the philosophical schools, by cultural and social movements, strives to help man in this condition. Generally, the ' religions ' evade the issue by dividing up man's need and seeking salvation for the so-called higher nature of man (his soul) in another world. This different world may be a transcendent ' space,' which is symbolically conceived, or an illusionary Paradise, supposed either before time began, or at the end of time. Not only the religions, but also the other forms which the message of deliverance may assume, fill the mind with hope directed either towards an ideal world or towards the future.

The Gospel does not belong to this category of panaceas, although it used to be proclaimed in similar ways. ' The hidden glory of Christ and its coming revelation ' is rightly understood not as a reference to another world but as the highest possible *interpretation of the present moment*. The message of the Gospel is that in spite of sin and death, which hold us in bondage from the beginning to the end of our lives, the almighty God who sustains every living thing wills that we should be saved. His glory makes its dwelling within the word of grace that He may reach us men who sin and die. We are to be saved *in this world, not outside it*. While now we wither and die, leading a life which bears upon it the marks of sin and death, we shall become new creations indeed, ' co-workers with God ' towards the new world of His power, having our part in the creative activities of God which are not shadowed by sin and death. We shall be brought back from meaningless work into the sure purposes of God, from the flux of time which we bitterly apprehend as change and decay into the creative process culminating in the new heaven and the new earth, from the kingdom of obscurity (hidden glory) into the kingdom of His beloved Son (revealed glory).

This is possible only through faith, through trustful receptivity of spirit and obedient learning of the message of God's grace. The believer in this sense does not live in another world, but in this world. His communion of spirit with all men, indeed with all living creatures, is not broken : on the contrary, it now becomes complete for the first time. For faith is directed to the one Lord of heaven and earth, not to a special Saviour-God to be distinguished from the Creator-God, or to special soteriological aspects of the Deity, whose personal character may be reabsorbed into the ultimate being of the Almighty which is indifferent to the salvation of men. Certainly this present existence, this life characterised by sin and death, is apprehended by faith to be time, which is the field of *God's creative activity*, which He extends in the interests of man in order to save him.

This point of view relieves us of a mass of difficulties which occur when, instead of a dynamic ontology, we affirm the objectivity of persons and things which are customarily described by means of static spatial pictures. Simultaneously the ' three in one '—Father, Son, and Spirit, creation, redemption, and sanctification as the prime wonder of life—is seen to be a tenable doctrine. The Almighty Creator as ground of all being, Christ as the gracious condescension of the Father to us in the present age, the Spirit as the power of God which brings forth here and now the first-fruits of the coming age, is a consistent train of thought.

Most important, however, for the present, are the consequences which follow from the above point of view when applied to the *ethical attitude of Christianity*. As soon as it is understood that all life hastens to the day of Christ's revelation, a real reconciliation of nature and grace is needed—and is possible, in the sense of proclaiming and representing the world to come. An ethic of boundless hope which is free of impatience and illusion arises from our Christology.

It is free from impatience because we do not yet know

the final date of the end. The Church did well to restrain the mistaken zeal of those who kept stressing the *speedy* return of Christ, the end of the world in their generation ! When this emphasis was made, the heart of the eschatological message was misunderstood. The official teaching of Christianity erred, however, in so far as it pushed into the background the idea of waiting for the end of the world. The affirmation of a coming revelation of the now hidden glory is the kernel of all ethic which is inspired by faith. Only thus may faith become fact.

The accomplishment of this fact without illusion is a necessary postulate because hope in the Coming One who is to return in glory is inspired by Him and is no spontaneous movement on our part. Thus we ought not to speak of ' building the Kingdom of God ' as though it were our own affair. He only is the Builder, and it is better to speak of His Kingdom as ' coming to us.'

What, then, ought we to do ? We ought to proclaim the Kingdom. The ethic of Christianity must correspond to the ' sign ' of the prophets : the transformation of earth into the image of heaven, an expression of the spiritual message of the coming day of God in terms of physical liberation. The meaning and the end of the Christian life cannot be other than to *announce the hidden glory of Christ and its coming revelation.*

But only to announce, not to fulfil ! ' To reign in glory ' is reserved for the coming age. Now we may only await in patience. Real waiting in patience, however, is certainly not inactivity or just empty speech, but a limitless, potent transforming work applied to this present world. So transforming is it that all reality becomes a proclamation of the message, a visible word of God, a token of the coming Kingdom. Sense of reality *and* vigorous idealism, untiring patience *and* courageous readiness for change are implied in the idea of ' waiting.' *Luther's teaching of justification by faith alone and the best impulses of the Social Gospel* are seen from this point of view to be not two opposed conceptions, nor again are they two shades of belief between which we have to choose, but they are just differently accented expressions of the same reality, as we see when we follow both trains of thought to their logical conclusion.

This has always been understood in the best periods of Protestant history. We may close with two illustrations, from Luther and Zinzendorf. Both pictures describe *at the same time* the complete moderation and great tension of the Christian life. They demand an ethic which comprehends in one patience and creative activity. They involve a Christian conviction of the hidden glory of Christ and its coming revelation.

Luther [1] says : 'Meanwhile Christians must remain quiet. They must consent to be trampled upon, and have patience. For in the realm of faith Christ will seem weak ; but in the kingdom of sight He will be not weak but strong. . . . We must wait, that is hope for the appearance and revelation of His almighty wisdom, glory, strength and power. Now the kingdom of this world appears before our eyes, the enemy of the kingdom of Christ. Hence it is necessary to hold fast to the word and to strengthen our souls in faith, patience, and hope until the hour comes of His glory and power and of our release : as a husbandman must endure the winter in hope and wait for his corn until it springs up from the earth in spring, and grows into the laden ear.'

Zinzendorf,[2] speaking of missionary work, says : ' It is only a foretaste of what is to come, a gracious earnest for our exertions. It is an undecided conflict, a dim struggle between the light of dawn and the darkness lingering on from night. As the beauty of the day *will* come, the heralding light greets the eyes of men early or late. We do not know how far it is still to the glow of morning, for we do not belong to the Apocalyptici.'

The pictures of waiting for the spring and of dawn are as far from illusion as they are near to the Gospel, for they depict as one single process the hiddenness of Christ's glory in the present and its coming revelation. In both of them the spirit of the early Christian prayer lives : ' Thy Kingdom come ! Maranatha ! '

---

[1] *W.A.*, vol. 34, II. p. 131.
[2] *Neue Allgemeine Missionszeitschrift*, 1924, p. 145.

THE CHURCH AND THE THEOLOGIAN
BY GEORGE KENNEDY ALLEN BELL

XII

THE CHURCH AND THE THEOLOGIAN

THEOLOGY has for centuries been honoured in the Church as the mistress of the sciences. Like the other sciences, theology also is a special science, but at least in former days she also held a place above the rest as their queen. To the student of theology so high a regard seems as natural now as it certainly was to his predecessor many centuries ago. But it is impossible to deny that in fact—whatever the theories may be—theology does not at present receive the tribute which is her due from the ordinary churchman or perhaps even from the authorities of the Church. Moreover, side by side with this insufficient regard on the part of the Church, it is sometimes said that the theological student is too little concerned to keep his own studies and his own work in touch with the life of the Church.

At the close of a volume of essays on the Mystery of Christ—all written by professional teachers or students of theology—it may therefore not be out of place to devote a few pages to the consideration of the mutual relations of the theologian and the Church. It is, so it seems to me, of the utmost danger to the Christian Religion that the two should remain apart. It is of the highest importance that the Doctor of Theology and the Priest, or Pastor, with his cure of souls, should not only understand one another, but support one another in their respective spheres, and join their forces in their common task of revealing the message of Jesus Christ to a world which needs Him so supremely.

At no time was there so great a necessity for systematic thought about the meaning of Christianity. The extraordinary development of science in the last hundred years has given a special urgency to such a task ; and in an age where the range of education is steadily increasing, it stands to reason that a new challenge is given to the teachers of religious faith. I do not mean that this challenge is the challenge of attack, though that may often be the case. Rather, when so many new things are being discovered, new facts about the beginning of the world, about the origin of the human species, about the antiquity and yet the youth of the world, a fresh stimulus comes to the teacher of religion as he is invited to relate his facts to all these, and to show in what ways his doctrine of the invisible and eternal for which religion stands is affected by the ever widening scale of the visible universe around us. Does the invisible wane as the visible waxes? or do the results of ever fresh research about, say, the basis of religious experience, or the historic setting of the Christian religion, or the new light thrown on Christian origins or human belief by the modern study of anthropology or comparative religion or psychology, put in jeopardy the fundamental conviction for which the worshipper of God in Christ must stand? It is for the theologian (in the widest sense) to answer each question, and to give the assurance which the Christian, or the non-Christian man in the street, desires—and very foolish is the Church or the minister of the Church who does not ask for the fullest help from the theologian in meeting these calls. I use theology as denoting systematic thought about the Christian religion; and I should wish to include thought about whatever that religion includes, whether philosophy, Biblical interpretation, Church history or the development of doctrine, or religious origins. For minds able to give themselves to such studies as these, to be single-minded in the research which these subjects involve and to teach, or help others to teach, the fruits of their learning, hardly any praise can be too high. It is in the realm of thought that the Christian conflict is raging to a peculiar degree to-day. And I venture to claim that there are thousands of unnecessary losses to the Christian faith and the Christian Church which are due to a misunderstanding of the Christian religion which more theology and more instructive teaching and a clearer and deeper exposition of the fundamentals of Christianity would prevent.

When we describe the teaching of the Church as Orthodoxy we ought to mean that it is right-thinking and right-teaching, and we should maintain that the Church can no more teach that which is rationally indefensible that it can teach heresy. A particular minister may do the Church untold disservice and involve untold loss by teaching things which are not only foolish or false, but permanently misleading. Christianity is Truth. What is alien from the truth is not Christian. Rightly held and rightly interpreted, with a full sense of what the complete life means, the Christian teaching must be the crown of all other teaching, and its truth in tune with that on which all seekers after truth are bent. The theologian is the Church's agent for unfolding and expounding the Christian truth and for relating it to all aspects of life and thought. Truly then ought the Church to honour the theologian, and the pastor in his turn should seek the aid of the theologian in answering the questions or meeting the doubts which the layman raises, and in teaching the faith of the Church.

But, it may be said, there are theologians *and* theologians. It is agreed that truth is the interest of all as it is most certainly the interest of the Church. Yet it is human to err, and theologians are human. Are we to give *carte blanche* to any learned doctor to research as he will and to teach as he will, and all in the name of the Church? Perhaps the theologian (as well as the parish priest), will talk nonsense. We know only too well that learned theologians, like other learned men, differ amongst themselves; that there are rival opinions and that the conflict between the schools is often fierce. How is the poor layman to learn which is speaking sense, which tells the truth, which is the proper representative of the orthodox faith? Are we to think that it is only those who teach some new thing that are right? Are we to rule out the fundamentalist and the reactionary from the start, with the ruthless sentence, ' Sir, he is no theologian ' ? Or are we, on the contrary, to affirm that the greater the approximation in *form* of Dr. Jones's theology now to Dr. Paley's of the last century, the more likely is Dr. Jones to be the man for us?

The question is not only fair but inevitable. And the answer is not quite simple. It is certain we can do nothing without trouble ; and we shall never (I think) be saved the trouble of thinking for ourselves. A modern writer, Mr. Aldous Huxley, quotes Heracleitus of Ephesus in the following way :

'Homer was wrong in saying : "Would that strife might perish from among gods and men ! " He did not see that he was praying for the destruction of the universe ; for if his prayer was heard, all things would pass away.'

And Mr. Huxley comments thus : ' These are words which the superhumanists should meditate. Aspiring towards a consistent perfection, they are aspiring towards annihilation.'[1] It is a very narrow interpretation of ' strife ' which such a comment could possibly have in view. But I quote the sentence now in order to emphasise the point, that without some ἔρις, some clash or ' strife,' we should certainly make very little progress in thinking or in theology, and that in course of that ' strife ' no doubt false and even mischievous things will be spoken and written. But if it be understood that each theologian has full liberty to speak for himself, and does not in each utterance represent, nor perhaps even wish to represent, the Church, should not the Church be content, believing that out of and in the strife the truth will in the end be made clear ? It is, I believe, of very poor service to religion to censor all theological utterances, or, what comes to the same thing, simply to denounce as scandalous and disloyal some unusual theological opinions or some new book which runs atilt against any known orthodoxy, instead of meeting the new opinions with arguments. The Church has no reason to be afraid ; and Church authorities have, alas, often only made themselves foolish by violent and unthinking attack on some new thing. The witness of the Church to faith or morals is embarrassed by the rash utterance of a foolish or perverse divine. Often the new opinions die without trouble, for they have no permanent force, but sometimes they become the correct opinion, the orthodoxy of to-morrow. It is, I am convinced, worth while to take risks. The taking

[1] Aldous Huxley, *Do What You Will*, p. 74.

of risks may indeed be described as part of the price of faithful witness to the truth in succeeding generations.

But, I may be pressed to say, is there no limit, no check? Must error be encouraged that theology may abound? By no means. I would give great liberty, as well as great honour, to the theologian, and encourage him to ever fresh endeavour and ever new research. But he is, after all, the servant of the Church, and it is the faith of the Church speaking through the ages that he studies and expounds. He may be endowed with such insight that he perceives an aspect unperceived before in some Christian doctrine. He may find a new and true way of interpreting *Mysterium Christi* to his own generation. Or he may have the genius which is able to relate fundamental Christian theology to modern categories of science and philosophy. If this be so, sooner or later (and if the Church is truly living in the Spirit sooner rather than later), his contribution will be taken in and absorbed, his new light will become a permanent part of the Church's faith. But at first he offers it as something that he has been taught, offers it to Christian opinion, offers it to the study and criticism of other theologians. It is his gift, his work, the best contribution he can make at this very moment to the common faith. Time and reason will show just where it fits in. And there is this further point. All the time that the theologian is exploring, there are certain great landmarks by which he is guided. He believes in Christ and in the guidance of the Spirit. He cannot and he does not wish to ignore the many-coloured experience of Christian believers throughout the ages. He hears the witness which they give that God is in Christ reconciling the world to himself. Not only is he unable and unwilling to deny this, but he will welcome these great and historic landmarks as guides to his own thought. To vary the metaphor, he is out at sea, but there are certain stars by which his course is guided : he has the whole ocean before him, but there are certain signs which it is shipwreck to ignore. He may find all sorts of new things, he may be led to the conclusion that certain passages in his scriptures hold a different sense from that which his contemporaries attach to them, or that psychological or anthropological considerations ignored by former students involve a radically different construction of certain things in the records. But the fundamental faith to which the creeds give witness must be his. The experience of life in Christ which is so real and so indisputable he will recognise to the full. To all this he must relate himself and his views and discussions, so that in the light he seeks to bring to that fundamental faith he may always subdue himself to things—*se rebus subjungere conetur*. He theologises as a debtor to Christ, as a servant of the Church. He may surprise and even startle contemporary churchmen by the new language he employs or by his attitude to conventional teaching. But there must be something wrong with his theology if in the last resort it involves a denial that God revealed himself uniquely in Jesus Christ, who is in some real sense the eternal Son of God—that is to say, ultimately of the same essence and nature as God. No restatement of the Christian doctrine can be satisfactory which does not conserve the religious valuation to which the Christian Church has always borne witness as faithfully as did that of the fourth century.[1] Given this presupposition of the theologian's thinking and the assumption of his faith in Christ, the churchman will be wise in allowing an ample liberty to theological study and writing, for he will recognise that in modern days, in which discussion abounds and there is so much attack upon the very bases of the Christian religion, a bold and fearless theology is a powerful ambassador for Christ. Indeed, more than this, the Church should not only tolerate the theologian but seek most earnestly to help him and reward him as one of the most honourable of her sons.

Yet if the Church, with special reference to the rulers and leaders of the Church, has a duty to the theologian, the converse is no less true. It cannot be too emphatically affirmed that theology is a very serious science and ought to be very seriously supported by the Church. The theologian has his own special duty to the Church. It is unfortunately true that a gulf does often separate the

---

[1] Wheeler Robinson, *The Christian Experience of the Holy Spirit*, p. 257.

professional student and teacher from the pastor. This
is the loss of both : certainly the loss of the pastor and of
those to whom the pastor daily ministers, but also the loss
of the divine. The duty of the theologian to the Church
may, I suggest, be regarded from two points of view. On
the one hand, he ought to seek for some personal contact
with the parish priest or pastor and the tasks in which he is
daily engaged. He must not dwell altogether apart from
the turmoil of the market or the shop, or regard its
problems or the work of the clergy ministering in that turmoil as no concern of his. The divine must, even for the
sake of his divinity, study how human beings face the
ordinary problems of life and, not least, the socially complex
life of the present day. He, too, must learn from men
that he may the better teach them. Indeed, Christian
theologians are bound by the very principle of the Incarnation to make an effort to enter into the world's affairs.
And besides this, the theologian ought to take the world
of man into his purview from the strictly scientific point
of view : the thoughts, feelings, and activities of men to
whom God comes and who enjoy, or may enjoy, a religious
experience, form a part (however small in a particular
instance) of his material. The theologian has, as it were,
to organise all his material and relate each of the many
parts to the rest. And as the theologian is a man who
communicates his results to men it is necessary that he be
alive to other men's thoughts and affairs. Indeed, in some
branches of theology, where the theologian is in a special
degree the interpreter of the religious experience of
human beings, he may have the same sort of relation
to that experience as the musician who sets his songs to
music has to the poet who makes those songs. He may not
only follow the words, understanding and realising them
as well as he can, but he may also express what he feels
about them as a theologian, and add a new force and
fire to those words—the religious experience of human
beings.

So the theologian owes it to theology to maintain his
human kinship with the pastor, and while he must be a
student and therefore reserve both much time and much

thought for the fulfilment of his vocation he owes it to live as near as he can to ordinary human affairs.

There is another debt which the theologian owes to the Church in the parish, to the pastor doing his everyday ministerial work. Let me call it patience. Nothing matters so much as the truth. But somebody has said that it takes two persons to tell the truth, the speaker and the hearer. The theologian, enthusiastic with some new discovery as yet untested, should not hasten to announce that the discovery is the true teaching to which the Church at last must yield or be discredited for ever. And the theologian must remember that after all he is an individual, and, in addition, the servant of the Church, which is greater than he. The theologian in his ardour has sometimes done harm to his case and even postponed the acceptance of his work by the Church at large through a rash denunciation of well-tried doctrines or the proclamation of debatable suggestions as ascertained truths. There is a difference which both the Church and the theologian should bear in mind between the opinion uttered by a scholar as a personal opinion which he believes to be true and the assertion of that opinion, at present unconfirmed by the convictions and studies of others as learned and competent in other ways, as the doctrine which is or ought to be the doctrine of the Church. Personal opinion is one thing, but teaching in the name of the Church is another ; and it is a distinction to be observed by all. Time and reason will perform the due process of sifting. Every Church, especially in these days, has its problems in the intellectual field, and every Church has need to be patient just as the theologian has need to be patient. That the theologian, the pastor and the layman will increasingly work together as servants of the Church must be the earnest wish of all those to whom the Christian faith is of supreme concern. The Church is greater than each and embraces them all. Neither the layman nor the pastor nor the divine can live by himself or to himself alone, as each learns more truly to love, and more perfectly and humbly to adore, *Mysterium Christi*.

INDEX

Printed in Great Britain at THE BALLANTYNE PRESS
SPOTTISWOODE, BALLANTYNE & CO. LTD.
Colchester, London & Eton